Hands-On Standards, Deluxe Edition

The First Source™ for Introducing Math Manipulatives

(Grades 3–4)

ETA/Cuisenaire®

Vernon Hills, IL 60061-1862

Hands-On Standards, Deluxe Edition
The First Source™ for Introducing Math Manipulatives (Grades 3–4)

Product Development Manager: Mark Schmit
Project Editor: Kathleen Bowler
Design and Production: Schawk, Inc., Evanston, IL

Hands-On Standards, Deluxe Edition
The First Source™ for Introducing Math Manipulatives (Grades 3–4)

ETA 43044

ISBN: 978-0-7406-1779-9

ETA/Cuisenaire®
Vernon Hills, IL 60061-1862
800-445-5985
www.etacuisenaire.com

07 08 09 10 11 12 13 14 15   10 9 8 7 6 5 4

Contents

Introduction

How can we make sure that students grasp the real meaning behind mathematical concepts instead of just memorizing numbers and repeating them back on tests? How can we help students develop an in-depth mathematical understanding?

Hands-On Standards, Deluxe Edition: The First Source™ for Introducing Math Manipulatives (Grades 3–4) provides teachers with easy-to-access ways to help students "visualize mathematics." This 200-page manual delivers 76 age-appropriate lessons designed to engage teachers and students in meaningful, authentic learning. Each lesson defines the specific concepts and skills that students will be taught and includes step-by-step procedures for students to use in solving a problem that easily links math to their day-to-day lives. Full-color photographs highlight the steps used in hands-on learning. Because it is important to reinforce learning, each lesson provides additional ways to practice the concepts.

Hands-On Standards is divided into five sections—Number and Operations, Geometry, Algebra, Measurement, and Data Analysis and Probability. These sections are based on National Council of Teachers of Mathematics (NCTM) concept strands. Each NCTM-focused lesson provides a structured framework for teachers to use manipulatives as tools to move students from the concrete to the abstract so that students can achieve understanding and succeed on standardized tests.

Each lesson in this book uses one of the following manipulatives:
Write-On/Wipe-Off Clocks • Color Tiles • Cuisenaire® Rods • Attribute Blocks • Fraction Circles • Fraction Tower® Equivalency Cubes • Geoboards • Three Bear Family® Counters • Relational Geosolids® • Pattern Blocks • Bucket Balance • Tangrams • Two-Color Counters • Base Ten Blocks • Centimeter Cubes • XY Coordinate Pegboard

Read on to find out how *Hands-On Standards, Deluxe Edition: The First Source™ for Introducing Math Manipulatives (Grades 3–4)* can help the students in your class master beginning math concepts and build a foundation for future math success!

Research on the Benefits of Manipulatives

History of Manipulatives

Since ancient times, people of many different civilizations have used physical objects to help them 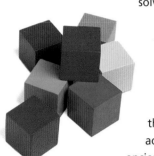 solve everyday math problems. The ancient civilizations of Southwest Asia (the Middle East) used counting boards. These were wooden or clay trays covered with a thin layer of sand. The user would draw symbols in the sand to tally, for example, an account or take an inventory. The ancient Romans modified counting boards to create the world's first abacus. The Chinese abacus, which came into use centuries later, may have been an adaptation of the Roman abacus.

Similar devices were developed in the Americas. The Mayans and the Aztecs both had counting devices that featured corn kernels strung on string or wires that were stretched across a wooden frame. The Incas had their own unique counting tool—knotted strings called *quipu.*

The late 1800s saw the invention of the first true manipulatives—maneuverable objects that appeal to several different senses and are specifically designed for teaching mathematical concepts. Friedrich Froebel, a German educator who, in 1837, started the world's first kindergarten program, developed different types of objects to help his kindergartners recognize patterns and appreciate geometric forms found in nature. In the early 1900s, Italian-born educator Maria Montessori further advanced the idea that manipulatives are important in education. She designed many materials to help preschool and elementary school students discover and learn basic ideas in math and other subjects.

Since the early 1900s, manipulatives have come to be considered essential in teaching mathematics at the elementary-school level. In fact, for decades, the National Council of Teachers of Mathematics (NCTM) has recommended the use of manipulatives in teaching mathematical concepts at all grade levels.

Manipulatives and Curriculum Standards

The NCTM calls for manipulatives to be used in teaching a wide variety of topics in mathematics.

- sorting—a pre-mathematical skill that aids in comprehension of patterns and functions
- ordering—a pre-mathematical skill that enhances number sense and other math-related abilities
- distinguishing patterns—the foundation for making mathematical generalizations
- recognizing geometric shapes and understanding relationships among them
- making measurements, using both nonstandard and standard units with application to both two- and three-dimensional objects
- understanding the base-ten system of numbers
- comprehending mathematical operations—addition, subtraction, multiplication, division
- recognizing relationships among mathematical operations
- exploring and describing spatial relationships
- identifying and describing different types of symmetry
- developing and utilizing spatial memory
- learning about and experimenting with transformations
- engaging in problem-solving
- representing mathematical ideas in a variety of ways
- connecting different concepts in mathematics
- communicating mathematical ideas effectively

Different states across the nation have also mandated the use of manipulatives for teaching math. These have included California, North Carolina, Texas, and Tennessee, among others. In addition, many local school districts mandate or strongly suggest manipulatives be used in teaching math especially for mathematics teaching at the elementary level.

Manipulative use is recommended because it is supported by both learning theory and educational research in the classroom.

Concrete stage	Representational stage	Abstract stage
A mathematical concept is introduced with manipulatives; students explore the concept using the manipulatives in purposeful activity.	A mathematical concept is represented using pictures of some sort to stand for the concrete objects (the manipulatives) of the previous stage; students demonstrate how they can both visualize and communicate the concept at a pictorial level.	Mathematical symbols (numerals, operation signs, etc.) are used to express the concept in symbolic language; students demonstrate their understanding of the mathematical concept using the language of mathematics.

How Learning Theory Supports the Use of Manipulatives

The theory of experiential education revolves around the idea that learning is enhanced when students acquire knowledge through active processes that engage them (Hartshorn and Boren, 1990). Manipulatives can be key in providing effective, active, engaging lessons in the teaching of mathematics.

Manipulatives help students learn by allowing them to move from concrete experiences to abstract reasoning (Heddens, 1986; Reisman, 1982; Ross and Kurtz, 1993). Experts in education posit that this learning takes place in three stages.

The use of manipulatives helps students hone their mathematical thinking skills. According to Stein and Bovalino (2001), "Manipulatives can be important tools in helping students to think and reason in more meaningful ways. By giving students concrete ways to compare and operate on quantities, such manipulatives as pattern blocks, tiles, and cubes can contribute to the development of well-grounded, interconnected understandings of mathematical ideas."

To gain a deep understanding of mathematical ideas, students need to be able to integrate and connect a variety of concepts in many different ways. Clements (1999) calls this type of deep understanding "Integrated-Concrete" knowledge. The effective use of manipulatives can help students connect ideas and integrate their knowledge so that they gain a deep understanding of mathematical concepts.

Teachers play a crucial role in helping students use manipulatives successfully, so that they move through the three stages of learning and arrive at a deep understanding of mathematical concepts.

How Research from the Classroom Supports the Use of Manipulatives

Over the past four decades, studies done at all different grade levels and in several different countries indicate that mathematics achievement increases when manipulatives are put to good use (Canny, 1984; Clements and Battista, 1990; Clements, 1999; Dienes, 1960; Driscoll, 1981; Fennema, 1972, 1973; Skemp, 1987; Sugiyama, 1987; Suydam, 1984). Additional research shows that use of manipulatives over the long-term provides more benefits than short-term use does (Sowell, 1989).

With long-term use of manipulatives in mathematics, educators have found that students make gains in the following general areas (Heddens; Picciotto, 1998; Sebesta and Martin, 2004):

- verbalizing mathematical thinking
- discussing mathematical ideas and concepts
- relating real-world situations to mathematical symbolism
- working collaboratively
- thinking divergently to find a variety of ways to solve problems
- expressing problems and solutions using a variety of mathematical symbols
- making presentations
- taking ownership of their learning experiences
- gaining confidence in their abilities to find solutions to mathematical problems using methods that they come up with themselves without relying on directions from the teacher

Studies have shown that students using manipulatives in specific mathematical subjects are more likely to achieve success than students who don't have the opportunity to work with manipulatives. Following are some specific areas in which research shows manipulatives are especially helpful:

Counting   Some children need to use manipulatives to learn to count (Clements, 1999).

Place Value   Using manipulatives increases students' understanding of place value (Phillips, 1989).

Computation   Students learning computational skills tend to master and retain these skills more fully when manipulatives are used as part of their instruction (Carroll and Porter, 1997).

Problem Solving   Using manipulatives has been shown to help students reduce errors and increase their scores on tests that require them to solve problems (Carroll and Porter, 1997; Clements, 1999; Krach, 1998).

Fractions   Students who have appropriate manipulatives to help them learn fractions outperform students who rely only on textbooks when tested on these concepts (Jordan, Miller, and Mercer, 1998; Sebesta and Martin, 2004).

Ratios   Students who have appropriate manipulatives to help them learn fractions also have significantly improved achievement when tested on ratios when compared to students who do not have exposure to these manipulatives (Jordan, Miller, and Mercer, 1998).

Algebraic Abilities   Algebraic abilities include the ability to represent algebraic expressions, to interpret such expressions, to make connections between concepts when solving linear equations, and to communicate algebraic concepts. Research indicates that students who used manipulatives in their mathematics classes have higher algebraic abilities than those who did not use manipulatives (Chappell and Strutchens, 2001).

Manipulatives have also been shown to provide a strong foundation for students mastering the following mathematical concepts (The Access Center, October 1, 2004):

- number relations
- measurement
- decimals
- number bases
- percentages
- probability
- statistics

Well-known math educator Marilyn Burns considers manipulatives essential for teaching math to students of all levels. She finds that manipulatives help make math concepts accessible to almost all learners, while at the same time offering ample opportunities to challenge students who catch on quickly to the concepts being taught. Research indicates that using manipulatives is especially useful for teaching low achievers, students with learning disabilities, and English language learners (Marsh and Cooke, 1996; Ruzic and O'Connell, 2001).

Research also indicates that using manipulatives helps improve the environment in math classrooms. When students work with manipulatives and then are given a chance to reflect on their experiences, not only is mathematical learning enhanced, math anxiety is greatly reduced (Cain-Caston, 1996; Heuser, 2000). Exploring manipulatives, especially self-directed exploration, provides an exciting classroom environment and promotes in students a positive attitude toward learning (Heuser, 1999; Moch, 2001). Among the benefits several researchers found for using manipulatives was that they helped make learning fun (Moch, 2001; Smith et. al, 1999).

Summary

Research from both learning theory and classroom studies shows that using manipulatives to help teach math can positively affect student learning. This is true for students at all levels and of all abilities. It is also true for almost every topic covered in elementary school mathematics curricula. Papert (1980) calls manipulatives "objects to think with." Incorporating manipulatives into mathematics lessons in meaningful ways helps students grasp concepts with greater ease, making teaching most effective.

Reference Citations

The Access Center, http://coe.jme.edu/mathvidsr/disabilities.htm (October 1, 2004)

Cain-Caston, M. (1996). Manipulative queen. *Journal of Instructional Psychology,* 23(4): 270–274.

Canny, M. E. (1984). The relationship of manipulative materials to achievement in three areas of fourth-grade mathematics: Computation, concept development, and problem solving. *Dissertation Abstracts International,* 45A: 775–776.

Carroll, W. M. & Porter, D. (1997). Invented strategies can develop meaningful mathematical procedures. *Teaching Children Mathematics,* 3(7): 370–374.

Chappell, M. F. & Strutchens, M. E. (2001). Creating connections: Promoting algebraic thinking with concrete models. *Mathematics Teaching in the Middle School.* Reston, VA: National Council of Teachers of Mathematics.

Clements, D. H. (1999). "Concrete" manipulatives, concrete ideas. *Contemporary Issues in Early Childhood,* 1(1): 45–60.

Clements, D. H. & Battista, M. T. (1990). Constructive learning and teaching. *The Arithmetic Teacher,* 38: 34–35.

Dienes, Z. P. (1960). *Building up mathematics.* London: Hutchinson Educational

Driscoll, M. J. (1984). What research says. *The Arithmetic Teacher,* 31: 34–35.

Fennema, E. H. (1972). Models and mathematics. *The Arithmetic Teacher,* 19: 635–640.

———. (1973). Manipulatives in the classroom. *The Arithmetic Teacher,* 20: 350–352.

Hartshorn, R. & Boren, S. (1990). Experiential learning of mathematics: Using manipulatives. *ERIC Clearinghouse on Rural Education and Small Schools.*

Heddens, J. W. (1986). Bridging the gap between the concrete and the abstract. *The Arithmetic Teacher,* 33: 14–17

———. Improving mathematics teaching by using manipulatives. Kent State University, accessed at www.fed.cubk.edu.hk.

Heuser, D. (1999). Reflections on teacher philosophies and teaching strategies upon children's cognitive structure development—reflection II; Pennsylvania State University, accessed at http://www.ed.psu.edu/CI/Journals/1999AETS/Heuser.rtf

———. (2000). Mathematics class becomes learner centered. *Teaching Children Mathematics,* 6(5): 288–295.

Jordan, L., Miller, M., & Mercer, C. D. (1998). The effects of concrete to semi-concrete to abstract instruction in the acquisition and retention of fraction concepts and skills. *Learning Disabilities: A Multidisciplinary Journal,* 9: 115–122.

Krach, M. (1998). Teaching fractions using manipulatives. *Ohio Council of Teachers of Mathematics,* 37: 16–23.

Maccini, P. & Gagnon, J. A. (2000, January). Best practices for teaching mathematics to secondary students with special needs. *Focus on Exceptional Children,* 32 (5): 11.

Marsh, L. G. & Cooke, N. L. (1996). The effects of using manipulatives in teaching math problem solving to students with learning disabilities. *Learning Disabilities Research & Practice,* 11(1): 58–65.

Martino, A. M. & Maher, C. A. (1999). Teacher questioning to promote justification and generalization in mathematics: What research practice has taught us. *Journal of Mathematical Behavior,* 18(1): 53–78.

Moch, P. L. (Fall 2001). Manipulatives work! *The Educational Forum*

Nunley, K. F. (1999). *Why hands-on tasks are good.* Salt Lake City, UT: Layered Curriculum.

Papert, S. (1980). *Mindstorms,* Scranton, PA: Basic Books.

Phillips, D. G. (1989). The development of logical thinking: A three-year longitudinal study. Paper presented to the National Council of Teachers of Mathematics, Orlando, FL.

Picciotto, H. (1998). Operation sense, tool-based pedagogy, curricular breadth: a proposal, accessed at http://www.picciotto.org.

Pugalee, D. K. 1999. Constructing a model of mathematical literacy. *The Cleaning House* 73(1): 19–22.

Reisman, F. K. (1982). *A guide to the diagnostic teaching of arithmetic* (3rd ed.). Columbus, OH: Merrill.

Ross, R. & Kurtz, R. (1993). Making manipulatives work: A strategy for success. *The Arithmetic Teacher* (January 1993). 40: 254–258.

Ruzic, R. & O'Connell, K. (2001). Manipulatives. *Enhancement Literature Review,* accessed at http://www.cast.org/ncac/Manipulatives1666.cfm.

Sebesta, L. M. & Martin, S. R. M. (2004). Fractions: building a foundation with concrete manipulatives. *Illinois Schools Journal,* 83(2): 3–23.

Skemp, R. R. (1987). *The psychology of teaching mathematics* (revised American edition). Hillsdale, NJ: Erlbaum.

Smith, N. L., Babione, C., & Vick, B. J. (1999). Dumpling soup: Exploring kitchens, cultures, and mathematics. *Teaching Children Mathematics,* 6: 148–152.

Sowell, E. (1989). Effects of manipulative materials in mathematics instruction. *Journal for Research in Mathematics Edcuation,* 20: 498–505.

Stein, M. K. & Bovalino, J. W. (2001). Manipulatives: One piece of the puzzle. *Mathematics Teaching in Middle School,* 6(6): 356–360.

Sugiyama, Y. (1987). Comparison of word problems in textbooks between Japan and the U.S. in J. P. Becker & T. Miwa (eds), *Proceedings of U.S.-Japan Seminar on Problem Solving.* Carbondale, IL: Board of Trustees, Southern Illinois University.

Suydam, M. (1984). Research report: manipulative materials. *The Arithmetic Teacher,* 31: 27.

How to Use This Book

The goal of *Hands-On Standards, Deluxe Edition: The First Source™ for Introducing Math Manipulatives (Grades 3–4)* is to transition students from informal, concrete strategies to more formal, abstract ones. This book is based on the use of manipulatives, which are perfect tools for teaching and reinforcing learning. Manipulatives

- are meaningful to students;
- provide students with control and flexibility;
- mirror cognitive and mathematical structures in meaningful ways; and
- help students in connecting different types of knowledge.

Built around the manipulatives are activities that engage memory so that students more readily retain the mathematical concepts they learn.

The First Step

Before even opening the book, create a learning environment in which your students are excited about embarking on their mathematics adventure.

- First, take time to become familiar with the manipulatives and the lessons in which they are used.
- The lessons have been written to be used with common manipulatives. However, depending on the resources available, you may need to substitute one manipulative with another.
- Introduce your students to the manipulatives they will encounter. Have them investigate the manipulative kits in an unstructured way so that they will become familiar with all of the manipulative shapes and textures.
- Allow your students the time to discover the relationships between sizes and shapes. Let them have fun.
- Keep the manipulative kits in a special place. Make sure students know where the manipulatives are stored so that they can easily access them during math time and classroom free time.

Getting Ready

Once students have had time to use the manipulatives, walk them through a sample lesson.

- You might want to model an activity so that students can see how you use the manipulatives.
- Make sure students know that there is a trial-and-error process that they must go through so that they aren't self-conscious if they make errors.
- Tell students that you will all talk about the activities afterward and that they will be able to write about the activities as well.

Using the Manual

The lessons in *Hands-On Standards* have been organized so that you can make an easy progression through the book. However, feel free to teach the lessons in any order to maximize students' learning. Following is a suggested plan for teaching each lesson:

- Read the story problem to students. Ask them if they have ever had a similar problem. Let them tell you their experiences.
- Define any necessary vocabulary. Give students ways to use the words so they become familiar with the concepts.
- Divide the class into groups or pairs, depending on the directions. Show students the manipulatives they will be using. Give them a few minutes to get their supplies ready.
- While the lessons have been designed for use with individual students, pairs, or small groups, they can easily be adapted to meet your own classroom organization or teaching preference. Lessons can be used in centers or in a more traditional classroom setting.
- Lessons have been written for a fairly broad age range, for example, grades 3–4. While the lessons serve as a guide, you should feel free to adapt data, vocabulary, and complexity to what you consider developmentally appropriate for your students.

- Help students perform the **Try It!** activity. Make sure they are having success as they work to understand the concept and develop an answer to the problem.

- Discuss the activity with students when they are finished. For suggestions, see the **Talk About It** section.

- Ask students to follow up the discussion by using the prompt in the **Solve It** section.

- Finally, have students work the problem in the **Standardized Practice** section without using manipulatives.

However you decide to use these lessons, make this manual your own. Use the ideas as jumping off points to enhance your teaching style and your existing math curriculum.

Hands on Standards, Deluxe Edition: The First Source™ for Introducing Math Manipulatives includes a CD-ROM, containing the following:

- **Blackline Masters for Hands-On Math, Deluxe Edition:** All the blackline masters from all three books are included on the CD.

- **Additional Blackline Masters:** These selections will assist in using the manipulatives. Many of these blackline masters will assist students with the creation of their representations of the concrete manipulatives, thus helping students to connect the concrete to the abstract mathematical concept. For more information see our Grids 'N' Graphs book and CD, product number 40964.

- **Essays about the seven core manipulatives:** These essays from The Super Source® will help you to understand the use and the importance of these manipulatives. These informative essays will provide you with information on the use of Geoboards, Tangrams, Pattern Blocks, Snap Cubes®, Cuisenaire® Rods, Color Tiles, and Base Ten Blocks.

- **Activities from The Super Source®:** These sample activities will give you a taste of what lies within Super Source as you continue to increase student conceptual knowledge through the use of hands-on activities.

  Grades K–2
  Base Ten Blocks: Sum It Up
  Cuisenaire Rods: Challenge Match
  Pattern Blocks: Look How I'm Growing
  Color Tiles: What's in the Bag?
  Geoboard: All About Squares
  Snap Cubes: Two-Color Patterns
  Tangrams: The Great Triangle Coverup

  Grades 3–4
  Base Ten Blocks: Even It Up
  Cuisenaire Rods: Shorter Trains
  Pattern Blocks: What's Next?
  Color Tiles: Sides and Angles
  Geoboard: Tessellating the Geoboard
  Snap Cubes: Loose Caboose
  Tangrams: Design It With Symmetry

- **Report on the benefits of using manipulatives:** This research paper will give you more evidence and support on the importance of implementing manipulatives in your classroom.

A Walk Through a Lesson

Each lesson in *Hands-On Standards* includes many features, including background information, objectives, pacing and grouping suggestions, discussion questions, and ideas for further activities, all in addition to the step-by-step, hands-on activity instruction. Take a walk through a lesson to see an explanation of each feature.

Lesson Introduction
A brief introduction explores the background of the concepts and skills covered in each lesson. It shows how they fit into the larger context of students' mathematical development.

Try It! Arrow
In order to provide a transition from the introduction to the activity, an arrow draws attention to the Try It! activity on the next page. When the activity has been completed, return to the first page to complete the lesson.

Objective
The **Objective** summarizes the skill or concept students will learn through the hands-on lesson.

Skills
The **Skills** box lists the top three mathematical skills that students will use in each lesson.

NCTM Expectations
Each lesson has been created to align with one or more of the grade-level expectations set by the National Council of Teachers of Mathematics (NCTM) in their *Principles and Standards for School Mathematics* (2000).

Talk About It
The **Talk About It** section provides post-activity discussion topics and questions. Discussion reinforces activity concepts and provides the opportunity to make sure students have learned and understood the concepts and skills.

Solve It
Solve It gives students a chance to show what they've learned. Students are asked to return to and solve the original word problem. They might summarize the lesson concept through drawing or writing, or extend the skill through a new variation on the problem.

More Ideas
More Ideas provides additional activities and suggestions for teaching about the lesson concept using a variety of manipulatives. These ideas might be suggestions for additional practice with the skill or an extension of the lesson.

Standardized Practice
Standardized Practice allows students to confront the lesson concept as they might encounter it on a standardized test.

LESSON 1

Number and Operations

Writing Numbers in Different Forms

In order for students to work flexibly with numbers, they need to understand different representations of numbers, including standard form, expanded form, and word form. Understanding multiple representations of numbers sets the stage for multiplication and division of numbers as well as understanding and comparing fractions and decimals.

Try It! Perform the Try It! activity on the next page.

Objective
Model, read, and write one-through four-digit numbers in standard notation, expanded notation, and in words.

Skills
- Modeling numbers
- Reading numbers
- Writing numbers

NCTM Expectations
Number and Operations
- Understand the place-value structure of the base-ten number system and be able to represent and compare whole numbers and decimals.
- Recognize equivalent representations for the same number and generate them by decomposing and composing numbers.

Talk About It
Discuss the Try It! activity.
- **Ask:** *How did you show 1,342 using the Base Ten Blocks?* Have students describe the blocks they used.
- **Ask:** *How did you write 1,342 in standard notation? How did you write it in expanded notation?* Have students compare their Number Forms Recording Sheets (BLM 1).
- **Ask:** *How did you know how to separate the different parts of 1,342 when you wrote it in expanded form?* Discuss with students how they separated the number into thousands, hundreds, tens, and ones.

Solve It
With students, reread the problem. Have students explain in writing the four ways that Mr. Mancetti's students could represent the number 1,342. **Say:** *The next day, a group had to represent the number 2,511 four ways.* Have students complete a new copy of the Number Forms Recording Sheet for 2,511.

More Ideas
For other ways to teach about modeling and writing numbers—
- Establish a learning center with Base Ten Blocks. Have students take turns working at the center in pairs to play a game with blocks. One student will say a four-digit number. Then the other student builds the number with blocks.
- Use Cuisenaire® Rods to model different numbers, and have students write the numbers in the three different forms.

Standardized Practice
Have students try the following problem.

Which shows the word form of 5,892?

A. Five thousand eight hundred ninety
B. Five thousand eight hundred two
C. Five thousand eight hundred ninety-two
D. Five hundred nine hundred eighty-two

16

8

Try It!

The **Try It!** activity opens with **Pacing** and **Grouping** guides. The **Pacing** guide indicates about how much time it will take for students to complete the activity, including the post-activity discussion. The **Grouping** guide recommends whether students should work independently, in pairs, or in small groups.

Next, the **Try It!** activity is introduced with a real-world story problem. Students will "solve" the problem by performing the hands-on activity. The word problem provides a context for the hands-on work and the lesson skill.

The **Materials** box lists the type and quantity of materials that students will use to complete the activity, including manipulatives such as Color Tiles and Pattern Blocks.

This section of the page also includes any instruction that students may benefit from before starting the activity, such as a review of foundational mathematical concepts or an introduction to new ones.

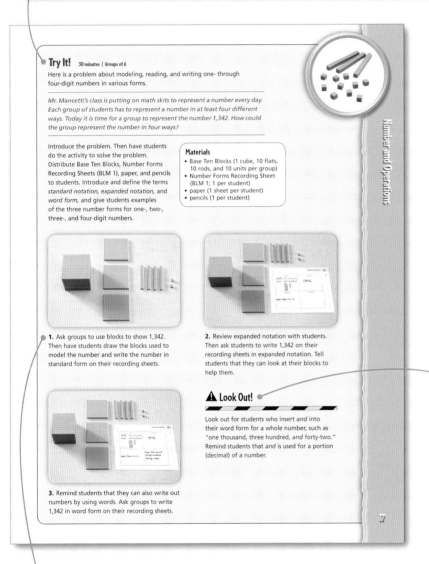

Try It! 30 minutes | Groups of 6

Here is a problem about modeling, reading, and writing one- through four-digit numbers in various forms.

Mr. Mancetti's class is putting on math skits to represent a number every day. Each group of students has to represent a number in at least four different ways. Today it is time for a group to represent the number 1,342. How could the group represent the number in four ways?

Introduce the problem. Then have students do the activity to solve the problem. Distribute Base Ten Blocks, Number Forms Recording Sheets (BLM 1), paper, and pencils to students. Introduce and define the terms *standard notation, expanded notation,* and *word form,* and give students examples of the three number forms for one-, two-, three-, and four-digit numbers.

Materials
• Base Ten Blocks (1 cube, 10 flats, 10 rods, and 10 units per group)
• Number Forms Recording Sheet (BLM 1; 1 per student)
• paper (1 sheet per student)
• pencils (1 per student)

Number and Operations

1. Ask groups to use blocks to show 1,342. Then have students draw the blocks used to model the number and write the number in standard form on their recording sheets.

2. Review expanded notation with students. Then ask students to write 1,342 on their recording sheets in expanded notation. Tell students that they can look at their blocks to help them.

⚠ **Look Out!**

Look out for students who insert *and* into their word form for a whole number, such as "one thousand, three hundred, *and* forty-two." Remind students that *and* is used for a portion (decimal) of a number.

3. Remind students that they can also write out numbers by using words. Ask groups to write 1,342 in word form on their recording sheets.

Look Out!

Look Out! describes common errors or misconceptions likely to be exhibited by students at this age dealing with each skill or concept and offers troubleshooting suggestions.

Step-by-Step Activity Procedure

The hands-on activity itself is the core of each lesson. It is presented in three—or sometimes four—steps, each of which includes instruction in how students should use manipulatives and other materials to address the introductory word problem and master the lesson's skill or concept. An accompanying photograph illustrates each step.

NCTM Correlation Chart

*NCTM Standards/Expectations	Lessons
Number and Operations	
Understand numbers, ways of representing numbers, relationships among numbers, and number systems.	
Understand the place-value structure of the base-ten number system and be able to represent and compare whole numbers and decimals.	NUM-1; NUM-2; NUM-3; NUM-12; NUM-23; NUM-24
Recognize equivalent representations for the same number and generate them by decomposing and composing numbers.	NUM-1; NUM-2; NUM-3
Develop understanding of fractions as parts of unit wholes, as parts of a collection, as locations on number lines, and as divisions of whole numbers.	NUM-15; NUM-16; NUM-17; NUM-19; NUM-21; NUM-22
Use models, benchmarks, and equivalent forms to judge the size of fractions.	NUM-15; NUM-16; NUM-17; NUM-18; NUM-20; NUM-21; NUM-22
Recognize and generate equivalent forms of commonly used fractions, decimals, and percents.	NUM-17; NUM-18; NUM-20; NUM-21; NUM-22; NUM-23
Explore numbers less than 0 by extending the number line and through familiar applications.	
Describe classes of numbers according to characteristics such as the nature of their factors.	
Understand meanings of operations and how they relate to one another.	
Understand various meanings of multiplication and division.	NUM-5; NUM-6; NUM-7; NUM-8; NUM-9; NUM-10; NUM-11; NUM-12; NUM-13; NUM-14
Understand the effects of multiplying and dividing whole numbers.	NUM-5; NUM-6; NUM-7; NUM-8; NUM-9; NUM-10; NUM-11; NUM-12; NUM-13; NUM-14
Identify and use relationships between operations, such as division as the inverse of multiplication, to solve problems.	NUM-11
Understand and use properties of operations, such as the distributivity of multiplication over division.	
Compute fluently and make reasonable estimates.	
Develop fluency with basic number combinations for multiplication and division and use these combinations to mentally compute related problems, such as 30×50.	
Develop fluency in adding, subtracting, multiplying, and dividing whole numbers.	NUM-3; NUM-4; NUM-5; NUM-6; NUM-7; NUM-8; NUM-9; NUM-10; NUM-11
Develop and use strategies to estimate the results of whole-number computations and to judge the reasonableness of such results.	NUM-4
Develop and use strategies to estimate computations involving fractions and decimals in situations relevant to students' experience.	

Number and Operations Continued	
Use visual models, benchmarks, and equivalent forms to add and subtract commonly used fractions and decimals.	NUM-20; NUM-24
Select appropriate methods and tools for computing with whole numbers from among mental computation, estimation, calculators, and paper and pencil according to the context and nature of the computation and use the selected method or tool.	NUM-4

*NCTM Standards/Expectations	Lessons
Geometry	
Analyze characteristics and properties of two- and three-dimensional geometric shapes and develop mathematical arguments about geometric relationships.	
Identify, compare, and analyze attributes of two- and three-dimensional shapes and develop vocabulary to describe the attributes.	GEO-1; GEO-2; GEO-3; GEO-4; GEO-5; GEO-8
Classify two- and three-dimensional shapes such as triangles and pyramids.	GEO-1; GEO-2; GEO-3; GEO-4; GEO-8
Investigate, describe, and reason about the results of subdividing, combining, and transforming shapes.	GEO-2; GEO-3; GEO-5; GEO-10; GEO-11; GEO-13
Explore congruence and similarity.	GEO-8
Make and test conjectures about geometric properties and relationships and develop logical arguments to justify conclusions.	
Specify locations and describe spatial relationships using coordinate geometry and other representational systems.	
Describe location and movement using common language and geometric vocabulary.	GEO-6; GEO-7
Make and use coordinate systems to specify locations and to describe paths.	GEO-6; GEO-7, GEO-17
Find the distance between points along horizontal and vertical lines of a coordinate system.	GEO-7; GEO-18
Apply transformations and use symmetry to analyze mathematical situations.	
Predict and describe the results of sliding, flipping, and turning two-dimensional shapes.	GEO-3; GEO-9; GEO-10; GEO-11; GEO-12; GEO-14, GEO-19
Describe a motion or a series of motions that will show that two shapes are congruent.	GEO-9; GEO-10
Identify and describe line and rotational symmetry in two- and three-dimensional shapes and designs.	GEO-9; GEO-15; GEO-16
Use visualization, spatial reasoning, and geometric modeling to solve problems.	
Build and draw geometric objects.	GEO-3; GEO-5; GEO-12
Create and describe mental images of objects, patterns, and paths.	GEO-11

Geometry Continued	
Identify and build a three-dimensional object from two-dimensional representations of that object.	GEO-5
Identify and build a two-dimensional representation of a three-dimensional object.	
Use geometric models to solve problems in other areas of mathematics, such as number and measurement.	
Recognize geometric ideas and relationships and apply them to other disciplines and to problems that arise in the classroom or in everyday life.	GEO-8

*NCTM Standards/Expectations	Lessons
Algebra	
Understand patterns, relations, and functions.	
Describe, extend, and make generalizations about geometric and numeric patterns.	ALG-1; ALG-2; ALG-3; ALG-4; ALG-10; ALG-13
Represent and analyze patterns and functions, using words, tables, and graphs.	ALG-1; ALG-2; ALG-3; ALG-4; ALG-10; ALG-13
Represent and analyze mathematical situations and structures using algebraic symbols.	
Identify such properties as commutativity, associativity, and distributivity and use them to compute with whole numbers.	ALG-5; ALG-6; ALG-7; ALG-8; ALG-9
Represent the idea of a variable as an unknown quantity using a letter or a symbol.	ALG-6; ALG-7; ALG-8
Express mathematical relationships using equations.	ALG-11; ALG-12
Use mathematical models to represent and understand quantitative relationships.	
Model problem situations with objects and use representations such as graphs, tables, and equations to draw conclusions.	ALG-11; ALG-12; ALG-13
Analyze change in various contexts.	
Investigate how a change in one variable relates to a change in a second variable.	ALG-13
Identify and describe situations with constant or varying rates of change and compare them.	

*NCTM Standards/Expectations	Lessons
Measurement	
Understand measurable attributes of objects and the units, systems, and processes of measurement.	
Understand such attributes as length, area, weight, volume, and size of angle and select the appropriate type of unit for measuring each attribute.	MEA-6; MEA-7; MEA-8; MEA-9; MEA-10; MEA-11
Understand the need for measuring with standard units and become familiar with standard units in the customary and metric systems.	MEA-3; MEA-4; MEA-5; MEA-6; MEA-7; MEA-8; MEA-11
Carry out simple unit conversions, such as from centimeters to meters, within a system of measurement.	

Measurement Continued

Understand that measurements are approximations and understand how differences in units affect precision.	MEA-11
Explore what happens to measurements of a two-dimensional shape such as its perimeter and area when the shape is changed in some way.	MEA-5; MEA-9
Apply appropriate techniques, tools, and formulas to determine measurements.	
Develop strategies for estimating the perimeters, areas, and volumes of irregular shapes.	MEA-5; MEA-7; MEA-8
Select and apply appropriate standard units and tools to measure length, area, volume, weight, time, temperature, and the size of angles.	MEA-1; MEA-2; MEA-3; MEA-4; MEA-5; MEA-6; MEA-7; MEA-8; MEA-9; MEA-10; MEA-11
Select and use benchmarks to estimate measurements.	MEA-11
Develop, understand, and use formulas to find the area of rectangles and related triangles and parallelograms.	MEA-6; MEA-9
Develop strategies to determine the surface areas and volumes of rectangular solids.	MEA-10

*NCTM Standards/Expectations	Lessons
Data Analysis and Probability	
Formulate questions that can be addressed with data and collect, organize, and display relevant data to answer them.	
Design investigations to address a question and consider how data-collection methods affect the nature of the data set.	DAT-3; DAT-4
Collect data using observations, surveys, and experiments.	DAT-3; DAT-4; DAT-5; DAT-6; DAT-8
Represent data using tables and graphs such as line plots, bar graphs, and line graphs.	DAT-2; DAT-3; DAT-4; DAT-5; DAT-8
Recognize the differences in representing categorical and numerical data.	
Select and use appropriate statistical methods to analyze data.	
Describe the shape and important features of a set of data and compare related data sets, with an emphasis on how the data are distributed.	DAT-2; DAT-3; DAT-4; DAT-5; DAT-6
Use measures of center, focusing on the median, and understand what each does and does not indicate about the data set.	DAT-1
Compare different representations of the same data and evaluate how well each representation shows important aspects of the data.	
Develop and evaluate inferences and predictions that are based on data.	
Propose and justify conclusions and predictions that are based on data and design studies to further investigate the conclusions or predictions.	DAT-8
Understand and apply basic concepts of probability.	
Describe events as likely or unlikely and discuss the degree of likelihood using such words as *certain, equally likely,* and *impossible.*	DAT-7; DAT-9
Predict the probability of outcomes of simple experiments and test the predictions.	DAT-7; DAT-8; DAT-9
Understand that the measure of the likelihood of an event can be represented by a number from 0 to 1.	

Number and Operations

Number pervades all areas of mathematics and is, therefore, a cornerstone of elementary mathematics education. **Operations**–the use of numbers to add, subtract, multiply, and divide–give students the tools to solve real-life problems. Together, **Number and Operations** combine to form the core of elementary mathematics instruction to give students greater number sense and more fluency in performing arithmetic operations.

In Grades 3 and 4, developing number sense is still a main goal of mathematics instruction. Concepts such as even, odd, prime, composite, and square numbers are taught throughout the elementary grades. Students in the intermediate grades are expected to not only understand whole numbers, but also to understand and represent fractions in context. Representing numbers with manipulatives should continue to be a major part of mathematics instruction. Students' understanding of fractions and decimals will grow as they practice representing them with physical materials.

Building computational fluency is a second goal of mathematics instruction in Grades 3 and 4. The focus at the intermediate grades is on helping students understand the meaning of multiplication and division. Working with different representations of multiplication and division–manipulatives, drawings, etc.–helps students to develop an understanding of the relationship between the two operations. Students in grades 3 and 4 should develop fluency with basic multiplication facts and reliable algorithms to use with larger numbers.

The Grades 3–5 NCTM Standards for Number and Operations suggest that students should:

- Understand numbers, ways of representing numbers, relationships among numbers, and number systems
- Understand meanings of operations and how they relate to one another
- Compute fluently and make reasonable estimates

As third- and fourth-grade students develop an understanding of number and operations, they are building a foundation upon which future mathematical concepts can be built. Throughout these years, students should gain a better understanding of our base-ten number system through work with large numbers. They should be able to solve many problems mentally, recall basic facts with fluency, estimate a reasonable answer to a problem, and compute accurately with multidigit numbers. The following are activities involving manipulatives that third- and fourth-grade students can use to develop skills in **Number and Operations.**

Number and Operations

Contents

Number and Operations

Writing Numbers in Different Forms

In order for students to work flexibly with numbers, they need to understand different representations of numbers, including standard form, expanded form, and word form. Understanding multiple representations of numbers sets the stage for multiplication and division of numbers as well as understanding and comparing fractions and decimals.

Try It! *Perform the Try It! activity on the next page.*

Talk About It

Discuss the Try It! activity.

- **Ask:** *How did you show 1,342 using the Base Ten Blocks?* Have students describe the blocks they used.

- **Ask:** *How did you write 1,342 in standard notation? How did you write it in expanded notation?* Have students compare their Number Forms Recording Sheets (BLM 1).

- **Ask:** *How did you know how to separate the different parts of 1,342 when you wrote it in expanded form?* Discuss with students how they separated the number into thousands, hundreds, tens, and ones.

Solve It

With students, reread the problem. Have students explain in writing the four ways that Mr. Mancetti's students could represent the number 1,342. **Say:** *The next day, a group had to represent the number 2,511 four ways.* Have students complete a new copy of the Number Forms Recording Sheet for 2,511.

More Ideas

For other ways to teach about modeling and writing numbers—

- Establish a learning center with Base Ten Blocks. Have students take turns working at the center in pairs to play a game with blocks. One student will say a four-digit number. Then the other student builds the number with blocks.

- Use Cuisenaire® Rods to model different numbers, and have students write the numbers in the three different forms.

Standardized Practice

Have students try the following problem.

Which shows the word form of 5,892?

A. Five thousand eight hundred ninety
B. Five thousand eight hundred two
C. Five thousand eight hundred ninety-two
D. Five hundred nine hundred eighty-two

Objective

Model, read, and write one-through four-digit numbers in standard notation, expanded notation, and in words.

Skills

- Modeling numbers
- Reading numbers
- Writing numbers

NCTM Expectations

Number and Operations
- Understand the place-value structure of the base-ten number system and be able to represent and compare whole numbers and decimals.
- Recognize equivalent representations for the same number and generate them by decomposing and composing numbers.

Try It! 30 minutes | Groups of 6

Here is a problem about modeling, reading, and writing one- through four-digit numbers in various forms.

Mr. Mancetti's class is putting on math skits to represent a number every day. Each group of students has to represent a number in at least four different ways. Today it is time for a group to represent the number 1,342. How could the group represent the number in four ways?

Introduce the problem. Then have students do the activity to solve the problem. Distribute Base Ten Blocks, Number Forms Recording Sheets (BLM 1), paper, and pencils to students. Introduce and define the terms *standard notation, expanded notation,* and *word form,* and give students examples of the three number forms for one-, two-, three-, and four-digit numbers.

Materials

- Base Ten Blocks (1 cube, 10 flats, 10 rods, and 10 units per group)
- Number Forms Recording Sheet (BLM 1; 1 per student)
- paper (1 sheet per student)
- pencils (1 per student)

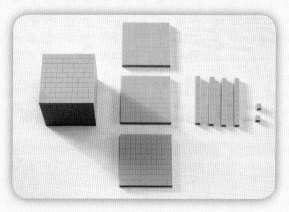

1. Ask groups to use blocks to show 1,342. Then have students draw the blocks used to model the number and write the number in standard form on their recording sheets.

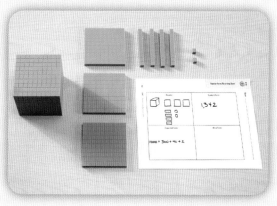

2. Review expanded notation with students. Then ask students to write 1,342 on their recording sheets in expanded notation. Tell students that they can look at their blocks to help them.

⚠ Look Out!

Look out for students who insert *and* into their word form for a whole number, such as "one thousand, three hundred, *and* forty-two." Remind students that *and* is used for a portion (decimal) of a number.

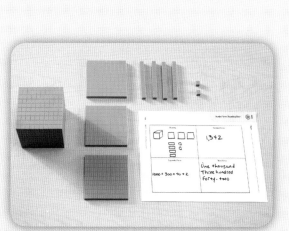

3. Remind students that they can also write out numbers by using words. Ask groups to write 1,342 in word form on their recording sheets.

Number and Operations

Comparing and Ordering Numbers

Comparing and ordering numbers requires a deep understanding of place value, which students will develop with sufficient work with multiple representations of numbers, including numbers in standard notation, expanded notation, word form, Base Ten Block representation, and on a number line. In order to compare and order numbers, students will also need to understand symbols used in comparing, including <, >, and =.

Try It! *Perform the Try It! activity on the next page.*

Objective

Compare and order one-through four-digit numbers using <, >, and =.

Skills

- Representing numbers
- Comparing numbers
- Ordering numbers

NCTM Expectations

Number and Operations
- Understand the place-value structure of the base-ten number system and be able to represent and compare whole numbers and decimals.
- Recognize equivalent representations for the same number and generate them by decomposing and composing numbers.

Talk About It

Discuss the Try It! activity.

- Write the numbers 1,394 and 1,439 on the board. *Ask: Which number is larger? How can you tell?*

- *Ask: If you were to order the numbers 1,394 and 1,439 from largest to smallest, which number would come first?*

- Write 1,394 < 1,439. *Ask: Can you write another statement about these numbers using the > sign? Can you write a statement using the = sign?*

Solve It

With students, reread the problem. Ask students to write a number sentence using < and > to compare the numbers. Then have students explain in writing which grade collected more cans.

More Ideas

For other ways to teach about comparing and ordering numbers—

- Have students work in pairs to play a game using Base Ten Blocks. One partner should come up with two numbers to compare. The other partner should compare the numbers using the correct sign. Students then model both numbers using blocks to see if the comparison was right.

- Set up a learning center with Base Ten Blocks and have pairs take turns using them. Have students model a number with the blocks and challenge their partners to model a number that is less than or greater than it.

Standardized Practice

Have students try the following problem.

Which is the correct symbol to fill in the box?

8,863 ☐ 8,683

A. <   B. >   C. =

Try It! 20 minutes | Groups of 6

Here is a problem about comparing and ordering numbers.

In one month, the third grade collected 1,378 cans for the school's recycling program. The fourth grade collected 1,783 cans in the same month. Which grade collected more cans in a month?

Introduce the problem. Then have students do the activity to solve the problem. Distribute Base Ten Blocks and Place-Value Charts (BLM 2) to students. Introduce the $<$, $>$, and $=$ signs to students, explain their meanings, and demonstrate their use by comparing one-, two-, three-, and four-digit numbers.

Materials

- Base Ten Blocks (1 cube, 10 flats, 10 rods, and 10 units per group)
- Place-Value Chart (BLM 2; 1 per student)
- paper (1 sheet per student)
- pencils (1 per student)

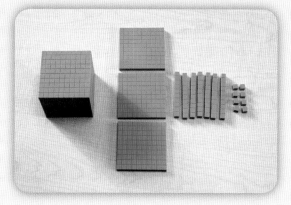

1. Say: *We are going to compare two numbers to find which is larger. Our first number is 1,378.* Have students use blocks to model 1,378. Then ask them to draw the blocks they used in the appropriate columns of the Place-Value Chart.

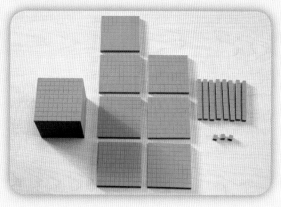

2. Say: *The second number is 1,783.* Have students model the number with blocks and then draw a picture of the blocks they used on the Place-Value Chart.

⚠ Look Out!

Look out for students who succeed with the Place-Value Chart but don't create the numbers correctly using the blocks. For example, a student may create the number 43 using 1 rod and 13 units. Assist students by helping them see that 10 units equal 1 rod. This will help them with their number sense.

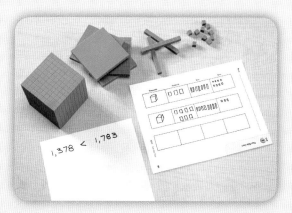

3. Have students write the numbers 1,378 and 1,783 side by side. **Say:** *Compare your drawings. Start at the thousands and move to the right until the drawings are different.* **Ask:** *How are they different?* Instruct students to place the appropriate symbol between the numbers.

Number and Operations

Adding and Subtracting

Learning how to add and subtract numbers up to four digits is an important skill both in mathematics and in everyday life. Addition and subtraction require students to be able to accurately represent numbers and understand the value of each. In this lesson, students will learn the fundamentals of adding and subtracting numbers up to four digits with and without regrouping.

Try It! *Perform the Try It! activity on the next page.*

Objective

Add and subtract numbers that have up to four digits, with and without regrouping, using Base Ten Blocks.

Skills

• Adding
• Subtracting
• Regrouping

NCTM Expectations

Number and Operations
• Understand the place-value structure of the base-ten number system and be able to represent and compare whole numbers and decimals.
• Recognize equivalent representations for the same number and generate them by decomposing and composing numbers.
• Develop fluency in adding, subtracting, multiplying, and dividing whole numbers.

Talk About It

Discuss the Try It! activity.

■ Write 289 and 319 on the board. **Ask:** *How can you write these numbers as an addition problem?* Help students line up the numbers so that they are ready to be added. Emphasize the importance of aligning place-value columns. Then add the numbers together as a class.

■ **Say:** *Sometimes when we add numbers we find that we need to regroup.* **Ask:** *How do you know when you need to regroup? Which numbers did you need to regroup to solve this problem? How did you do it? How did you show regrouping using the blocks?*

■ As a class, write the problem 608 − 95, lining up the place-value columns correctly. **Ask:** *How did you regroup numbers to solve this problem? How is regrouping for subtraction different from regrouping for addition?*

Solve It

With students, reread the problem. Have students write two sentences telling the total number of pages read by Peggy and Rahul and how they used addition and subtraction with regrouping to find the answer.

More Ideas

For other ways to teach about adding and subtracting—

■ Have students put Centimeter Cubes in a paper bag and then draw out two handfuls. Students should count each handful of cubes separately and then add the two numbers together.

■ Have students work in pairs to challenge each other to subtract two- and three-digit numbers. Each student makes up a subtraction problem. Then students use Base Ten Blocks to solve each other's subtraction problems.

Standardized Practice

Have students try the following problem.

Circle the correct answer.

$$
\begin{array}{r}
1{,}923 \\
+\ \ \ 411 \\
\end{array}
$$

A. 1,334 **B.** 1,534 **C.** 2,334 **D.** 2,134

Try It! 30 minutes | Groups of 6

Here is a problem about adding and subtracting.

Claire, Tim, Peggy, and Rahul keep track of the number of pages they read each month. Claire read 289 pages. Tim read 319 pages. Claire and Tim added their pages together to see how much they read altogether. Peggy and Rahul read 95 fewer pages. How many pages did Peggy and Rahul read?

Introduce the problem. Then have students do the activity to solve the problem. Distribute Base Ten Blocks and Place-Value Charts (BLM 2) to students.

Materials
- Base Ten Blocks (10 flats, 10 rods, and 20 units per group)
- Place-Value Chart (BLM 2; 2 per student)

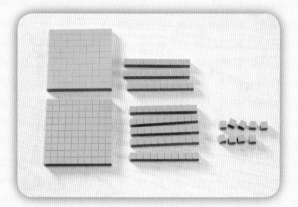

1. Say: *We are going to add together 289 and 319. First model 289 with blocks. Then draw the blocks you used on the chart and draw a plus sign below them.* Have students set the blocks they used to the side.

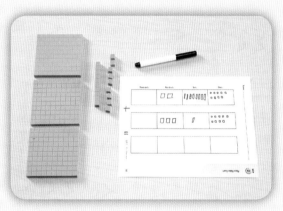

2. Say: *Now we will use new blocks to model 319.* Have students model the number and then draw the blocks they used in the second row on the chart. Students should draw an equal sign below the second addend.

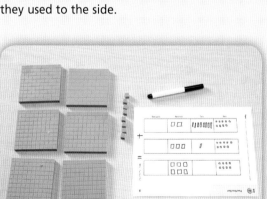

3. Say: *Now we will put the blocks together to help us add.* Explain to students that they will need to regroup to solve the problem by exchanging units for rods and rods for flats. Then have them draw the blocks that show the sum (608) on their charts.

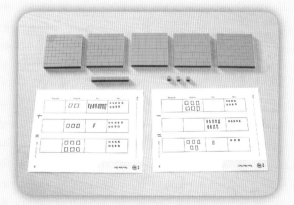

4. Say: *Transfer your sum to the second chart and subtract 95 from 608.* Assist students in exchanging blocks to regroup.

Number and Operations

Estimating the Sum or Difference

As students become more familiar with adding and subtracting, they come to understand that sometimes a situation calls for an estimate rather than an exact answer. Estimates are helpful when dealing with very large numbers and save time when an exact answer is not needed.

Try It! *Perform the Try It! activity on the next page.*

Talk About It

Discuss the Try It! activity.

- **Ask:** *When is an estimate enough information to solve a problem?* Guide students to understand that when a problem asks for "about" how many, they can use an estimate.

- **Ask:** *What number did you round 104 to? How did you know to round down instead of up? What about 328? How did you know to round up?*

- **Ask:** *Was your estimate close to the exact answer? Will rounding always give you an estimate that is close to the exact answer? What if you rounded the same numbers to the closest hundred?*

Solve It

With students, reread the problem. Have students write to describe how they used Base Ten Blocks to help them estimate 104 + 328. They should then write a sentence telling whether the class will have enough labels for a new computer.

More Ideas

For other ways to teach about estimating sums and differences—

- Have students use Base Ten Blocks to estimate differences. Give students a subtraction problem. Then ask them to round the numbers in the problem and subtract to find an estimate.

- Give students sample addition and subtraction word problems. Some problems should ask for an exact answer, while others should indicate that they require an estimate by using phrases such as "about how many." Have students decide for each problem whether an exact answer or an estimate is needed. For problems requiring an estimate, have students estimate using mental math first. Then have them use Base Ten Blocks to check their answers.

Standardized Practice

Have students try the following problem.

Find the difference between 812 and 489. What is the answer rounded to the nearest 10?

A. 300   **B.** 320   **C.** 420   **D.** 480

Objective

Estimate the sum or difference in addition and subtraction problems.

Skills

- Adding
- Subtracting
- Estimating

NCTM Expectations

Number and Operations
- Develop fluency in adding, subtracting, multiplying, and dividing whole numbers.
- Develop and use strategies to estimate the results of whole-number computations and to judge the reasonableness of such results.
- Select appropriate methods and tools for computing with whole numbers from among mental computation, estimation, calculators, and paper and pencil according to the context and nature of the computation and use the selected method or tool.

Try It! 25 minutes | Groups of 3

Here is a problem about estimating a sum.

Mrs. Vasquez's class is collecting box top labels for a new computer. The class collects 104 labels in September and 328 labels in October. They need 500 labels for a new computer. Can the students find out if they have enough labels without counting them or adding 104 + 328?

Introduce the problem. Then have students do the activity to solve the problem. Distribute Base Ten Blocks to students. Introduce the concept of rounding to students, and explain how they can use rounding to estimate sums and differences. With students, practice rounding one-, two-, three-, and four-digit numbers using 5 as the benchmark. Write the addition problem 104 + 328 on the board.

Materials
- Base Ten Blocks (5 flats, 10 rods, and 10 units per group)
- paper (1 sheet per group)
- pencils (1 per group)

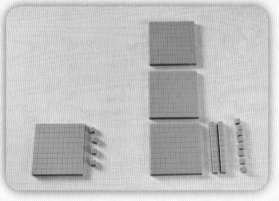

1. Have students model the numbers 104 and 328 using blocks. Have students use these models to assist them in rounding to the tens place.

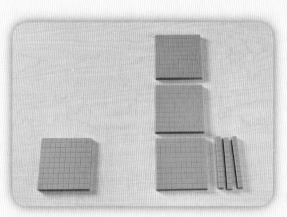

2. Students should then model the rounded numbers using blocks. Ask students to add the rounded numbers to find the sum. Have students write down the rounded sum.

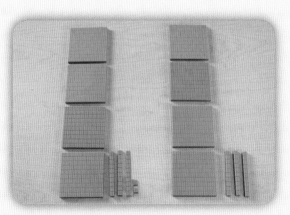

3. Now ask students to find the exact answer using blocks. Have students write down their exact answer and compare it to their estimated answer.

⚠ Look Out!

Students may feel compelled to find an exact answer every time. Brainstorm with students to identify situations in which they need an estimate rather than an exact answer. Also, for students who are confused about when to round up or down, you may wish to draw a blank ten-frame on paper and use counters to illustrate the rule that numbers under 5 are rounded down, while numbers 5 and above are rounded up.

Number and Operations

Multiplying With Arrays

Arrays are arrangements of equal groups that can be used to show repeated addition and multiplication. Arrays can be made from Color Tiles or units of Base Ten Blocks but are also found in everyday objects, such as the arrangement of cans in a six-pack or eggs in a carton. They can be especially helpful as students learn multiplication facts.

Try It! *Perform the Try It! activity on the next page.*

Talk About It

Discuss the Try It! activity.

- **Ask:** *How did the array help you solve the problem?* Discuss with students how they used the array and repeated addition to solve the problem.

- **Ask:** *If you made 4 rows of 8 and added 8 + 8 + 8 + 8, would you get the same answer?* Have students model 4 × 8 and compare the 2 arrays side by side.

- **Ask:** *If you wanted to find 8 × 3 instead of 8 × 4, how would you change the array you made?*

Solve It

With students, reread the problem. Have students draw a picture of the array of chairs. Then have them write the numerical representation as both repeated addition and multiplication.

More Ideas

For other ways to teach about relating arrays and repeated addition to multiplication—

- Have students work in pairs. One partner will create an array with Color Tiles. The other partner must then create an equation using repeated addition to represent the array. Both students should count the tiles to check the equation.

- Have students use Color Tiles to create an array using prime numbers. For example, ask students to make an array using 29 tiles. Challenge them to explain why this array can only be made as a straight line rather than a square or rectangle.

- Have students use Color Tiles to explore arrays of perfect squares. Ask students to explain why they can make a square array for 16 but not for 18.

Standardized Practice

Have students try the following problem.

Which number sentence describes the array?

A. 3 × 4   **C.** 4 + 4 + 4 + 4

B. 3 + 3 + 3   **D.** 4 + 3

Try It! 20 minutes | Pairs

Here is a problem about relating arrays and repeated addition to multiplication.

Mr. Booth asked a police officer to speak to his class and another fourth-grade class about summer safety. To make room for the other students, Mr. Booth arranged the chairs in his classroom into 8 rows and put 4 chairs in each row. How many chairs were there in all?

Introduce the problem. Then have students do the activity to solve the problem. Distribute Color Tiles, paper, and pencils to students.

Materials
- Color Tiles (40 per pair)
- paper (1 sheet per student)
- pencils (1 per student)

1. Tell students that one way to solve the problem is by using an array. **Say:** *Use the tiles to show 8 rows of 4 tiles.* Emphasize rows and columns in the array.

2. Ask: *How could we find the number of tiles in the array?* Point out that students can use the array they made to add 4 + 4 + 4 + 4 + 4 + 4 + 4 + 4.

3. Have students calculate the answer to the problem by adding. **Ask:** *What other ways can we find the answer?* Demonstrate that 8 × 4 is the same as 4 + 4 + 4 + 4 + 4 + 4 + 4 + 4.

⚠ Look Out!

Make sure students are aware of the difference between a row and a column. Additionally, students may not understand that they need to have the same number of tiles in each row. Reinforce that in order to use repeated addition for multiplication, they need the same number in each group. To increase students' understanding of the number sense behind multiplication, encourage them to use skip counting for repeated addition before they start to memorize multiplication facts. This will give them a deeper understanding of what multiplication is, rather than merely encouraging rote memorization.

Number and Operations

Multiply With a One-Digit Multiplier

Students build on and practice with the multiplication concept of repeated addition by using Base Ten Blocks to multiply a one-digit number by a two-digit number. This practice is important for students to build fluency in multiplication. This lesson provides students with a foundation for later lessons on multiplying by 5, by 10, and by larger numbers.

Try It! *Perform the Try It! activity on the next page.*

Talk About It

Discuss the Try It! activity.

- **Say:** *You arranged 3 groups of 21. Write a number sentence to show this problem.* **Ask:** *How else could you have modeled 3 × 21 using blocks?*

- **Ask:** *What was the total number represented by your blocks?* **Say:** *Write a number sentence to show this multiplication problem with its answer.*

- **Ask:** *How would you use the blocks to solve the problem 2 × 28?* Students should note that they will regroup the 16 units into 1 rod and 6 units. Explain how this regrouping is like "carrying" a number from the ones place to the tens place when multiplying on paper.

Solve It

With students, reread the problem. Have students draw a picture to show the number of leaves Ms. Parson's class will collect during the entire month. Ask students to write a number sentence to show the multiplication problem, including the answer, and explain in writing how they solved the problem.

More Ideas

For other ways to teach about multiplying with a one-digit multiplier—

- Write several multiplication problems on the board for students to solve. Provide one-digit by one-digit problems, then have students move on to one-digit by two-digit problems. Have pairs of students use Color Tiles to model and solve the problems.

- Write 3 × 16, 2 × 32, and 4 × 19 on the board. Ask small groups of students to use Cuisenaire® Rods to model and solve each problem.

Standardized Practice

Have students try the following problem.

Each of Mr. Carrido's 23 students brought 2 snacks to take on their field trip. How many snacks did the students have altogether?

A. 25   **B.** 46   **C.** 54   **D.** 68

Objective

Solve a multiplication problem with a one-digit multiplier using Base Ten Blocks.

Skills

- Representing numbers
- Multiplying numbers
- Identifying factors and products

NCTM Expectations

Number and Operations
- Understand various meanings of multiplication and division.
- Understand the effects of multiplying and dividing whole numbers.
- Develop fluency in adding, subtracting, multiplying, and dividing whole numbers.

Try It! 20 minutes | Groups of 4

Here is a problem about multiplying with a one-digit multiplier.

Ms. Parson's class collects 3 different types of leaves every day to study during science. Brian calculates that the class will have 21 days of class this month. How can Brian find the total number of leaves the class will collect this month?

Introduce the problem. Then have students do the activity to solve the problem. Distribute Base Ten Blocks and Place-Value Charts (BLM 2) to groups of students.

Materials
- Base Ten Blocks (30 units and 15 rods per group)
- Place-Value Chart (BLM 2; 1 per group)

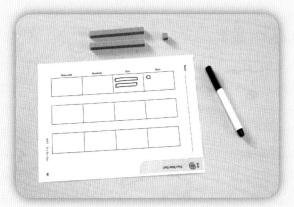

1. Have students model 21 with the blocks. Instruct students to represent this number on their Place-Value Chart.

2. Say: *We want to make 3 groups of 21. Arrange two more groups of 21 with blocks, then draw them on your Place-Value Charts.*

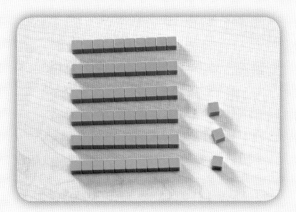

3. Have students find the total number represented by all the blocks. **Say:** *Count all of your blocks.* **Ask:** *What number do you have?*

⚠ Look Out!

Look out for students who don't grasp the concept of multiplication as repeated addition. Write 2 × 12 on the board. **Say:** *You need to find the number 12 "two times." So multiplying 12 by 2 is the same as adding 2 groups of 12 together.* Have students model 2 × 12 with blocks and then on their Place-Value Charts. Point out to students that they have made a group of 12 *two times.* Then have students add to find the total.

Multiply by 5

Students may already be familiar with counting by 5s from counting their fingers to make 10 and 20. Also, students are familiar with grouping manipulatives to multiply by single-digit numbers. Multiplying by 5 and skip counting teach students that patterns can help them remember number facts.

Objective

Multiply a number by 5 using grouping and skip counting.

Skills

- Representing numbers
- Counting numbers
- Multiplying numbers

NCTM Expectations

Number and Operations
- Understand various meanings of multiplication and division.
- Understand the effects of multiplying and dividing whole numbers.
- Develop fluency in adding, subtracting, multiplying, and dividing whole numbers.

Try It! *Perform the Try It! activity on the next page.*

Talk About It

Discuss the Try It! activity.

- **Ask:** *Did you get the same answer for 4 × 5 when you used the Two-Color Counters to multiply as you did when you skip counted on the Hundred Chart?*

- **Ask:** *Was it easier to count all the counters one by one to solve 4 × 5, or to skip count by 5s?*

- **Ask:** *What do you notice about your answers to all of the multiplication facts of 5? Do you think this still would be true if we multiplied a larger number like 5 × 17? What about 2,378 × 5? Can we use this pattern to help us solve any multiplication problem that uses 5?*

Solve It

With students, reread the problem. Have students write a short paragraph summarizing how they know 4 groups of 5 paint brushes will be a number ending in 5 or 0. Then have them explain how they can solve 4 × 5 as proof. Encourage them to describe using a counter array or Hundred Chart as support.

More Ideas

For other ways to teach about multiplying by 5—

- Have students work in groups to create number lines from 1 to 50 on paper. Have students use Centimeter Cubes to show skip counting by 5s on the number line and explain how it relates to multiplication facts involving 5.

- Challenge groups of students to model multiples of 5 through 5 × 20 using Color Tiles to build arrays and skip count. Have students record the algorithms for these facts and discuss the patterns involved.

Standardized Practice

Have students try the following problem.

In gym class, there are 5 teams with 5 players on each team. How many students are in the gym?

A. 15   **B.** 20   **C.** 25   **D.** 30

Try It! 20 minutes | Pairs

Here is a problem about multiplying by 5.

The art teacher divided the class into 4 equal-sized groups. Each group needs 5 paintbrushes. How many paintbrushes are needed in all?

Introduce the problem. Then have students do the activity to solve the problem. Distribute Two-Color Counters, Hundred Charts (BLM 3), pencils, and paper to each pair of students.

Materials
- Two-Color Counters (50 per pair)
- Hundred Chart (BLM 3; 1 per pair)
- pencils (1 per pair)
- paper (2 sheets per pair)

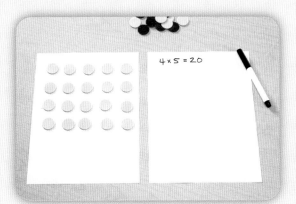

1. Direct students to divide counters into 4 rows of 5 counters, all yellow-side up. Have students represent the model by writing the multiplication sentence 4 × 5. Have students solve the problem 4 × 5 by counting each individual counter (1 to 20).

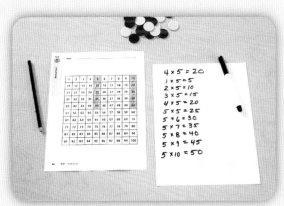

3. Have students continue skip counting on their Hundred Charts to complete multiples of 5 through 50. Discuss the pattern of numbers when skip counting or multiplying by 5s (the place value of ones is 5 or 0). Challenge students to use their completed charts to create multiplication sentences for facts up to 5 × 10.

2. Have students repeat counting and flip over every fifth counter to red as they count. Then have students transfer the value the red counters represent to their Hundred Charts by circling or shading appropriate values (5, 10, 15, 20). Discuss the pattern created on the Hundred Chart and its link to the array of counters. **Ask:** *How many rows are in the counter array? How many numbers did we shade on our Hundred Chart? How many counters are in each row? How much does the value of each shaded number on the chart increase each time?*

⚠ Look Out!

Watch out for students who can complete multiplication facts involving 5, but cannot represent multiples of 5 with an array or a Hundred Chart. This is an indication that rote memory has been used to solve the facts, but that the solid number sense driving the algorithms is not yet understood. Provide guided assistance to make sure students can model multiplication facts as well as solve their algorithms.

Objective

Multiply with a two-digit number.

Skills

- Representing numbers
- Understanding relationships between operations
- Multiplying numbers

NCTM Expectations

Number and Operations
- Understand various meanings of multiplication and division.
- Understand the effects of multiplying and dividing whole numbers.
- Develop fluency in adding, subtracting, multiplying, and dividing whole numbers.

Number and Operations

Multiplying With a Two-Digit Number

Students in earlier lessons used strategies such as modeling an array, grouping Base Ten Blocks, and skip counting on a hundred chart to multiply with smaller numbers. In this lesson, students return to using blocks to model and solve more complicated multiplication problems involving two-digit multipliers and three-digit products. It is important for students to have a solid foundation of knowledge in multiplication before they move on to exploring division problems in later lessons, so that they can see the relationship between the two.

Try It! *Perform the Try It! activity on the next page.*

Talk About It

Discuss the Try It! activity.

- Discuss the terms *factor* and *product*. **Ask:** *Which blocks show the factors? Which show the product?*

- **Ask:** *How did you use the model to find the answer?* Guide students to discuss how they used the model to break down the two factors into smaller numbers. Students should explain that they multiplied the smaller numbers, then added to find the total.

- **Ask:** *How could we model the problem if we change it to 13 × 25?*

Solve It

With students, reread the problem. Have students draw a picture to show how to use blocks to solve the problem. Then have them label their drawing to show which blocks represent the factors and which show the product.

More Ideas

For other ways to teach about multiplying with a two-digit number—

- Set up a learning center with Two-Color Counters and a list of problems such as 33 × 12, 20 × 25, and 15 × 37. Challenge students to model and solve the problems using counters.

- Have students work in groups to make up two-digit number multiplication problems and use Base Ten Blocks and repeated addition to solve each problem.

Standardized Practice

Have students try the following problem.

Samantha is making goody bags for her birthday party. She is making 15 bags, and each bag will have 11 items in it. Which expression can be used to find how many items she needs?

A. 11 + 15   **B.** 11 − 15   **C.** 11 × 15   **D.** 11 ÷ 15

Try It! 30 minutes | Groups of 4

Here is a problem about multiplying with a two-digit number.

Rita's class is having a bake sale. Each student in Rita's class will bring in 12 treats to sell. There are 25 students in Rita's class. How many treats will the class bring in altogether?

Introduce the problem. Then have students do the activity to solve the problem. Distribute Base Ten Blocks, two long pieces of masking tape, paper, and pencils to groups. Write 12 × 25 on the board. Explain to students that they will multiply 12 × 25 by building rectangles and squares using blocks.

Materials
- Base Ten Blocks (5 flats, 15 rods, and 30 units per group)
- masking tape (2 pieces per group)
- paper (1 sheet per group)
- pencils (1 per group)

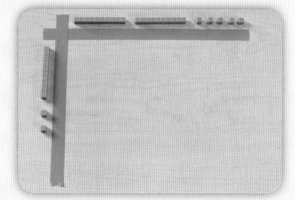

1. Have students represent 25 with blocks by placing them horizontally along the top of their grid. Then have students represent 12 along the vertical side of their grid.

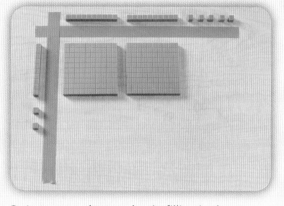

2. Instruct students to begin filling in the intersection of each row and column using a block that has the same dimensions as the one on the horizontal and the vertical portion of the grid. Assist students in completing their grids.

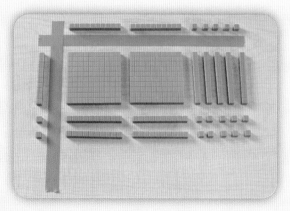

3. Say: *Count the total number of flats, rods, and units to find the answer to 12 × 25.* Have students write down the number they find.

 Look Out!

Look out for students who don't properly complete the array. For example, students might think they are done after completing only one row. Give students two more pieces of masking tape to complete a rectangular field for their answer. **Say:** *When you've multiplied all the numbers, the blocks in your answer should form a large rectangle.*

Number and Operations

Multiply by 10

Multiplying by 10 will illustrate the patterns in multiplication in a more obvious way than multiplying by other numbers. Students need to know that multiplying by 10 will result in a 0 in the ones place in the product. Through using manipulatives such as Base Ten Blocks, students will understand the patterns involved in multiplication.

Try It! *Perform the Try It! activity on the next page.*

Talk About It

Discuss the Try It! activity.

- Display a Place-Value Chart (BLM 2) and show a 1 in the ones place. **Ask:** *What do we get when we multiply by 10?* Students should explain that the 1 moves to the tens place, and a 0 is placed in the ones place. **Ask:** *How can we use the Place-Value Chart to show 13 × 10 = 130?*

- **Say:** *When you multiply by a multiple of 10, your answer will always have a 0 in the ones place.* **Ask:** *Why do you think this is true?* Have students skip count by 10 on a number line to reinforce this concept.

- **Ask:** *If you had 15 teams with 20 students on each team, how could you find the total number of students?*

Solve It

With students, reread the problem. Have students write a short paragraph to explain how they can use place value to multiply 13 × 10 by adding a 0 to 13.

More Ideas

For other ways to teach about multiplying by 10—

- Have groups of students make stacks of 10 Color Tiles and use them to multiply various numbers by 10. After multiplying, students can check their work by counting the tiles. Have them record their answers to reinforce the pattern and conclude that in each case they added a 0 to the number they multiplied by 10.

- Have students work in groups using Base Ten Blocks to multiply larger multiples of 10. Supply a series of problems, such as 4 × 40, 4 × 50, 4 × 60, and 4 × 70. Help students see the pattern of multiplying and then adding 0—for example, 4 × 40 is solved by multiplying 4 × 4 and adding 0.

Standardized Practice

Have students try the following problem.

Mrs. McMahon wants to prepare a copy of a test for each of the 20 students in her class. The test is 3 pages long. How many pages will she prepare altogether?

A. 6   **B.** 30   **C.** 60   **D.** 120

Objective

Identify the effect of multiplying by 10.

Skills

- Representing numbers
- Multiplying numbers
- Identifying patterns

NCTM Expectations

Number and Operations
- Understand various meanings of multiplication and division.
- Understand the effects of multiplying and dividing whole numbers.
- Develop fluency in adding, subtracting, multiplying, and dividing whole numbers.

Try It! 30 minutes | Groups of 4

Here is a problem about multiplying by 10.

On Olympics Day at Baker Elementary School, students divide into 13 teams. Each team has 10 students. What is the total number of students?

Introduce the problem. Then have students do the activity to solve the problem. Distribute Base Ten Blocks to groups and explain that they will use them to multiply 13 × 10.

Materials

- Base Ten Blocks (30 rods and 30 units per group)

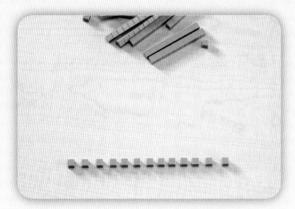

1. Write 13 × 10 on the board. Tell students to model 13 using 13 units.

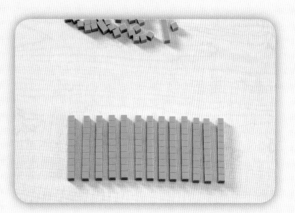

2. Have students multiply 13 × 10 by replacing each unit with a rod. Have them count the rods to find the total. **Say:** *When you multiply by a 10, you can add a 0 to the other factor to find the product.*

Invite students to model other problems, such as 8 × 10 or 15 × 10.

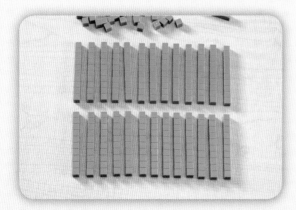

3. Ask: *How can you multiply 13 × 20?* Guide students to line up 2 rows of 13 units each, then to replace each unit with a rod. Explain that this is the same as multiplying 13 × 2, then adding a 0 to the product.

⚠ Look Out!

Students may not understand why multiplying by 10 will automatically result in a product with a 0 in the ones place. Have them create arrays for 1 × 10, 2 × 10, and so on through 10 × 10 to show how the number in every new row adds 10. Have students map this pattern on a Hundred Chart (BLM 3) to reinforce.

Number and Operations

Finding Factor Pairs

Finding factor pairs allows students to deepen their understanding of division as they learn about factors and divisibility rules. To find all the factor pairs of a number, students should be encouraged to proceed in an ordered fashion by finding the factor pair of 1, then 2, then 3, then 4, and so on. This will help them avoid skipping any factor pairs, which is a common mistake if students try to haphazardly identify factor pairs. Factor pairs also allow students to understand the difference between prime and composite numbers.

Try It! *Perform the Try It! activity on the next page.*

Objective

Identify the factors and factor pairs of a number.

Skills

- Identifying factors
- Representing numbers
- Identifying patterns

NCTM Expectations

Number and Operations
- Understand various meanings of multiplication and division.
- Understand the effects of multiplying and dividing whole numbers.
- Develop fluency in adding, subtracting, multiplying, and dividing whole numbers.

Talk About It

Discuss the Try It! activity.

- **Ask:** *Why do we call the sets of numbers we found the "factor pairs" of 10? What do all the pairs have in common?*

- **Ask:** *How many factor pairs are there for 9? How many are there for 7?* Explain that 7 is a prime number whose only factors are 1 and itself. **Ask:** *Will all prime numbers have only one factor pair? Why?*

- **Ask:** *What if you put two orange Cuisenaire® Rods together? What number would you have then?* Have students use Rods to find the new number. **Ask:** *What factor pair of 20 does the train of two orange Rods show?*

Solve It

With students, reread the problem. Have students use Rods to model the factor pairs for 10. They should then write a sentence telling who was correct, Lisa or Adrienne, and how they used Rods to find the answer.

More Ideas

For other ways to teach about identifying the factors of a number—

- Have students use a complete set of Cuisenaire® Rods, or two sets combined, to model factor pairs of larger numbers. For example, ask students to use Rods to model the number 18 showing two different factor pairs.

- Write the following numbers on the board: 25, 36, 50, and 63. Ask groups of students to work together to make arrays for each number using Color Tiles. Students should discover that the number of rows and the number of columns in the array represent a factor pair for the product shown.

Standardized Practice

Have students try the following problem.

Which of the following are factors of 40?

A. 3 and 15   **B.** 4 and 10   **C.** 8 and 6   **D.** 7 and 7

Try It! 30 minutes | Groups of 6

Here is a problem about identifying factor pairs.

Mr. Robinson's fourth-grade class is using Cuisenaire® Rods to show the factors of different numbers. Lisa says that the number 10 has one pair of factors. Adrienne says that the number 10 has two pairs of factors. Who is correct?

Introduce the problem. Then have students do the activity to solve the problem. Distribute Rods and Factor Pairs Worksheets (BLM 4) to students. Tell students that each Rod corresponds to a number from 1 to 10 and they can find the number a Rod represents by counting how many white Rods make up the larger Rod.

Materials
- Cuisenaire® Rods (1 set per group)
- Factor Pairs Worksheet (BLM 4; 1 per group)
- crayons or pencils (several per group)

1. Instruct students to find the orange Rod.
Ask: *What number does the orange Rod show?*
Students should use white Rods to measure, if necessary. Then have students make a train the same size using Rods of only one color.

2. Ask: *What size Rod did you use? How many Rods did you use?* Tell students that these two numbers represent a factor pair for the number 10. Students should transfer their trains to the worksheet.

3. Ask students to find another factor pair for 10 and model it two different ways using Rods. Students should write the factor pairs and draw the Rod trains on the Factor Pairs Worksheet. Repeat with other values.

⚠ Look Out!

Some students may make trains out of different colors of Rods. Emphasize that trains of Rods must be made of only one color to show multiplication. If trains are made up of more than one color, they show addition, not multiplication. Reinforce that two factors must be multiplied to equal the target product.

Number and Operations

Exploring Division

Exploring ideas visually and kinesthetically helps students learn new concepts. When students reach grade 3, the emphasis on operations switches from addition and subtraction to multiplication and division. Using concrete models to solve division problems allows students to see the meaning of the different parts of the division problem and how the numbers are tied together.

> **Try It!** Perform the Try It! activity on the next page.

Talk About It

Discuss the Try It! activity.

- **Ask:** *How many groups of Two-Color Counters did you get when you divided 24 into equal groups of 4? How many groups were there when you divided 24 counters into equal groups of 8?*

- **Ask:** *What do you notice about the division sentences you wrote when you divided 24 into equal groups of 2 and equal groups of 12? How can you use what you know about multiplication to help you solve a division problem?*

- **Ask:** *Will you always have equal parts when you divide something? Why or why not?*

Solve It

With students, reread the problem. Have students write about how they can use what they know about arrays and multiplication to solve division problems.

More Ideas

For other ways to teach about exploring division—

- Sort Centimeter Cubes and paper cups into evenly divisible groups for a variety of division problems. Present a problem to students, such as *21 divided into equal groups of 3.* Then have students model the problem by placing the correct number of cubes into each cup.

- Have students work in pairs using Color Tiles. One student will make an array using the tiles, and the other student must come up with a multiplication sentence and a division sentence that matches the array. Students take turns creating arrays and multiplication and division sentences.

Standardized Practice

Have students try the following problem.

Which grouping of tally marks shows 24 ÷ 3?

A. |||||||| |||||||| ||||||||

B. ||| ||| ||| ||| ||| |||

C. |||||||| |||||||| ||||||||

D. ||| ||| ||| ||| ||| ||| ||| ||| |||

Objective

Explore the meaning of division.

Skills

- Dividing
- Counting
- Representing numbers

NCTM Expectations

Number and Operations
- Understand various meanings of multiplication and division.
- Understand the effects of multiplying and dividing whole numbers.
- Identify and use relationships between operations, such as division as the inverse of multiplication, to solve problems.
- Develop fluency in adding, subtracting, multiplying, and dividing whole numbers.

Try It! 30 minutes | Pairs

Here is a problem about exploring division.

There are 24 students in Mrs. Lopez's class. Mrs. Lopez divided the class into groups of 4 students. How many groups are there?

Introduce the problem. Then have students do the activity to solve the problem. Pass out Two-Color Counters and Division Recording Sheets (BLM 5) to students.

Materials
- Two-Color Counters (24 per pair)
- Division Recording Sheet (BLM 5; 1 per student)
- paper (1 sheet per student)
- pencils (1 per student)

1. Say: *We are going to divide our counters into equal groups of 4.* Tell students that this is one way to show 24 divided into equal groups of 4. **Ask:** *What division sentence are we modeling?*

2. Have students use their groups to construct an array to show the product of 6 and 4. **Ask:** *What multiplication sentence is displayed?* Have students fill out the Division Recording Sheet, using counters to assist them.

⚠ Look Out!

If students have difficulty using arrays to perform division, you may wish to show them a multiplication array. Point out that they need 4 columns, and they have 24 counters to use up. Have students put 1 counter in each column, adding rows until the counters have all been used. Also, watch for students who can divide using paper and pencil but cannot display the operation using manipulatives. This may indicate that the student lacks number sense and is relying on the memorization of facts.

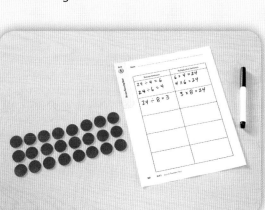

3. Have students use arrays of counters to model the other ways of dividing 24 into equal groups. They should write a division and multiplication sentence for the models they built on the recording sheet.

L E S S O N

12

Objective

Solve division problems with
one-digit divisors, with and
without remainders, using
Base Ten Blocks.

Skills

- Counting
- Dividing
- Representing numbers

NCTM Expectations

Number and Operations
- Understand the place-value
  structure of the base-ten
  number system and be able
  to represent and compare
  whole numbers and decimals.
- Understand various meanings
  of multiplication and division.
- Understand the effects of
  multiplying and dividing
  whole numbers.

Number and Operations

Dividing With One-Digit Divisors

Once students have a basic understanding of division concepts such as "equal
shares," they can move on to more complex division problems, including those
with remainders. Students should be introduced to the idea of remainders
through hands-on exploration and real-life situations.

> **Try It!** *Perform the Try It! activity on the next page.*

Talk About It

Discuss the Try It! activity.

- **Ask:** *Why was it necessary to trade in a Base Ten Block rod for units in order
  to complete the division problems?*
- **Ask:** *When you divided 67 by 5, why were there 2 units left over?* Explain
  that these leftover units are called a *remainder.* **Ask:** *Why do you think
  leftover numbers are called "remainders"? Why did we have a remainder
  in the second problem but not in the first?*
- **Say:** *Suppose we wanted to divide 125 by 5.* **Ask:** *What blocks would we
  use? Would we have to exchange any of them while solving the problem?*

Solve It

With students, reread the problem. Have students write a short explanation
of what answer they found and why it did or did not include a remainder.

More Ideas

For other ways to teach about dividing with one-digit divisors—

- Have partners make arrays with Color Tiles. For example, tell students to
  make an array with 8 rows using 24 tiles. Ask them to find how many tiles
  are in each row and then write a division sentence to tell about the array.
- Give pairs of students 20 index cards, and have them write the divisors 2–9 on
  8 of the cards and random numbers between 20 and 100 on the remaining
  cards. Direct students to take turns selecting one card from each pile to make
  a division problem and use Centimeter Cubes to solve the problems.

Standardized Practice

Have students try the following problem.

*There were 42 hot dogs left after the baseball game. The 4 people selling hot
dogs divided them up to take home. Each took 10 home. How many hot dogs
were left over?*

A. 2   **B.** 3   **C.** 4   **D.** 1

Try It! 30 minutes | Groups of 4

Here is a problem about dividing with one-digit divisors.

There are 52 students in each lunch period at Whittier Elementary School. The students are divided evenly between 4 large lunch tables. How many students eat lunch at each table?

Introduce the problem. Then have students do the activity to solve the problem. Distribute Base Ten Blocks to students.

Materials
- Base Ten Blocks (20 units and 10 rods per group)

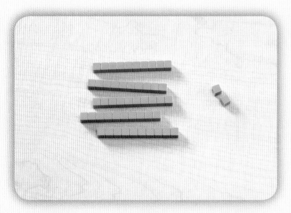

1. Have students use blocks to build the number 52.

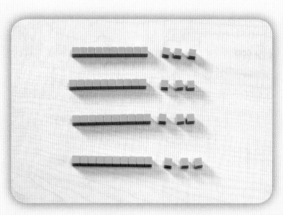

2. Say: *Divide these into 4 equal groups to represent the students at each lunch table.* Direct students to divide up the rods first. Students should discover that they must exchange the fifth rod for 10 units, and divide the total of 12 units evenly. Have students write down the number of students who eat at each table.

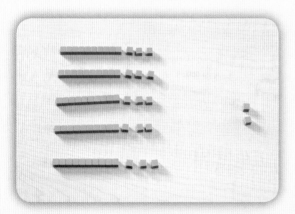

3. Ask: *What if there were 67 students divided evenly among 5 tables in the lunchroom?* Direct students to use the same strategy to divide 67 by 5.

⚠ Look Out!

Students may not include the remainder in their solution to a problem. **Say:** *If you have 4 groups of 10, you have 40. If you have 4 groups of 10 with a remainder of 1, you have 41. It is important to always include the remainder in your final answer to a problem.* As students work with blocks to solve division problems, remind them to keep the remainder blocks near the other groups of blocks so they don't forget to include them. Also, encourage students to check their division by performing the related multiplication operation. This will help them understand the connection between multiplication and division.

Number and Operations

Dividing With Two-Digit Divisors

Dividing larger numbers with a two-digit divisor is most often done using a tool such as an algorithm or a calculator. Before students can use these tools, they need to observe how a number is divided visually. Otherwise, the process is too abstract for students to understand due to the size of the numbers involved.

Try It! *Perform the Try It! activity on the next page.*

Objective

Divide by a two-digit number.

Skills

- Dividing
- Counting
- Problem solving

NCTM Expectations

Number and Operations
- Understand various meanings of multiplication and division.
- Understand the effects of multiplying and dividing whole numbers.

Talk About It

Discuss the Try It! activity.

- **Ask:** *How many Centimeter Cubes and index cards would you need if you wanted to divide 78 by 15? How do you know?*

- Have groups compare their answers. **Ask:** *Did you end up with a remainder? How can you tell? Is it possible to have a remainder when you divide by a two-digit number?*

- Direct students to look at the division sentence they wrote. **Ask:** *Which number did you show using cubes? Which number did you show using index cards?*

Solve It

With students, reread the problem. Have students draw a picture showing how the cherries in the bowl were divided up, then write the corresponding division sentence under the picture.

More Ideas

For other ways to teach about dividing by a two-digit number—

- Have students use Two-Color Counters as units for the dividend in a division problem with a two-digit divisor. Students should begin with all counters flipped to the same color side. As they begin to divide the units into groups, they can flip the counters over to help keep track of which counters still need to be grouped.

- Have students practice writing word problems involving division. Then invite students to partner up and solve each other's division problems using Base Ten Blocks.

Standardized Practice

Have students try the following problem.

The Science Club earned 42 Fun Fair tickets for planting flowers around the school. There are 14 students in the club. How many tickets will each student get?

A. 3   **B.** 4   **C.** 5   **D.** 6

Try It! 25 minutes | Groups of 4

Here is a problem about dividing by a two-digit number.

There are 13 students in the dance club that meets after school. The end of the school year is tomorrow, so Juan brought in a large bowl of cherries to share with the other students in the club. The bowl has 52 cherries in it. How many cherries will each student get?

Introduce the problem. Then have students do the activity to solve the problem. Distribute Centimeter Cubes and index cards to groups of students.

Materials
- Centimeter Cubes (60 per group)
- index cards (13 per group)

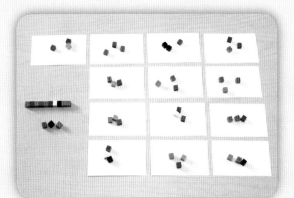

1. Say: *You need to divide 52 by 13.* Have students count out 52 cubes. Tell students that it may be easier to count out the cubes by placing them in groups of 10.

2. Direct students to place their 13 index cards on the desk or table so that all are visible and there is space between them. Have students divide the 52 cubes evenly, placing them on the 13 index cards until all the cubes are gone.

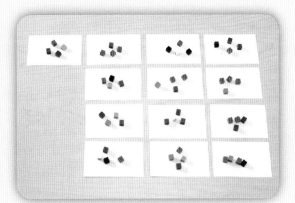

3. Tell students to count the cubes on each index card. **Ask:** *How can you show what you just did as a division sentence?* Help students write the division sentence 52 ÷ 13 = 4.

⚠ Look Out!

Watch for students who confuse two-digit dividends and divisors. Help students stress key words. For example, remind students that they want to divide 52 *by* 13, so they should separate 52 cubes into 13 groups.

Number and Operations

Divide by Multiples of 10

Once students have explored division by multiples of 10 visually, they can learn the process of solving the algorithm through simplifying. This idea, however, is too abstract without a student being able to see the division process modeled in a concrete way. It is important for students to experience the concept before moving to paper and pencil. In this lesson, students will use Base Ten Blocks to solve division problems with multiples of 10.

> **Try It!** *Perform the Try It! activity on the next page.*

Objective

Divide by multiples of 10.

Skills

- Dividing
- Counting
- Representing numbers

NCTM Expectations

Number and Operations
- Understand various meanings of multiplication and division.
- Understand the effects of multiplying and dividing whole numbers.

Talk About It

Discuss the Try It! activity.

- **Ask:** *How many groups of Base Ten Block rods and units did you make for the first problem, 22 ÷ 2? How many rods and units were in each group?*

- **Ask:** *How many groups did you make for the second problem, 220 ÷ 20? How many were in each group?*

- **Ask:** *What do you multiply 22 by to get 220? What do you multiply 2 by to get 20? Tell students that these numbers are called multiples of 10.*

- **Ask:** *Can you think of a rule to use when you are dividing and both numbers are multiples of 10? Does this rule make dividing big numbers easier? How?*

Solve It

With students, reread the problem. Have students write a sentence telling how they solved the problem and draw a picture to show the number of rows in the auditorium.

More Ideas

For other ways to teach about dividing by multiples of 10—

- Have students use Centimeter Cubes to model dividing by multiples of 10. Give groups 100–200 cubes and have them practice dividing the total by different multiples of 10, such as 20, 30, and 40. Remind students that it's okay to have a remainder.

- Write *100 ÷ 20, 150 ÷ 30, and 200 ÷ 40* on the board. Have students use Base Ten Blocks to solve the problems. For an extra challenge, have students work on problems with four-digit dividends, such as 1,200 ÷ 30; 1,500 ÷ 50; and so on.

Standardized Practice

Have students try the following problem.

Andy wants to give away his basketball cards to his friends. He has 10 friends and 200 cards. How many cards will each friend get?

A. 2   **B.** 10   **C.** 12   **D.** 20

Try It! 20 minutes | Groups of 4

Here is a problem about dividing by multiples of 10.

An auditorium in the school holds 220 people in all. Each row has 20 seats. How many rows are there in all?

Introduce the problem. Then have students do the activity to solve the problem. Distribute Base Ten Blocks to groups of students. Write the division sentences 22 ÷ 2 and 220 ÷ 20 on the board. Students should notice that the numbers in the problems are similar except for the number of zeros they contain. Remind students of the pattern they see when multiplying 22 × 1, 22 × 10, 22 × 100, and so on.

Materials
• Base Ten Blocks (2 flats, 30 rods, and 30 units per group)

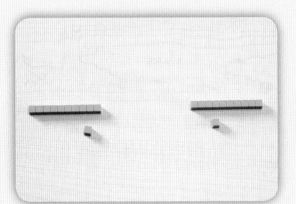

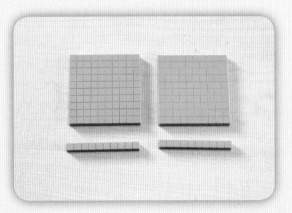

1. Say: *First, let's divide 22 by 2.* Have students use 2 rods and 2 units to model 22. Then have them divide the blocks into 2 equal groups. Write the answer, 11, on the board.

2. Now have students use flats and rods to build 220. **Say:** *We need to divide 220 into 20 equal groups.* Students should exchange each flat for 10 rods and make 20 groups of 1 rod each. They should then exchange the remaining 2 rods for 20 units and place 1 unit with each rod.

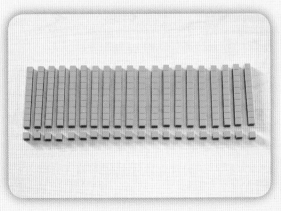

3. Write the answer for the second problem, 11, on the board. **Ask:** *What do you notice about the answers you got for the two problems?* Have students check their answers using multiplication.

⚠ Look Out!

Watch for students who count the number of rods as their answer instead of the number of groups. Have students go back and reread the question and check to see if their answer makes sense. Also, watch for students who conclude that they can remove common last digits in all division problems, thinking for example that 121 ÷ 11 is the same as 12 ÷ 1. Have students work out problems like these to discover that they will get two different answers.

Number and Operations

Identify and Write Fractions

Students have explored fractions in earlier grades and by this time should understand that a fraction shows a part of a whole. Here, students begin to divide that whole into smaller pieces. Identifying and writing fractions in this lesson will lay the foundation for students' work identifying fractions as parts of sets and finding equivalent fractions.

Try It! *Perform the Try It! activity on the next page.*

Talk About It

Discuss the Try It! activity.

- **Ask:** *What does the bottom number, or denominator, mean in our fraction? What about the top number?*

- **Say:** *We use fractions to show a part or parts of a whole.* **Ask:** *Do you think it is important that all the parts of a fraction—like all 6 parts in the circle—are equal? Why or why not?*

- **Ask:** *What other fractions could you show using the sixths fraction circle? How would you show one whole using the sixths fraction circle?*

Solve It

With students, reread the problem. Have students trace the 6 parts of the circle onto white paper. Then have them label 2 pieces of the circle to show the slices of pizza William ate. Below the picture, they should write $\frac{2}{6}$.

More Ideas

For other ways to teach about identifying and writing fractions—

- Use Pattern Blocks to help build fraction sense. For example, have students select a hexagon and several triangles. Ask students to cover the hexagon with triangles. Then ask students to show $\frac{1}{6}$ of the hexagon using the triangles, then $\frac{2}{6}$, and so on. Repeat with the trapezoid.

- Have students use Fraction Circles to create their own fraction models. Have students trace a whole circle, then use smaller pieces to trace within the circle, dividing it into equal parts. Students should then color some of the pieces to show a fraction of their choice.

- Have students use geoboards to show fractions. Students should create a rectangle or square, then divide it evenly using other rubber bands.

Standardized Practice

Have students try the following problem.

What fraction of the circle is shaded?

A. $\frac{3}{5}$ **B.** $\frac{2}{5}$ **C.** $\frac{2}{3}$ **D.** $\frac{1}{3}$

Objective

Identify and write fractions to name equal parts of regions (thirds, fourths, fifths, sixths, and eighths).

Skills

- Dividing
- Representing rational numbers
- Problem solving

NCTM Expectations

Number and Operations
- Develop understanding of fractions as parts of unit wholes, as parts of a collection, as locations on number lines, and as divisions of whole numbers.
- Use models, benchmarks, and equivalent forms to judge the size of fractions.

Try It! 25 minutes | Groups of 4

Here is a problem about identifying and writing fractions.

William's class had a pizza party on the last day of school. One of the pizzas was divided into 6 pieces. William ate 2 of the pieces. What fraction of the pizza did William eat?

Introduce the problem. Then have students do the activity to solve the problem. Pass out Fraction Circles, paper, and pencils to groups of students.

Materials
- Fraction Circles (1 set per group)
- paper (1 sheet per group)
- pencils (1 per group)

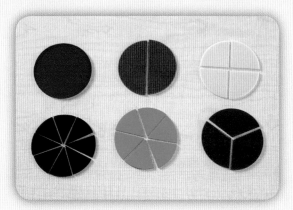

1. Say: *In the problem above, the pizza is divided into 6 pieces. Find the circle that is divided into 6 sections, or "sixths."* Have students look at the various circles and select the one that is divided into 6 sections.

2. Have students count the number of pieces in the fraction and write it on their paper. **Say:** *This number will become the denominator, or the bottom number of our fraction.*

⚠ Look Out!

Watch for students who mistakenly think they are "taking away" pieces of the circles. Have students trace the circles onto paper and color 4 of the pieces blue and 2 of the pieces yellow to represent $\frac{2}{6}$.

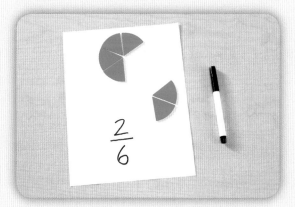

3. Ask students to find 2 slices of the sixths fraction circle to show the 2 slices of pizza that William ate. **Say:** *This will become the numerator, or the top number of our fraction.* Instruct students to draw a line over the 6 on their paper and write a 2 on top of it.

Number and Operations

Fractional Parts

Understanding fractional parts is the springboard to understanding decimals and percents. Students will use their knowledge of fractional parts when they begin to deal with money and when they organize and interpret data. In this lesson, students use Two-Color Counters to identify and represent fractions as parts of sets. Students also begin to see that when fractional parts are added together, they equal a whole set or one of something.

Objective

Identify fractions as parts of sets.

Skills

- Representing rational numbers
- Counting
- Dividing

NCTM Expectations

Number and Operations

- Develop understanding of fractions as parts of unit wholes, as parts of a collection, as locations on number lines, and as divisions of whole numbers.
- Use models, benchmarks, and equivalent forms to judge the size of fractions.

Try It! *Perform the Try It! activity on the next page.*

Talk About It

Discuss the Try It! activity.

- Review the terms *numerator* and *denominator* with students and have them identify the numerators and denominators in a few example fractions. **Ask:** *How did you determine the denominator of your fraction?*

- **Ask:** *When you flipped over 2 counters, what fraction did the red counters show? What fraction was shown by the remaining yellow counters?*

- **Say:** *Your counters show that 2 fractions can make up a whole or a set. In this case, $\frac{2}{6}$ and $\frac{4}{6}$ make up a set.* **Ask:** *Can you think of when it might be useful to show what 2 fractions make up a set?*

Solve It

With students, reread the problem. Have students draw a picture to show the total number of games played and the number won by each team. Then ask students to label the picture by writing the fractions in numeric form.

More Ideas

For other ways to teach about identifying fractions as parts of sets—

- Have groups of students build a family, or set, of 8 Three Bear Family® Counters of various sizes and colors. Then have students identify several fractions, such as the fraction of Bears that are blue or the fraction that are Baby Bear™ Counters.

- Students can use geoboards to identify fractions as parts of sets. Have students work in small groups to count the pegs to find the total number in the set. Then one student can mark off a number of pegs with a rubber band. The rest of the group should identify the fraction of pegs inside the rubber band and the fraction outside it.

Standardized Practice

Have students try the following problem.

There are 6 boys and 4 girls on the basketball team. What fraction of the team is boys?

A. $\frac{6}{10}$ B. $\frac{4}{6}$ C. $\frac{5}{8}$ D. $\frac{10}{4}$

Try It! 25 minutes | Pairs

Here is a problem about identifying fractional parts.

Students played dodgeball last Tuesday in gym class. They were divided into 2 teams: a red team and a yellow team. During class, they played 6 games. The red team won 2. What fraction of the games did the red team win?

Introduce the problem. Then have students do the activity to solve the problem. Give students Two-Color Counters, paper, and a pencil.

Materials
- Two-Color Counters (10 per pair)
- paper (2 sheets per pair)
- pencils (1 per pair)

1. Say: *Count out 6 counters.* Explain that the 6 counters represent the total number of games played, which is the "whole" or "set." Make sure students begin with all counters flipped yellow-side up.

2. Ask: *How can we show 2 out of 6?* Direct students to flip over 2 of the counters. **Say:** *We still have 6 counters, but now 2 of them are red.* Guide students to see that the 6 counters still represent the total number of games, and the 2 red counters represent the 2 games out of 6 that the red team won. Introduce the terms *numerator* and *denominator* and help students write the fraction $\frac{2}{6}$ as a number. Challenge students to find a fraction to show how many games the yellow team won, and write it as a number.

3. Have students use the counters to create a set of 8 and then flip them to find different fractional parts of that set, such as $\frac{2}{8}$ and $\frac{6}{8}$ or $\frac{5}{8}$ and $\frac{3}{8}$. Have students write each fraction they find in number form.

⚠ Look Out!

Watch for students who confuse regional fractions with set fractions. Have students think of how a six-pack of soda is a whole or set. Explain that the six-pack is "1 whole" and that students would count the cans of soda to find part of the whole, such as 2 cans out of 6 cans in the whole set.

Number and Operations

Equivalent Fractions

When students look at equivalent fractions in written form, such as $\frac{1}{2}, \frac{2}{4}, \frac{3}{6}$, it is hard for them to understand that they are looking at the same fraction. When students divide an object several ways, they can see that the overall size of the object does not change—it just has a different number of equal-sized units.

Try It! *Perform the Try It! activity on the next page.*

Talk About It

Discuss the Try It! activity.

■ **Ask:** *What fraction was left when you took away 3 pieces from the Fraction Circle made of 6 equal parts?*

■ Explain to students that the fractions they made that cover the same part of the circle are called *equivalent fractions*. **Ask:** *What were some equivalent fractions for $\frac{3}{6}$?* Make sure students are able to list $\frac{1}{2}, \frac{2}{4}$, and $\frac{4}{8}$. **Say:** *"Equivalent" means "same" or "equal."* **Ask:** *How do you know that the fractions you found are equivalent?*

■ **Ask:** *What fraction did you have when you removed 1 piece of the circle made of 3 equal parts? What equivalent fractions did you find for $\frac{2}{3}$?*

■ **Ask:** *Can you think of a situation in which you might want to know fractions that are equivalent to one another?*

Solve It

With students, reread the problem. Have students trace the circle pieces to show the different equivalents for $\frac{3}{6}$. Ask them to label each drawing with the fraction shown, drawing an equal sign between each equivalent fraction.

More Ideas

For other ways to teach about equivalent fractions—

■ Have students use Fraction Tower® Equivalency Cubes to make equivalent fractions. Give students a problem such as: *Sue had a granola bar. She divided it into 5 equal parts and ate 2 of them. Use Cubes to show the fraction of granola bar that was left. Then find 1 equivalent fraction.*

■ Have students work in groups using geoboards to find other ways to make equivalent fractions. Ask students to show a fraction on the geoboard, and then ask them to find an equivalent fraction.

Standardized Practice

Have students try the following problem.

Mrs. Daniel cut a pizza into 8 slices. The students ate 4 slices. The fractional part of the remaining pizza is $\frac{4}{8}$. Which fraction below means the same as $\frac{4}{8}$?

A. $\frac{2}{8}$ B. $\frac{1}{2}$ C. $\frac{4}{4}$ D. $\frac{8}{4}$

Try It!   25 minutes | Groups of 4

Here is a problem about equivalent fractions.

It is Darnell's birthday, so his mother brought a birthday cake to his after-school class for him to share with his friends. The cake was cut into 6 equal slices. If Darnell and his friends ate 3 of the 6 slices, what fraction of the cake was left over?

Introduce the problem. Then have students do the activity to solve the problem. Pass out a set of Fraction Circles to each group.

Materials
- Fraction Circles (1 set per group)

1. Have students assemble all of the circles in the set and explore how each circle is divided into different numbers and sizes of pieces.
Say: *Find the fraction pieces that make a circle out of 6 equal parts.* Make sure students use sixths to make a circle. Explain that the 6 pieces match the 6 equal pieces of the cake in the problem, and that combined, the 6 equal pieces make up 1 whole.

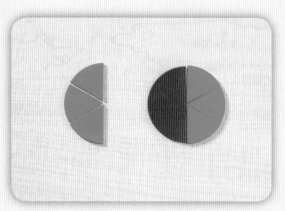

2. Say: *Let's take away the 3 pieces eaten by the kids.* **Ask:** *What is the fraction of the circle that is left? Can we use any other fractional parts to cover the $\frac{3}{6}$ that is left to make another fraction that means the same thing?* Students should find the equivalent fractions $\frac{1}{2}$, $\frac{2}{4}$, and $\frac{4}{8}$.

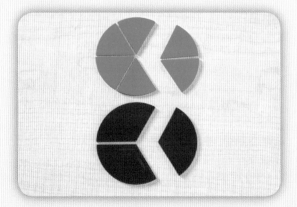

3. Have students create other equivalent fractions using circles. **Say:** *A pie is divided into 3 slices. One slice is removed. What fraction of the pie is left?* Then have students build models to show $\frac{2}{3}$ and then $\frac{4}{6}$.

⚠ Look Out!

Stress that when finding equivalent fractions, students need to use the same size of the fractional parts. Watch for students who try to put together $\frac{1}{3}$ and $\frac{1}{6}$ to show $\frac{1}{2}$. Although these two fractions added together equal $\frac{1}{2}$, they are not creating an equivalent fraction for $\frac{1}{2}$. Stress the one-to-one correspondence of equivalent fractions: $\frac{1}{2} = \frac{3}{6}$. Although $\frac{1}{3} + \frac{1}{6} = \frac{1}{2}$ is true, it is an addition sentence, not a set of equivalent fractions.

18

Comparing and Ordering Fractions

When students begin to compare and order fractions, they need to develop benchmarks in their mind to draw upon. It helps if they are able to create mental number lines on which to place these reference points. Often they use $\frac{1}{2}$ as a comparison to other fractions, asking themselves whether the other fraction is more or less than $\frac{1}{2}$.

Try It! *Perform the Try It! activity on the next page.*

Objective

Compare and order fractions.

Skills

- Comparing
- Ordering numbers
- Representing numbers

NCTM Expectations

Number and Operations
- Use models, benchmarks, and equivalent forms to judge the size of fractions.
- Recognize and generate equivalent forms of commonly used fractions, decimals, and percents.

Talk About It

Discuss the Try It! activity.

- **Ask:** *When two fractions have the same denominator, how can you tell which fraction is larger?* Guide students to understand that if fractions have the same denominator, the fraction with the larger numerator will be greatest.

- **Ask:** *Which fraction was larger, $\frac{1}{5}$ or $\frac{1}{6}$? What guess can you make about other fractions that have the same numerator but different denominators?* Help students understand that when fractions have the same numerator, the one with the smaller denominator will always be the larger of the two.

Solve It

With students, reread the problem. Have students draw a picture of a snack bar and divide it to show the sizes of the pieces eaten by Kari, Eva, and Nai. Ask students to label each piece with its numeric fraction and the name of the student who ate it. Then have students explain in writing who ate the largest piece of the snack bar and who ate the smallest.

More Ideas

For other ways to teach about comparing and ordering fractions—

- Have students work in groups and use Fraction Circles. Give students a list of fractions to compare and order, and have them use the circles to model.

- Have students play a game using Fraction Tower® Equivalency Cubes. One student will list two fractions. The other will try to guess which is larger. Then students will build the fractions using Cubes to find out if the guess was correct.

Standardized Practice

Have students try the following problem.

Which fraction is the largest?

A. $\frac{1}{3}$　　B. $\frac{1}{4}$　　C. $\frac{1}{5}$　　D. $\frac{1}{6}$

Try It! 30 minutes | Groups of 4

Here is a problem about comparing and ordering fractions.

Kari brought a snack bar to share with two friends, Eva and Nai. Kari ate $\frac{1}{3}$ of the snack bar, Eva ate $\frac{6}{12}$, and Nai ate $\frac{1}{6}$. Who ate the largest piece of the snack bar? Who ate the smallest?

Introduce the problem. Then have students do the activity to solve the problem. Pass out a set of Fraction Tower® Equivalency Cubes to each group of students.

Materials
- Fraction Tower® Equivalency Cubes (1 set per group)

1. Write *Kari: $\frac{1}{3}$, Eva: $\frac{6}{12}$,* and *Nai: $\frac{1}{6}$* on the board. **Say:** *We are going to use the Cubes to compare these fractions.* Have students build $\frac{1}{3}$, $\frac{6}{12}$, and $\frac{1}{6}$ with the Cubes.

2. Say: *Compare the sizes of these three fractions.* **Ask:** *Which is largest? Which is smallest? Which is in between?* Have students order the fractions left to right, from largest to smallest.

⚠ Look Out!

Watch for the student who thinks that because a fraction has a bigger numerator, it is the largest. You can use the example $\frac{1}{2}$ and $\frac{4}{12}$ to illustrate that this is not always the case. Explain that finding the greater numerator works only when the denominators are the same.

3. Now have students compare and order other fractions. **Ask:** *What if Kari ate $\frac{3}{10}$, Eva ate $\frac{1}{5}$, and Nai ate $\frac{2}{4}$ of the snack bar?* Have students use the Cubes to compare and order the three new fractions from left to right, greatest to least.

19

Number and Operations

Mixed Numbers

Mixed numbers show how whole numbers and rational numbers can be stated together to represent amounts greater than 1. Students need to understand how improper fractions can be converted to a mixed number to more easily show whole and fractional parts. This will help students begin to create a mental number line in which they can see that a mixed number falls between two whole numbers.

Try It! *Perform the Try It! activity on the next page.*

Talk About It

Discuss the Try It! activity.

- **Ask:** *What is a mixed number?* Review with students that a mixed number is a whole number combined with a fraction.

- **Ask:** *Is $\frac{7}{6}$ a mixed number?* Review with students that an improper fraction is one with a numerator that is greater than its denominator, such as $\frac{7}{6}$. **Ask:** *How would we show $\frac{7}{6}$ as a mixed number?*

- **Ask:** *Where would the mixed number $1\frac{1}{6}$ fall on a number line?* Guide students to understand that $1\frac{1}{6}$ would fall between 1 and 2.

Solve It

With students, reread the problem. Have students trace circles divided into sixths to represent the pizzas. Then have them convert $\frac{13}{6}$ to a mixed number to find how many whole pizzas would be left.

More Ideas

For other ways to teach about mixed numbers—

- Continue the activity by providing several examples of improper fractions, and having pairs work together using Fraction Circles to identify the equivalent mixed number. Then provide several examples of mixed numbers, and have pairs find their equivalent improper fractions.

- Have students use Cuisenaire® Rods to investigate improper fractions and mixed numerals. Let the brown Rod have a value of 1. Direct students to build an equivalent train of white Rods below the brown one. Then have them place the blue Rod below. **Ask:** *What fractional part of 1 brown Rod is 1 blue Rod?* Repeat with other Rods.

Standardized Practice

Have students try the following problem.

Andrew had $\frac{3}{4}$ of his candy bar left and Sue had $\frac{2}{4}$ of her candy bar left. How many whole candy bars could be made from the parts left over?

A. $\frac{5}{8}$ **B.** $1\frac{1}{4}$ **C.** $1\frac{2}{4}$ **D.** $1\frac{5}{6}$

Try It! 30 minutes | Groups of 4

Here is a problem about modeling, identifying, and writing mixed numbers.

Ana's class had a pizza party. Students bought 5 pizzas and each pizza was cut into 6 equal slices. After the party, there were 13 slices left. How many whole pizzas can be made with the leftover slices?

Introduce the problem. Then have students do the activity to solve the problem. Distribute Fraction Circles, paper, and pencils to students.

Materials
- Fraction Circles (1 set per group)
- paper (1 sheet per group)
- pencils (2 per group)

1. Say: _A mixed number is made up of a whole number and a fraction. Let's use the circles to show a mixed number._ Have students put together one whole circle with a fraction such as $\frac{2}{3}$. **Say:** _The circles show $1\frac{2}{3}$. This is a mixed number._

2. Say: _Suppose you had 3 circles, and all the circles were divided into sixths, like the pizzas in the problem. Then you took away all except for 11 pieces. Use circles to show the pieces that are left._ Have students trace 3 circles onto paper, each circle divided into sixths, and shade 11 pieces.

⚠ Look Out!

Watch for students who struggle with converting improper fractions to mixed numerals. Assist these students by showing $2\frac{1}{6}$ as an addition problem: $2 + \frac{1}{6}$.

3. Say: _Now count the sixths that are shaded._ Students should count 11 sixths. Explain that this number can be expressed as $\frac{11}{6}$ and that it is called an _improper fraction_ because the numerator is larger than the denominator. Then have students count the number of shaded whole circles and the number of shaded sixths to find the mixed number $1\frac{5}{6}$.

Number and Operations

Add and Subtract Fractions

Students will need to add and subtract fractions when they begin working with measurements. Sometimes the fractions will have like denominators and other times they will have unlike denominators. When dealing with unlike denominators, students need to draw upon knowledge of equivalent fractions to create like denominators.

Try It! *Perform the Try It! activity on the next page.*

Talk About It

Discuss the Try It! activity.

- **Ask:** *How do we add or subtract fractions when they have like denominators? What do we do when we see unlike denominators?*
- **Ask:** *Can we use subtraction to check our work when adding fractions? How do you know?*
- **Ask:** *When you add fractions will you always get a fraction?* Show students how they can get a whole number or mixed number.

Solve It

With students, reread the problem. Have students draw a rectangle to represent the mural. Then have them label the sections that the third and fourth graders will paint. Have students write a number sentence showing how to find the fraction of the mural that the third and fourth graders are painting altogether, and solve.

More Ideas

For other ways to teach about adding and subtracting fractions—

- Give students a problem that involves adding or subtracting fractions with like or unlike denominators. Students can use Fraction Circles to help them solve the problem.
- Have students grab eight random Color Tiles from a bag or box, then come up with a fraction to represent one of the colors of tiles, such as "$\frac{2}{8}$ of the tiles are red." Then have students use addition and subtraction to model the pile based on that color tile, for example, "$\frac{8}{8} - \frac{2}{8} = \frac{6}{8}$ of my group is not red." Challenge students to use addition to check their problems, for example, "$\frac{2}{8} + \frac{6}{8} = \frac{8}{8}$."

Standardized Practice

Have students try the following problem.

Tenysha has $\frac{1}{6}$ of her muffin left. Anna has $\frac{3}{6}$ of her muffin left. Between the two of them, what fraction of a muffin do they have?

A. $\frac{4}{12}$ B. $\frac{2}{6}$ C. $\frac{4}{6}$ D. $\frac{5}{6}$

Objective

Add and subtract fractions with like and unlike denominators.

Skills

- Adding rational numbers
- Subtracting rational numbers
- Representing rational numbers

NCTM Expectations

Number and Operations

- Use models, benchmarks, and equivalent forms to judge the size of fractions.
- Recognize and generate equivalent forms of commonly used fractions, decimals, and percents.
- Use visual models, benchmarks, and equivalent forms to add and subtract commonly used fractions and decimals.

Try It! 30 minutes | Groups of 4

Here is a problem about adding and subtracting fractions.

The third, fourth, and fifth graders at Liberty Elementary School are painting a mural to celebrate school spirit. The third graders will paint $\frac{1}{6}$ of it, and the fourth graders will paint $\frac{2}{6}$ of it. What fraction of the mural are the third and fourth graders painting altogether?

Introduce the problem. Then have students do the activity to solve the problem. Distribute Fraction Tower® Equivalency Cubes to students.

Materials
- Fraction Tower® Equivalency Cubes (1 set per group)

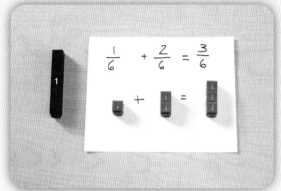

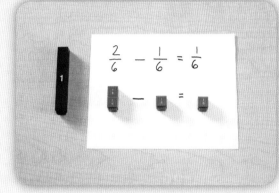

1. Write $\frac{1}{6} + \frac{2}{6}$ on the board. Have students model the problem with one $\frac{1}{6}$ Cube and a tower of two $\frac{1}{6}$ Cubes. Explain that when the denominator is the same, students should just add the numerators. Have students solve the problem using Cubes.

2. Ask: *How much more of the mural are the fourth graders painting?* Write $\frac{2}{6} - \frac{1}{6}$ on the board. Tell students that when the denominators are the same, they can just subtract the numerators. Have students solve the problem using Cubes.

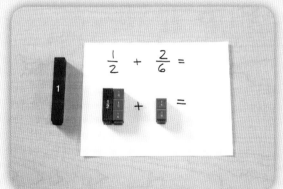

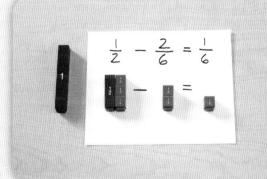

3. Say: *The fifth graders are painting $\frac{1}{2}$ of the mural.* **Ask:** *What fraction of the mural are the fourth and fifth graders painting altogether?* Write $\frac{1}{2} + \frac{2}{6}$ on the board. Ask students to model the fractions with Cubes. Explain that one or both denominators must be changed so that the denominators are alike. Have students substitute $\frac{3}{6}$ for $\frac{1}{2}$ and add to solve.

4. Say: *Now let's find how much more of the mural the fifth graders are painting than the fourth graders.* Write $\frac{1}{2} - \frac{2}{6}$ on the board. **Ask:** *Do we need to change one or both of the denominators?* Have students model $\frac{1}{2} - \frac{2}{6}$ with Cubes to see that they cannot subtract without finding a common denominator. Have students substitute $\frac{3}{6}$ for $\frac{1}{2}$ and subtract to solve.

Number and Operations

Fractions and Decimals

In this lesson, students will explore the relationship between fractions and decimals. Fundamental to this is the concept that decimals, like fractions, can be used to show a value that is part of one whole. This lays the foundation for students' exploration of equivalent fractions and decimals and their formation of a deeper understanding of the relationships between numbers.

Try It! *Perform the Try It! activity on the next page.*

Talk About It

Discuss the Try It! activity.

■ Draw a number line on the board and guide students to see that the fractions and decimals they are working with represent numbers that are less than 1. Draw students' attention to benchmark fractions such as $\frac{1}{4}$ and $\frac{1}{2}$ and their decimal equivalents.

■ Point out that when you talk about money, you are often using decimals. Remind students that there are 100 cents in a dollar. **Ask:** *How much of a dollar is $\frac{1}{2}$, or 0.5? How much is $\frac{1}{10}$, or 0.1? What about $\frac{1}{4}$, or 0.25?*

■ **Ask:** *What if someone had 75 cents? How could you show 75 cents as a decimal? How could you show it as a fraction?* Help students model 0.75 and $\frac{3}{4}$ using Fraction Tower® Equivalency Cubes and Base Ten Blocks.

Solve It

With students, reread the problem. Have students draw pictures or pie charts to represent the three fractions, and use the Cubes to label each with a fraction and decimal. Then have students write a paragraph to explain how they know which student brought in the correct amount of money.

More Ideas

For other ways to teach about relating fractions and decimals—

■ Use Fraction Circles to show a fraction to the class. Have students name the fraction and find the corresponding decimal on Fraction Tower Equivalency Cubes.

■ Have students work in pairs using the $\frac{1}{2}$, $\frac{1}{4}$, $\frac{1}{5}$, and $\frac{1}{10}$ Fraction Tower Equivalency Cubes and Base Ten Block flats, rods, and units. One student names a fraction that can be shown using Cubes. The student's partner uses Cubes to model the fraction. Students then work together to model the fraction's decimal equivalent using rods and units placed on top of the flat.

Standardized Practice

Have students try the following problem.

Mariah ate $\frac{1}{5}$ of her sandwich at lunch. What decimal shows the part of the sandwich she ate?

A. 0.2   **B.** 0.25   **C.** 0.4   **D.** 0.5

Objective

Relate fractions and decimals.

Skills

• Fractions
• Decimals
• Comparing values less than 1

NCTM Expectations

Number and Operations

• Develop understanding of fractions as parts of unit wholes, as parts of a collection, as locations on number lines, and as divisions of whole numbers.
• Use models, benchmarks, and equivalent forms to judge the size of fractions.
• Recognize and generate equivalent forms of commonly used fractions, decimals, and percents.

Try It! 20 minutes | Groups of 4

Here is a problem about relating fractions and decimals.

Miss Kott asked each student to bring in 0.25 of a dollar for a field trip. Greta brought in $\frac{1}{2}$ of a dollar, Dylan brought in $\frac{1}{10}$ of a dollar, and Jan brought in $\frac{1}{4}$ of a dollar. Who brought exactly the right amount?

Introduce the problem. Then have students do the activity to solve the problem. Distribute Fraction Tower® Equivalency Cubes and Base Ten Blocks to students. Explain that the hundred flat is one whole, and the rods and units are parts.

Materials
- Fraction Tower® Equivalency Cubes (1 set per group)
- Base Ten Blocks (1 flat, 5 rods, and 5 units per group)

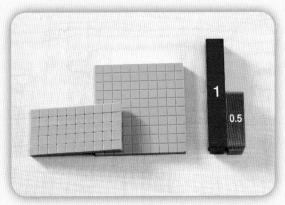

1. Have students compare the $\frac{1}{2}$ and one whole Cubes. Tell students to cover $\frac{1}{2}$ of the flat with rods. **Ask:** *How many parts out of 100 are covered?* $\left(\frac{50}{100}\right)$ **Say:** *We can show the number $\frac{1}{2}$ as $\frac{50}{100}$, 50 hundredths, or 0.50.* Have students rotate the Cube to show 0.5.

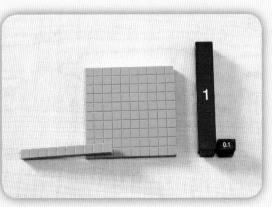

2. Ask: *Which Cube shows $\frac{1}{10}$?* Students should locate the purple $\frac{1}{10}$ Cube. **Say:** *$\frac{1}{10}$ is the same as $\frac{10}{100}$.* Use a rod to cover $\frac{10}{100}$ parts on the flat. Explain to students that this shows the decimal 0.10. Have them turn the Cube around to show 0.1.

3. Have students find the $\frac{1}{4}$ Cube. Then ask them to find how many squares of the flat they should cover to show $\frac{1}{4}$. **Say:** *$\frac{1}{4}$ is the same as $\frac{25}{100}$, or 25 hundredths. We can show this number as the decimal 0.25.* Have students model using blocks. Then have students rotate the Cube to show 0.25.

⚠ Look Out!

Students may expect that the digits in fraction and decimal equivalents will be the same (for example, $\frac{1}{2}$ should equal 0.1 or 0.2). Draw pie charts to show how 0.5 equals $\frac{5}{10}$ and $\frac{5}{10}$ equals $\frac{1}{2}$ to help students understand that decimals and fractions often use different numbers to express the same values.

Objective

Compare fractional and decimal equivalencies.

Skills

- Working with fractions
- Working with decimals
- Comparing fractions and decimals

NCTM Expectations

Number and Operations
- Develop understanding of fractions as parts of unit wholes, as parts of a collection, as locations on number lines, and as divisions of whole numbers.
- Use models, benchmarks, and equivalent forms to judge the size of fractions.
- Recognize and generate equivalent forms of commonly used fractions, decimals, and percents.

Number and Operations

Compare Fractions and Decimals

A central idea in the mathematical learning of students in grades 3–4 is equivalency. Students need to develop an understanding that the same amount can be represented in more than one way and be able to choose the most convenient representation to solve a particular problem. An effective way to help students make the connection between equivalent representations, such as fractions and decimals, is to teach these concepts simultaneously. Learning how to compare fractions and decimals will help students better understand fraction and decimal equivalencies.

Try It! Perform the Try It! activity on the next page.

Talk About It

Discuss the Try It! activity.

- **Ask:** *Which is more, 0.5 or $\frac{2}{5}$. How could you tell?*
- Write $\frac{3}{4}$, $\frac{1}{2}$, *0.75*, and *0.25* on the board. Have students model each using Fraction Tower® Equivalency Cubes. **Ask:** *Which two represent equivalent amounts? How can you tell?*
- **Say:** *Imagine that you found 80 cents on the way to school.* **Ask:** *What fraction of one dollar do you have? What decimal represents that amount?*

Solve It

With students, reread the problem. Then have students write a sentence summarizing how they were able to compare 0.5 and $\frac{2}{5}$ and explain whether or not Matthew had enough money to buy a postcard.

More Ideas

For other ways to teach about comparing fraction and decimal equivalencies—

- Tell students that 1 Base Ten Block flat represents one whole made up of 100 hundredths. Have students randomly select a handful of units and rods and determine what fraction of the flat they have selected. Then have them write the fraction and the decimal equivalent. For example, if a student selected 3 rods and 4 units, he or she would have $\frac{34}{100}$, or 0.34.
- Have students work with partners at a center. One student will show a fraction using Fraction Circles. The other partner will identify the fraction represented and use Fraction Tower® Equivalency Cubes to determine the decimal equivalent. Students will then switch roles.

Standardized Practice

Have students try the following problem.

Which is more, $\frac{7}{10}$ or 0.75?

Try It! 20 minutes | Groups of 4

Here is a problem about comparing fraction and decimal equivalencies.

Matthew has 50 cents to buy a postcard at the book fair. The librarian tells him that postcards cost $\frac{2}{5}$ of a dollar. Does Matthew have enough money to buy a postcard?

Introduce the problem. Then have students do the activity to solve the problem. Distribute Fraction Tower® Equivalency Cubes and Fraction Worksheets (BLM 6) to each group.

Materials
- Fraction Tower® Equivalency Cubes (1 set per group)
- Fraction Worksheet (BLM 6; 1 per group)
- colored pencils/crayons

1. Ask: *How would you show 50 cents as a decimal?* Remind students that there are 100 cents in a dollar, so 50 cents is $\frac{50}{100}$, or 0.50. Tell students that 0.50 is the same as 0.5. Have students find a Cube that shows 0.5 of one whole. Students should then trace the Cube onto the first blank one-whole Cube on the worksheet and write 0.5 on the first blank line.

2. Ask: *How can we find out if $\frac{2}{5}$ of a dollar is more than or less than 50 cents, or 0.5?* Have students find the one-fifth Cubes and use them to build $\frac{2}{5}$ of one whole. Students should then trace $\frac{2}{5}$ onto the second blank Cube on the worksheet. They should write $\frac{2}{5}$ on the second blank line below the Cubes and put the > sign between them.

⚠ Look Out!

Because $\frac{50}{100} = 0.50$, students may assume that $\frac{2}{5} = 0.20$. Explain that decimals always equate to tenths or hundredths, while the denominator of a fraction determines how many parts the fraction has in all. Finding equivalent fractions with 100 as the denominator may help students better understand converting fractions to decimals. For example, explain to students that the fraction $\frac{2}{5} = \frac{40}{100}$, or 0.40.

3. Have students compare another set of numbers including a fraction and a decimal, such as $\frac{1}{4}$ and 0.2. They should build each using Cubes and complete the third and fourth blank whole Cubes on the worksheet.

23

Number and Operations

Comparing Decimals

By this time, most third- and fourth-grade students are familiar with number lines and the representation of whole numbers. Students must expand this knowledge to include the representation and placement of decimals in relation to whole numbers. For students to understand the base-ten number system, they must have opportunities to use a variety of strategies to represent and learn about decimals.

Objective

Compare and order decimals.

Try It! *Perform the Try It! activity on the next page.*

Talk About It

Discuss the Try It! activity.

- **Ask:** *Which Base Ten Block did you use to show one whole in this activity?* Make sure students understand that the flat represents one whole. **Ask:** *What rods and units did you use to show 0.8? What about 0.67?*

- **Ask:** *Which is greater, 0.8 or 0.67? How do you know?*

- **Ask:** *When you put the decimals on the number line, is 0.8 to the right or to the left of 0.67? Why? If you were going to put the two decimals in order from greatest to least, which would you put first?*

Skills

- Comparing decimals
- Ordering decimals
- Representation of numbers less than 1

NCTM Expectations

Number and Operations
- Understand the place-value structure of the base-ten number system and be able to represent and compare whole numbers and decimals.
- Recognize and generate equivalent forms of commonly used fractions, decimals, and percents.

Solve It

With students, reread the problem. Have students write a sentence telling which is larger, 0.8 or 0.67, and ask them to explain how they know.

More Ideas

For other ways to teach about comparing and ordering decimals—

- Tell students that a Base Ten Block flat equals one whole, or $\frac{100}{100}$. Have pairs of students randomly select a handful of base ten rods and units and arrange them on the table. Then ask students to determine the decimal represented by each partner's selection, and write both decimals and < or > to compare them.

- Explain to struggling students that one Base Ten Block flat represents one whole. Then guide them to arrange a random number of base ten rods and units on top of a flat to show that the flat is a whole and the rods and units are parts of the whole. Explain that the amount selected is less than one whole flat and that decimals represent numbers that are less than 1. Assist students in writing the number as both a fraction and a decimal.

Standardized Practice

Have students try the following problem.

Which shows the numbers in order from least to greatest?

A. 0.9, 0.72, 0.61, 0.4   **C.** 0.4, 0.61, 0.72, 0.9
B. 0.4, 0.9, 0.61, 0.72   **D.** 0.61, 0.4, 0.72, 0.9

Try It! 20 minutes | Groups of 3

Here is a problem about comparing and ordering decimals.

Brandon is weighing rocks during science class. The first rock weighs 0.67 pounds. The second weighs 0.8 pounds. Which rock weighs more?

Introduce the problem. Then have students do the activity to solve the problem. Distribute Base Ten Blocks to students. Explain that a flat is equal to one whole, and that $1.0 = \frac{100}{100}$ and also $\frac{10}{10}$. Tell students that they will be comparing two decimals, 0.67 and 0.8, to see which is larger. Write the numbers on the board and label their place values.

Materials
- Base Ten Blocks (1 flat, 20 rods, and 20 units per group)
- paper (1 sheet per group)
- pencil (1 per group)
- index cards

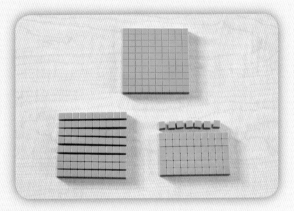

1. Instruct students to model 0.8 using base ten rods. Instruct students to model 0.67 beside their model of 0.8 using rods and units. Have students compare both numbers to the flat, which represents one whole.

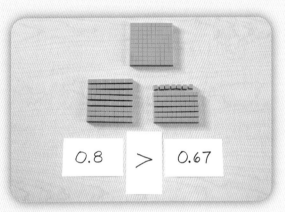

2. Instruct students to write 0.8 and 0.67. Tell them to write < or > between the numbers to show which decimal is greater. Tell students that they are deciding which represents more of the whole (flat), 0.8 or 0.67.

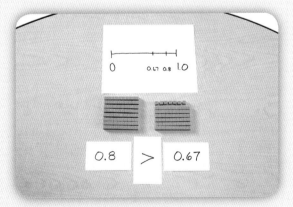

3. Have students draw a number line. Then have them locate and mark 0.8 and 0.67 on the number line. Repeat steps 1–3 using additional problems comparing and ordering decimals.

⚠ Look Out!

Students may believe that a decimal containing more digits is greater than a decimal with fewer digits. For example, they might think that 0.67 is greater than 0.8. For these students, emphasize the difference between the tenths and hundredths place. Add a 0 to the right of the final number in the decimal with fewer digits (for example, 0.8<u>0</u>). Then have students compare the decimals again.

Number and Operations

Add and Subtract Decimals

Students should be introduced to a variety of strategies for solving decimal problems, including models, pictures, estimation, and paper-and-pencil computing. The focus of adding and subtracting decimals should be on students' understanding of number sense and operations, rather than a specific computational process. Students use their knowledge of the base-ten number system to regroup decimals into whole numbers when adding.

Try It! *Perform the Try It! activity on the next page.*

Talk About It

Discuss the Try It! activity.

- Explain that the first place to the right of the decimal is "tenths." Write 1.2 on the board. **Ask:** *How do we read this number? How much is the 2 worth? How much is the 1 worth?*

- **Ask:** *In what situations would it be important to understand decimals? When might you need to add or subtract decimals?*

- **Ask:** *How are adding and subtracting decimals similar to adding and subtracting whole numbers? How are they different?*

Solve It

With students, reread the problem. Have students draw models of Makayla's two pieces of yarn and mark off each tenth. Then have students write a sentence to explain how they added the numbers together to get the total.

More Ideas

For other ways to teach about adding and subtracting decimals—

- Have students practice adding tenths using Two-Color Counters. Direct students to model two addends with the counters yellow-side up. As students count the tenths, they should flip the counters over to the red side and set them aside as a group every time they reach 10.

- Have students use a Place-Value Chart (BLM 2) and Centimeter Cubes to add decimals. Relabel the charts to show ones, tenths, and hundredths. Provide story problem scenarios, and have students model each addend on the chart. Tell students to model the sum in the bottom row of the chart, reminding them to regroup the tenths into whole ones if necessary.

Standardized Practice

Have students try the following problem.

Riana and Jake take turns feeding the class hamster. One week Jake gives the pet 0.7 cups of food, and the next week Riana gives him 0.8 cups of food. How much food in total did the hamster get during the two weeks?

A. 1.3 cups   **B.** 1.5 cups   **C.** 1.7 cups   **D.** 1.9 cups

Objective

Add and subtract decimals.

Skills

- Decimals
- Addition with regrouping
- Subtraction with regrouping

NCTM Expectations

Number and Operations
- Understand the place-value structure of the base-ten number system and be able to represent and compare whole numbers and decimals.
- Use visual models, benchmarks, and equivalent forms to add and subtract commonly used fractions and decimals.

Try It! 25 minutes | Pairs

Here is a problem about adding and subtracting decimals.

The art teacher, Mr. Davis, asked students to cut two different lengths of yarn to use in an art project. Makayla cut one piece of yarn that was 0.7 meters long and another that was 0.5 meters long. How much yarn did Makayla cut altogether?

Introduce the problem. Then have students do the activity to solve the problem. Distribute Base Ten Blocks to students.

Materials
- Base Ten Blocks (3 rods and 15 units per pair)

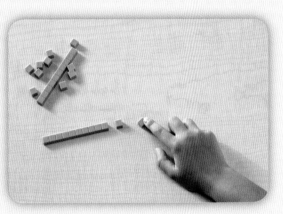

1. Say: *We want to add 0.7 and 0.5. Let's say that for this activity, a rod equals 1 and a unit equals 0.1.* Have students model 0.7 and 0.5 with the blocks.

2. Have students count the units. Then have students regroup the blocks to end up with 1 rod and 2 units. **Ask:** *What number do the blocks add up to?*

⚠ Look Out!

Watch out for students who express a sum greater than 1 in tenths or hundredths. Use Fraction Tower® Equivalency Cubes to reinforce the idea that a sum with 10 or more tenths must be regrouped into a whole number. For example, 0.5 + 0.9 = 1.4, not 0.14.

3. Ask: *What if we wanted to find the difference between 0.7 and 0.5?* Guide students to model 0.7 − 0.5 with the units. Remind them that they are using 1 rod to represent 1 whole.

Geometry

Geometry in the elementary grades allows students to learn about geometric shapes and structures and to analyze their characteristics and relationships. Spatial visualization is an important aspect of this learning. Through hands-on experiences, students learn to build and manipulate mental representations of geometric figures. These geometric skills and ideas are useful in determining area, identifying fractions, interpreting data, understanding algebra, and solving real-world problems.

Elementary-level geometry focuses on the properties of geometric figures and their relationship to one another. In Grades 3 and 4, the study of these properties becomes more abstract. At this level, students may use concrete objects to make generalizations about the properties of particular shapes. Problem-solving skills are encouraged through the use of visual and coordinate representations. At the intermediate level, this may mean using grids and arrays to solve multiplication problems.

The Grades 3 – 5 NCTM Standards for Geometry suggest that students should:

- Analyze characteristics and properties of two- and three-dimensional geometric shapes and develop mathematical arguments about geometric relationships
- Specify locations and describe spatial relationships using coordinate geometry and other representational systems
- Apply transformations and use symmetry to analyze mathematical situations
- Use visualization, spatial reasoning, and geometric modeling to solve problems

In Grades 3 and 4, students continue to use hands-on activities to develop a greater understanding of geometric principles. By sorting, modeling, drawing, measuring, and constructing geometric shapes, students at this level develop reasoning skills that allow them to make and justify conjectures about geometric relationships. Third- and fourth-grade students expand their vocabulary through discussion to more precisely identify and describe the properties of shapes. The following are activities involving manipulatives that third- and fourth-grade students can use to develop skills in **Geometry.**

Geometry

Contents

Objective

Identify and compare plane shapes.

Skills

- Analyzing characteristics of two-dimensional shapes
- Exploring geometric relationships
- Creating models of two-dimensional shapes

NCTM Expectations

Geometry
- Identify, compare, and analyze attributes of two- and three-dimensional shapes and develop vocabulary to describe the attributes.
- Classify two- and three-dimensional shapes according to their properties and develop definitions of classes of shapes such as triangles and pyramids.

Geometry

Plane Shapes

The reasoning skills that students develop at this age allow them to explore more complex geometric problems and properties. They should develop more precise ways to describe and classify shapes, with an emphasis on using the specialized vocabulary associated with the geometric attributes and properties. The words *parallel, perpendicular,* and *vertex* should be introduced and used repeatedly in context when discussing two-dimensional shapes.

Try It! *Perform the Try It! activity on the next page.*

Talk About It

Discuss the Try It! activity.

- Draw a triangle, circle, square, and rectangle on the board. Point to each shape. **Ask:** *How many vertices does this shape have? How many sides? How many parallel sides? What is the name of this shape?*

- Display one Attribute Block. **Ask:** *What shape is this? How can you tell?* Encourage students to describe the shape using the correct geometric vocabulary. Then challenge students to name correct shapes by giving them clues using attributes.

Solve It

With students, reread the problem. Have students draw the shape Nick and his friends were supposed to make. Instruct students to label each side and vertex and write a sentence telling how they knew which shape was being described. (square or rhombus)

More Ideas

For other ways to teach about identifying and comparing plane shapes—

- Name a two-dimensional shape, then have students build it on geoboards. Instruct students to compare results with a partner and explain the attributes of the shape. Point out that while the geoboard shapes may vary in size, side length, and position, they should all have the same number of sides, vertices, and so on.

- Play "What Shape Am I?" by telling riddles about two-dimensional shapes. For example, **say:** *I have 3 sides and 3 vertices. None of my sides are parallel.* **Ask:** *What shape am I?* Have students hold up a Pattern Block of that shape to show their answer.

Standardized Practice

Have students try the following problem.

Which shape has parallel lines?

A. △   B. ○   C. ▭   D. ◺

Try It! 20 minutes | Pairs

Here is a problem about identifying and comparing plane shapes.

Mr. Roberts asks Nick and his friends to help him get the playground ready for a game the class will play during recess. He asks the students to use chalk to make a large shape on the pavement. The shape should have two sets of parallel sides that are all the same length. It should have four corners. How can the boys figure out what shape Mr. Roberts is asking them to make?

Introduce the problem. Then have students do the activity to solve the problem. Distribute Attribute Blocks and Plane Shapes Recording Sheets (BLM 7) to students. Introduce and define the terms *vertex* (the point where two sides join), *perpendicular* (lines that intersect and form only right angles), and *parallel* (lines that never cross and stay the same distance apart at all points) for students.

Materials
- Attribute Blocks (1 circle, 1 square, 1 rectangle, and 1 triangle per student)
- Plane Shapes Recording Sheet (BLM 7; 1 per student)

1. Instruct students to select a circle, square, rectangle, and triangle block, and discuss similarities and differences between the shapes. Have students complete the first and second rows of the Plane Shapes Recording Sheet.

2. Explain that the plural of *vertex* is *vertices*. Instruct students to write the number of sides in the third row and the number of vertices in the fourth row for each shape.

3. Have students look for parallel sides in the shapes. Instruct students to write the number of parallel sides in the fifth row for each shape.

⚠ Look Out!

The geometric terms introduced in this lesson may be difficult to remember for some students. If so, draw a square or rectangle on the board. Write the terms *side, vertex, perpendicular,* and *parallel lines* on the board next to the shape, and draw arrows to parts of the shape to indicate examples of each term. Use colored chalk to emphasize the parallel and perpendicular lines on the shape. Then have students use tape to label the sides, vertices, perpendicular lines, and parallel lines on the blocks.

2

Geometry
Attributes of Geometric Shapes

Students need to be given opportunities to learn geometric properties by doing. Activities that allow students to manipulate shapes not only help students to maintain their interest and excitement about math, but also allow them to investigate and test relationships among shapes. Expanding their understanding of the properties of two-dimensional shapes will also prepare these students for the concepts of area and volume.

Objective

Recognize attributes of geometric shapes.

Try It! Perform the Try It! activity on the next page.

Skills

- Identifying attributes of two-dimensional shapes
- Composing models using two-dimensional shapes
- Spatial visualization

Talk About It

Discuss the Try It! activity.

- **Say:** *I am thinking of a shape that has four sides and four vertices (corners). Find that shape in your Pattern Blocks.* Discuss the four answers.

- **Say:** *Compare a square and a rhombus.* **Ask:** *How are they alike? How are they different?* Introduce the idea that each vertex starts either a big (90° or greater) or small (less than 90°) angle, and guide students to identify the sizes of different shapes' angles. **Say:** *Compare a trapezoid and a parallelogram.* **Ask:** *How are they alike? How are they different?* Students should note the sizes of their angles as well as how many pairs of parallel sides they have.

NCTM Expectations

Geometry
- Identify, compare, and analyze attributes of two- and three-dimensional shapes and develop vocabulary to describe the attributes.
- Classify two- and three-dimensional shapes according to their properties and develop definitions of classes of shapes such as triangles and pyramids.
- Investigate, describe, and reason about the results of subdividing, combining, and transforming shapes.

Solve It

With students, reread the problem. Then have them sort blocks into parallelogram and non-parallelogram groups. Students should then use the parallelogram blocks to spell the first letter of their names. Have them transfer this letter to paper by tracing each block, and then write a sentence telling how they knew which blocks to use.

More Ideas

For other ways to teach about recognizing attributes of geometric shapes—

- Have students build given geometric shapes, such as a rectangle or a large square, using Pattern Blocks. Then have them count the number of parallel sides in the shapes they used.

- Have students use geoboards to make shapes based on attributes. For example, tell students that you want them to build a shape with four vertices, four sides, and two pairs of parallel sides. Students should then build a shape to fit the description (rhombus, rectangle, or square).

Standardized Practice

Have students try the following problem.

Think about the attributes of each shape. Which shape does not belong?

A.   B.   C. ⬡   D. ▱

Try It! 30 minutes | Groups of 3

Here is a problem about attributes of geometric shapes.

Tonight is Parents' Night at school. Mrs. Matthews asked her students to use Pattern Blocks to spell out their names on their desks. That way, each student's parents can find where their child sits. Mrs. Matthews asked the students to only use shapes that have four vertices and two pairs of parallel sides. Which blocks should the students use?

Introduce the problem. Then have students do the activity to solve the problem. Distribute blocks and construction paper to each group.

Materials
- Pattern Blocks (50 assorted blocks per group)
- construction paper (1 large sheet per group)
- index cards with one alphabet letter on each (1 card per group)

1. Ask students to name each shape and note the number of sides and vertices of each shape. Record this data on a class chart. Point out that several of the shapes have four sides and four vertices. Discuss the differences between these shapes.

2. Give each group an index card with a letter of the alphabet on it. Instruct students to use the blocks to make the assigned letter on the paper, using any combination of shapes.

3. After making the letter, instruct students to trace around the blocks and color the shape the same color as the blocks. Have students write a sentence to describe the shapes used, such as "We used seven squares, four triangles, five hexagons, and eight trapezoids."

⚠ Look Out!

Trapezoids, squares, parallelograms, and rhombuses all have four sides and four corners. Look out for students who confuse these shapes. Help students distinguish these shapes by using tape and markers to label blocks. Guide students to distinguish these shapes by describing the size of their angles as well as how many pairs of parallel sides each has. Have the class brainstorm to describe each shape's angles. For example, "a square's angles are all the same size and it has two pairs of parallel sides," and "a trapezoid has two big angles and two small angles, and one pair of parallel sides."

Objective

Solve spatial visualization problems.

Skills

- Building models
- Analyzing geometric properties
- Spatial reasoning

NCTM Expectations

Geometry
- Identify, compare, and analyze attributes of two- and three-dimensional shapes and develop vocabulary to describe the attributes.
- Classify two- and three-dimensional shapes according to their properties and develop definitions of classes of shapes such as triangles and pyramids.
- Investigate, describe, and reason about the results of subdividing, combining, and transforming shapes.
- Predict and describe the results of sliding, flipping, and turning two-dimensional shapes.
- Build and draw geometric objects.

Geometry

Spatial Visualization

Opportunities to use shapes in a variety of ways will increase students' ability to visualize geometric relationships. Allowing them to explore geometry by sorting, building, modeling, constructing, and tracing a variety of shapes not only emphasizes geometric properties and increases their understanding of geometric concepts, but also provides an important opportunity for students to be actively involved in their own learning.

Try It! Perform the Try It! activity on the next page.

Talk About It

Discuss the Try It! activity.

- Have students discuss the shapes they built. **Ask:** *How many sides do your shapes have? How many vertices do they have? How many parallel sides? How are your two shapes alike? How are they different?*

- **Ask:** *In what situations could it be important to know how to divide a shape into smaller shapes? Why? When might you want to arrange smaller shapes into a larger shape?*

- **Ask:** *If I turn a trapezoid upside down, is it still a trapezoid? If I flip a parallelogram sideways, is it still a parallelogram? Why or why not?*

Solve It

With students, reread the problem. Then have students use the tangram pieces to identify, trace, and label the three, nameable geometric shapes Kendra could make with the tables. Have students write to describe the three shapes (rectangle, trapezoid, and parallelogram) to Kendra and tell her how to make them using the square and triangles. Have them label the shapes.

More Ideas

For other ways to teach about spatial visualization—

- Have students work in pairs to build larger shapes out of Pattern Blocks. Name a shape and invite students to build it. Then have them draw the shape on paper.

- Have students build shapes, such as rectangles, trapezoids, and pentagons, with Pattern Blocks. Then have partners identify and replicate the shapes on geoboards with rubber bands. Challenge students to use rubber bands to show the smaller shapes the larger shapes are built from.

Standardized Practice

Have students try the following problem.

Which shape can be made from two trapezoids?

A.   B.   C.   D.

Try It! 25 minutes | Independent

Here is a problem about spatial visualization.

There are three tables at the art center in Kendra's classroom. One table is a square and two are triangles. The teacher asked Kendra to plan three different ways to push the three tables together to make a different geometric shape. There should not be any space between the tables. How can Kendra arrange the tables to make three different shapes?

Introduce the problem. Then have students do the activity to solve the problem. Distribute tangrams and paper to students.

Materials
- Tangrams (1 set per student)
- paper (1 sheet per student)
- pencils (1 per student)

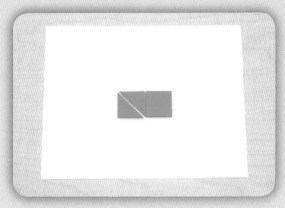

1. Instruct students to use the square and two small triangle tangram pieces to make a nameable geometric shape on their paper.

2. Instruct students to trace the tangram pieces as they are arranged on the paper. Have students identify and label the larger shape they made.

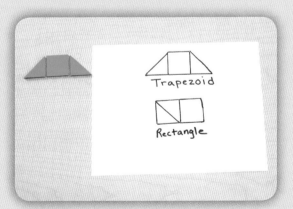

3. Challenge students to make a different shape using the same three pieces, and to trace and label this shape as well. Have students compare and discuss the two shapes each of them made. **Ask:** *Are you sure you made identifiable geometric shapes? How do you know? What are your shapes' names?*

⚠ Look Out!

Students may have difficulty remembering the names and properties of the shapes they create with the tangrams. Review the properties of a variety of shapes prior to the activity. Draw and label examples of each shape on the board or a chart.

Geometry

Classify Three-Dimensional Shapes

In order for students to develop their understanding of geometric properties, they need opportunities to compare and discuss the attributes of two- and three-dimensional shapes, classify these shapes, and develop definitions of each. It is important for them to have opportunities to examine the characteristics of a variety of two- and three-dimensional shapes and the relationships between them.

Try It! *Perform the Try It! activity on the next page.*

Perform the Try It! activity on the next page.

Objective

Classify three-dimensional shapes according to their attributes.

Skills

- Classifying
- Sorting according to predetermined characteristics
- Relating two- and three-dimensional shapes

NCTM Expectations

Geometry
- Identify, compare, and analyze attributes of two- and three-dimensional shapes and develop vocabulary to describe the attributes.
- Classify two- and three-dimensional shapes according to their properties and develop definitions of classes of shapes such as triangles and pyramids.

Talk About It

Discuss the Try It! activity.

- **Ask:** *Did any of the shapes have no faces? No edges? No vertices?*

- Review Euler's Formula. Have students look at their completed Geometric Solids Recording Sheets (BLM 8). **Say:** *If the formula worked, the same number should be on both sides of the equal sign, for example 14 = 14.* **Ask:** *Did this formula work for every shape? Which ones didn't it work for? Why?*

- **Ask:** *How can you use Euler's Formula to check if you counted a figure's vertices, edges, and faces correctly?*

Solve It

With students, reread the problem. Have students explain in writing what shapes (rectangular prism or cube) meet Mr. Keller's requirements, and why.

More Ideas

For other ways to teach about classifying three-dimensional shapes—

- Place each Relational Geosolid® (except the sphere, hemisphere, and hexagonal prism) in separate paper bags. Position each bag at a different station in the room. Have students identify the Geometric Solid at each station by placing their hand inside the bag and identifying, by feel, the number of vertices and edges and the number and shape of the faces.

- Distribute square, rectangular, circular, and triangular flat Attribute Blocks to groups of students. For each flat shape, have students list as many solid shapes as they can think of that have a face of that shape. Have groups compare their lists against the Relational Geosolids.

Standardized Practice

Have students try the following problem.

Which solid is shown?

A. cube   **B.** cylinder   **C.** pyramid   **D.** cone

Try It! 25 minutes | Groups of 4

Here is a problem about classifying three-dimensional shapes.

Mr. Keller asks his students to each bring in a box that has 6 faces, 8 vertices, and 12 edges. Students will use them to make dioramas. Tamyra isn't sure what shape the box should be. How can she find out?

Introduce the problem. Then have students do the activity to solve the problem. Distribute one set of Relational Geosolids® (without the sphere, hemisphere, and hexagonal prism) to be shared between two groups. Define the terms *prism, pyramid,* and *cone* for students and review the names of the Solids: cylinder, cube, rectangular prism, cone, triangular prism, triangular pyramid, and square pyramid.

Materials

- Relational Geosolids® (3 sets per class)
- Geometric Solids Recording Sheet (BLM 8; 1 per group)

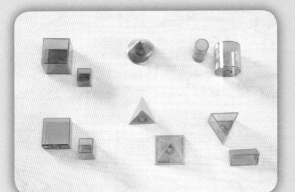

1. Have students sort the Solids into prisms, pyramids, and cones. **Say:** *Look at the top of each Solid.* **Ask:** *Is the face the same size and shape as the base? Is it a vertex or a point?*

2. Have each student select a Solid and find a face, an edge, and a vertex. Instruct groups to fill in the first four columns of their Geometric Solids Recording Sheet (BLM 8) with the name and the number of vertices, faces, and edges of each Solid they have.

⚠ Look Out!

Watch out for students who do not include the base when counting the faces of a solid figure. Reinforce with students that although not every face is a base, every base is a face. As students practice counting the faces of solid figures, have them count the bases first.

3. Introduce Euler's Formula: $(V + F) = (2 + E)$. Explain its variables: V = vertices, F = faces, and E = edges. **Say:** *Euler's Formula says that if a solid has flat faces that are polygons, the number of its vertices and faces is equal to the number of its edges plus 2.* Have students complete the chart by filling in the last column.

Geometry

Building Three-Dimensional Shapes

Students develop their knowledge of the attributes of three-dimensional solids—such as their faces, edges, and vertices—by looking at how two-dimensional shapes come together to form three-dimensional objects. Building three-dimensional models from two-dimensional shapes reinforces the link between two-dimensional and three-dimensional shapes.

Try It! *Perform the Try It! activity on the next page.*

Talk About It

Discuss the Try It! activity.

- Hold up a real-life example of a cube, such as a small square box. **Ask:** *What shapes do you see? What shapes are the faces? How many faces are there?*
- **Ask:** *If we were to take a cereal box apart by cutting along each edge, what shapes would we have? How do you know?*
- **Ask:** *What solid shape could we build with 4 triangles? What solid shape could we build with 1 square and 4 triangles?*

Solve It

With students, reread the problem. Have students identify the solid that Laura will build and draw a net for it.

More Ideas

For other ways to teach about building three-dimensional shapes—

- Challenge students to use blank paper, Two-Color Counters, and the small and large circle Attribute Blocks to build various sizes of cones and cylinders. Students will trace the manipulatives on paper and cut them out for bases. Then they should cut out sides from paper and tape the cones and cylinders together.
- Guide students to make nets to build geometric solids. Have students trace the base of one of the Relational Geosolids® onto construction paper. Then, without lifting the Solid, have students lay the object onto one of its faces and trace that side. Repeat until all faces have been traced. Students will cut out the outline, then fold the paper on the lines, marking the edges of each face to create three-dimensional representations of the Solids.

Standardized Practice

Have students try the following problem.

What solid can be built from this net?

A. triangular pyramid
B. triangular prism
C. rectangular pyramid
D. cylinder

Objective

Build a three-dimensional object from two-dimensional representations of that object.

Skills

- Composing three-dimensional shapes
- Spatial visualization
- Comparing two- and three-dimensional shapes

NCTM Expectations

Geometry
- Identify, compare, and analyze attributes of two- and three-dimensional shapes and develop vocabulary to describe the attributes.
- Investigate, describe, and reason about the results of subdividing, combining, and transforming shapes.
- Build and draw geometric shapes.
- Identify and build a three-dimensional object from two-dimensional representations of that object.

Try It! 20 minutes | Groups of 4

Here is a problem about building three-dimensional shapes.

Mrs. Grover's students made planters during art class, and Laura wants to give hers to her parents as a gift. She needs a box in which to wrap the planter. Mrs. Grover hands Laura 6 equal-sized squares of poster board. What solid shape can Laura build using all the squares?

Introduce the problem. Then have students do the activity to solve the problem. Have groups share sets of Relational Geosolids®. Distribute the Nets Worksheet (BLM 9) to students, and explain that a *net* is an arrangement of two-dimensional shapes that can be cut out and folded to form a three-dimensional solid.

Materials

- Relational Geosolids® (3 sets per class)
- Nets Worksheet (BLM 9; 1 per group)
- paper (1 sheet per group)
- pencils (1 per group)
- scissors
- tape

1. Have students study the shape and number of sides of each of the three nets on the Nets Worksheet and compare them to the Solids. Then have students predict and record which Solid each net will make.

2. Direct students to cut out the top net by cutting along only the dotted lines. **Ask:** *What Solid do you think this net will make? Why?* Have students fold along the solid lines and tape the net together, then compare it against the Solid they chose.

3. Have students cut out and assemble the other nets. **Ask:** *Were you able to predict what Solid these nets would make? What Solid was made from 6 equal-sized squares?*

⚠ Look Out!

Look out for students who have difficulty seeing how to make a three-dimensional solid from a net. They might not understand how to fold the paper to form a Solid. Encourage these students to select the Solid they think the net will make and then build the net around the Solid. Tell students that each dotted line on the net should correspond to one of the edges of the Solid.

Geometry

Points on a Coordinate Plane

Students have been learning about distance, location, and direction for some time now. Now they will build on their knowledge as well as deepen their understanding of these concepts. Students are ready to learn that the numbers of an ordered pair are used to identify specific points on a coordinate plane. Using ordered pairs to identify and name points on a coordinate grid prepares students to find and navigate distances between points on a coordinate plane.

Objective

Locate points on a coordinate plane.

Skills

- Spatial relationships
- Location of points on a plane
- Coordinate geometry

NCTM Expectations

Geometry
- Describe location and movement using common language and geometric vocabulary.
- Make and use coordinate systems to specify locations and to describe paths.

Try It! *Perform the Try It! activity on the next page.*

Talk About It

Discuss the Try It! activity.

- **Say:** *An ordered pair tells the location of a point on a grid.* **Ask:** *What does the first number tell us? What does the second number tell us?*

- **Ask:** *If two ordered pairs are (4, 3) and (3, 4), are they referring to the same location on the coordinate grid? Why or why not?*

- **Ask:** *What if a coordinate grid had the letters* A *through* D *along the side instead of numbers? How would that have changed the ordered pairs you named?*

Solve It

With students, reread the problem. Have them answer the question by writing a short paragraph. Tell students to be sure to use the term *ordered pair* and explain what it means in their answers by giving examples.

More Ideas

For other ways to teach about locating points on a coordinate plane—

- Have students use rubber bands to create simple shapes on geoboards and then write down the coordinates for each peg that the rubber band touches.

- Have students gently toss five Two-Color Counters onto a Coordinate Grid (BLM 10). Students will record the coordinates indicating the locations of the counters that landed red side up. If a counter does not land exactly on a point, tell students to find the pair closest to where the counter landed.

Standardized Practice

Have students try the following problem.

Which ordered pair tells the location of the triangle?

A. (2, 4)
B. (1, 3)
C. (3, 3)
D. (4, 2)

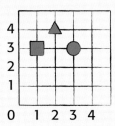

Try It! 20 minutes | Pairs

Here is a problem about locating points on a coordinate plane.

In the game Treasure Search, players mark secret spots on a grid where their treasure is. Then players take turns guessing the locations of their partner's treasure. If you are playing Treasure Search with a partner, how can you tell your partner which spot on the grid you are guessing without pointing to it?

Introduce the problem. Then have students do the activity to solve the problem. Distribute Centimeter Cubes, Coordinate Grids (BLM 10), and textbooks or folders to students.

Materials
- Centimeter Cubes (1 each of 3 different colors per student)
- Coordinate Grid (BLM 10; 2 per pair)
- large textbook or folder (1 per pair)

1. Say: *Ordered pairs tell you about locations on a grid. They have two numbers. The first one tells you how far right you should go. The second tells you how far up you should go.* Explain that ordered pairs always describe a location where two lines intersect. Have students find the ordered pair (2, 1) on their grids.

2. Instruct students to stand a textbook or folder on end between them and place their Coordinate Grids on either side of the book so that neither partner can see the other's grid. Have students place each of their three cubes at a different point on the grid and label that point with the correct ordered pair.

⚠ Look Out!

Students may have difficulty remembering which coordinate indicates the vertical position and which indicates the horizontal position on a plane. To help them remember to go over first and then up, relate the movements to climbing a tree. First, students must go *over* to the tree, and then they can climb *up* the tree.

3. Have pairs take turns guessing the locations of each other's cubes. Each time a student makes a guess, he or she should use an ordered pair to describe the location. Tell students that the partner who finds all three of his or her partner's cubes first wins the game.

Geometry

Location and Movement

Geometry is the means by which things that have shape and space are categorized and measured. Geometry is math for the "real world." Some students may already have an informal background in geometry from hobbies, sports, or play, while others will be realizing the connections between measurement and visualization for the first time. Using manipulatives and relating them to hands-on experiences enables students to connect math to their own lives.

Try It! *Perform the Try It! activity on the next page.*

Talk About It

Discuss the Try It! activity.

■ Discuss students' knowledge of ordered pairs. **Ask:** *How did you know where to put a point for (2, 1) and (3, 4)?*

■ **Ask:** *How did you choose the way to go? How many spaces do your rubber bands go in all? Is there another way to go that is the same length?*

■ Discuss the directions written by all the groups. Compare the language used and, as a class, determine which words and phrases were more precise in describing movement from one location to another.

Solve It

With students, reread the problem. Distribute a copy of the Coordinate Grid (BLM 10). Have students choose locations for Tom's house and Ling's house and show these on the grid. Then ask students to write directions that will help Ling find the shortest way home.

More Ideas

For other ways to teach about location and movement—

■ Create a "taxi cab" geometry exercise using geoboards. One student picks a starting point while a partner picks an intersection on the taxi driver's map (the geoboard). Students then find the number of blocks between the two points. Have students use compass directions north, east, south, and west, instead of right, left, up, and down.

■ Have students create a "connect the dots" picture using geoboards. Give students coordinate pairs to find on a grid. Then give them directions from one pair to another that they will connect to make a picture or shape.

Standardized Practice

Have students try the following problem.

Which ordered pair describes the location of the library?

A. (3, 4)   **B.** (2, 1)   **C.** (2, 4)   **D.** (4, 3)

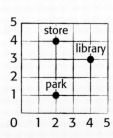

Objective

Create and follow directions on a coordinate system.

Skills

• Finding ordered pairs on a grid
• Comparing measurements
• Describing directional movement

NCTM Expectations

Geometry
• Describe location and movement using common language and geometric vocabulary.
• Make and use coordinate systems to specify locations and to describe paths.
• Find the distance between points along horizontal and vertical lines of a coordinate system.

Try It! *30 minutes | Pairs*

Here is a problem about creating and following directions on a coordinate system.

Ling rode her bike to Tom's house to play after school. Now she is going to be late for dinner if she does not get home quickly. How can Ling find the shortest way home?

Introduce the problem. Then have students do the activity to solve the problem. Distribute geoboards, rubber bands, paper, and pencils to students. On the board, draw a coordinate grid. Review finding and naming points on a grid with students.

Materials

- Geoboards (1 per pair)
- rubber bands (4 per pair)
- paper (1 sheet per student)
- pencils (1 per student)

1. Guide students in finding (2, 1) and (3, 4) on the geoboard. Remind them that the first number shows the horizontal movement and the second shows vertical movement.

2. Say: *Suppose you wanted to find how to get from one point to another on the geoboard.* **Ask:** *How would you do it?* Have students find the shortest route from (2, 1) to (3, 4) on their geoboards. Tell students that they may not travel diagonally on the geoboard. They should trace their route with rubber bands on their geoboards.

⚠ Look Out!

Watch for students who make errors in precision of direction. Use words such as *first, next,* and *then* to clarify the order of directions. Use words such as *left, right,* and *up* to clarify the direction in which you want students to go. Work with students using only coordinate pairs to give them a solid foundation for moving on a coordinate grid. For example, to find the pair (2, 1), tell students to first move two places to the right, then move up one.

3. Have students write directions for getting from (2, 1) to (3, 4) on paper, using the geoboard to help them. For example, if a rubber band stretches from (2, 1) to (3, 1), the directions should say "Go 1 right."

Geometry

Congruent and Similar Figures

Geometry is the branch of mathematics that deals with shape and size, and as such, its major topics include the relationships of points, angles, surfaces, straight lines, curves, and solids. Attributes are characteristics associated with an object. In this lesson, students will classify shapes as congruent (same size and shape) or similar (different size but same shape).

Objective

Identify congruent and similar figures.

Skills

- Identifying attributes
- Comparing and defining
- Classifying by size and shape

NCTM Expectations

Geometry
- Identify, compare, and analyze attributes of two- and three-dimensional shapes and develop vocabulary to describe the attributes.
- Classify two- and three-dimensional shapes according to their properties and develop definitions of classes of shapes such as triangles and pyramids.
- Explore congruence and similarity.
- Recognize geometric ideas and relationships and apply them to other disciplines and to problems that arise in the classroom or in everyday life.

Try It! *Perform the Try It! activity on the next page.*

Talk About It

Discuss the Try It! activity.

- **Ask:** *What makes two objects similar? Congruent?* Ask students to find things in the room that are congruent and others that are similar. Discuss what properties they can compare to help them make the distinction.

- Instruct students to arrange a pair of congruent blocks one next to the other. Then ask students to turn or flip the blocks. **Ask:** *When you turn the pairs sideways, are they congruent? When you turn them upside down, are they congruent?* Reinforce that congruent shapes can be turned or flipped, and they are still congruent.

- Stress the words *similar* and *congruent*. **Ask:** *How would it feel to ride in a car that had three congruent wheels and one smaller but similar wheel? Would the car look different from other cars? How?*

Solve It

With students, reread the problem. Have students draw four sailboats: two with congruent sails and two with similar sails. Have students label their drawings. Students can use triangle blocks to trace the sails on their boats. Then have students write a letter to Lucy, explaining how she can tell which boats should be in the race.

More Ideas

For other ways to teach about congruent and similar figures—

- Have students quiz each other on congruence and similarity using triangle tangram pieces. A student holds up two triangles, and his or her partner must say whether the triangles are congruent or similar.

- Place several congruent and similar Attribute Block shape pairs in a bag. Have students challenge each other to find congruent or similar pairs by feel.

Standardized Practice

Have students try the following problem.

Which shape is congruent to this triangle?

A.   B. ⬜   C.   D.

Try It! 30 minutes | Groups of 4

Here is a problem about congruent and similar figures.

Lucy is helping her dad check the miniature sailboats that will be raced in the school contest. To keep things fair, the sails of all boats must be congruent—not just similar. How can Lucy know which sailboats have sails that are similar and which have sails that are congruent?

Introduce the problem. Then have students do the activity to solve the problem. Distribute Attribute Blocks to each group.

Materials
• Attribute Blocks (2 of each size and shape, either all thick or all thin, per group)

1. Hold up two triangles that are exactly the same in size and shape. **Ask:** *How are these triangles alike?* Hold up a large triangle and a small triangle. **Ask:** *How are these different?* Repeat the sequence with other blocks.

2. Hold up two circles that are exactly the same size. **Say:** *These circles are congruent.* **Ask:** *What do you think the word* congruent *means?* Have students find congruent blocks. Guide students to place congruent blocks on top of each other to show that they are exactly the same size and shape.

3. Display one small and one large square block. **Say:** *These squares are similar.* Repeat with other similar shapes. Lead students to the conclusion that two things with exactly the same shape but different sizes are similar, not congruent. Challenge pairs to find two blocks that are the same shape but not the same size.

⚠ Look Out!

Some students may think that size and shape change with orientation. Emphasize that shapes are congruent when size and shape are the same, and that it does not matter how the shapes are positioned. Model this by showing students two congruent blocks that are oriented the same way. Move one block so that the shapes are oriented differently, telling students that the blocks are still congruent, even though the position of one block has changed.

LESSON 9

Geometry

Symmetrical Figures

Students in grades three and four are ready to explore congruency at the level of symmetry, recognizing points of regularity and visualizing a shape's transformation when it is rotated or reflected. Because relationships across a line of symmetry correspond exactly in terms of size, form, and arrangement, students can begin to develop a sense of formal balance, which will serve as a foundation for geometric equations.

Try It! *Perform the Try It! activity on the next page.*

Objective

Explore the meaning of symmetry and make symmetrical figures.

Skills

- Describing motions
- Predicting results
- Identifying symmetry

NCTM Expectations

Geometry
- Predict and describe the results of sliding, flipping, and turning two-dimensional shapes.
- Describe a motion or a series of motions that will show that two shapes are congruent.
- Identify and describe line and rotational symmetry in two- and three-dimensional shapes and designs.

Talk About It

Discuss the Try It! activity.

- **Say:** *An image that has symmetry can be divided into two halves that are mirror images of each other.* **Ask:** *What is a mirror image?*

- Draw two shapes on the board, one that is symmetrical and one that is not. Point to the symmetrical shape. **Ask:** *Is this shape symmetrical? How can you tell?* Point to the asymmetrical shape. **Ask:** *Is this shape symmetrical? How can you tell?*

- Point to the symmetrical shape. **Ask:** *If I turned this shape on its side, would it still be symmetrical? How can you tell? What if I turned it upside down?*

Solve It

With students, reread the problem. Have students create their own symmetrical masks by folding construction paper in the center and placing Pattern Blocks along the fold to make the first half of the mask. Students then trace the blocks and unfold the paper. Using blocks, they should complete the other half of the mask so that it is symmetrical and trace the other half.

More Ideas

For other ways to teach about symmetry—

- Have students work in pairs. Students should divide a geoboard in half with a rubber band. One student then makes a shape or pattern on one half of the geoboard. The other student must then make a mirror image of the first shape or pattern on the second half of the geoboard so that the design is symmetrical. Students then switch roles and repeat the activity.

- Have students make symmetrical designs out of Centimeter Cubes. Students can then use crayons to draw their designs on a Centimeter Grid (BLM 17).

Standardized Practice

Have students try the following problem.

Which shows a line of symmetry?

A.   B.   C.   D.

Try It!   30 minutes | Pairs

Here is a problem about symmetry.

Andrew wants to make a face mask of his favorite action hero to wear on the night of his class costume party. The mask he wore last year was torn in half, but Andrew is hoping to use it as a pattern. How can symmetry help Andrew create a whole face mask from the half he has?

Introduce the problem. Then have students do the activity to solve the problem. Give Pattern Blocks, crayons, and blank sheets of paper to each pair. Introduce and model the concept of symmetry.

Materials
- Pattern Blocks (50 assorted per pair)
- crayons (10 per pair)
- paper (5 sheets per pair)

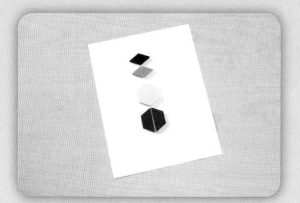

1. Take the blue rhombus. Use the green triangles to show a line of symmetry. Invite students to trace the blue rhombus and draw other lines of symmetry. Do the same with the yellow hexagon and red trapezoid.

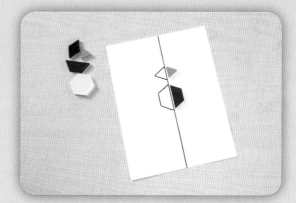

2. Say: *We can make a group of shapes that has symmetry, too.* Have one student in each pair create one half of a shape; then the other student should complete a symmetrical side. Have students draw a vertical line on their paper to help.

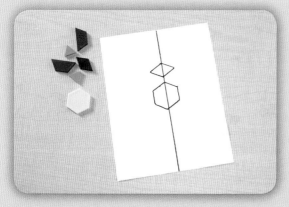

3. Students should trace their figures onto the paper and color the shapes. Have students check to make sure that they can draw a line of symmetry that will divide the design into two halves that are mirror images of each other. Partners then switch roles and repeat the activity.

⚠ Look Out!

Some students may try to complete the pattern by repeating the shapes (i.e., triangle, trapezoid, triangle, trapezoid) instead of creating a mirror image (triangle, trapezoid, trapezoid, triangle). You may wish to use a hand mirror or reflector to help students check their design for symmetry. Hold the mirror so that students can see half their design reflected along the line of symmetry. Then remove the mirror and have students check that the other half of the design matches what they just saw in the mirror.

Objective

Use translations, reflections, and rotations to solve a tangram puzzle.

Skills

- Combining shapes
- Applying and describing transformations
- Predicting results

NCTM Expectations

Geometry
- Investigate, describe, and reason about the results of subdividing, combining, and transforming shapes.
- Predict and describe the results of sliding, flipping, and turning two-dimensional shapes.
- Describe a motion or a series of motions that will show that two shapes are congruent.

Geometry

Tangram Puzzles

Students in grades 3 and 4 have learned to classify by shape, size, and properties—skills that will enable them to express relationships between objects in terms of corresponding physical characteristics. They are ready to put shapes together to form new ones, visualizing and predicting results as they transform their creations by the use of translations (slides), reflections (flips), and rotations (turns).

Try It! *Perform the Try It! activity on the next page.*

Talk About It

Discuss the Try It! activity.

- Discuss the tangram and its seven pieces. **Ask:** *Can you describe each of the seven tangram pieces?* Guide students to name the shapes. **Ask:** *What attributes did you use to identify the tangram pieces?*

- Review the terms *slide, flip,* and *turn.* Call for volunteers to demonstrate each one. **Ask:** *Does moving a tangram piece change its size or shape? Why does the piece look different when it is slid, flipped, or turned?*

- Tell students that these movements are also known as translations (slides), reflections (flips), and rotations (turns).

Solve It

With students, reread the problem. Have students move the tangram pieces to make a square half the size of the square that uses all seven pieces. Have students write the transformations they used to create the new shape.

More Ideas

For other ways to teach about tangram puzzles—

- Ask students to create their own tangram puzzles and challenge classmates to solve them using only slides, flips, and turns. Then have students explain how they transformed tangram pieces to solve the puzzles.

- Give students two tangram triangles that are oriented differently by one transformation, either a slide, flip, or turn. Have students move one triangle to match the other and then describe the transformation they used.

Standardized Practice

Have students try the following problem.

Which shows what the triangle will look like after it is flipped to the right?

A.   B.   C.   D.

Try It! 30 minutes | Pairs

Here is a problem about solving a tangram puzzle.

Peyton's class is studying slides, flips, and turns using tangrams. Peyton makes a square using all seven tangram pieces. Then the teacher asks Peyton if he can make a square that is half the size of the one he made. Peyton is only allowed to use slides, flips, and turns to make the new square. How can Peyton move the tangram pieces to make the smaller square?

Introduce the problem. Then have students do the activity to solve the problem. Distribute tangrams and Tangram Puzzles 1 and 2 (BLMs 11 and 12) to each pair of students. Review with students the meaning of the words *slide, flip,* and *turn.* Select a tangram piece and model each transformation for students.

Materials
- Tangrams (1 set per pair)
- Tangram Puzzle 1 (BLM 11; 1 per pair)
- Tangram Puzzle 2 (BLM 12; 1 per pair)

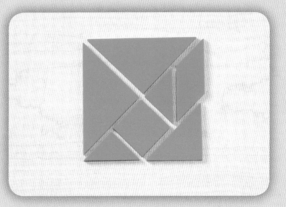

1. Explain to students that the tangram pieces are different shapes that can be put together to make a square or other shape. Have students place the pieces of their tangram on their desks so that the pieces are not overlapping.

2. Instruct students to assemble the tangram pieces into a square using slides, flips, and turns. As they move each tangram piece, they should use the words *slide, flip,* and *turn* to describe the transformation.

⚠ Look Out!

Some students may require extra help with the terms *slide, flip,* and *turn,* as they represent motions that are similar and closely related. Assist students by placing tangram pieces on their desks and modeling each term. To reinforce these concepts, play a call-and-response game in which you say the term and the students respond by performing the action.

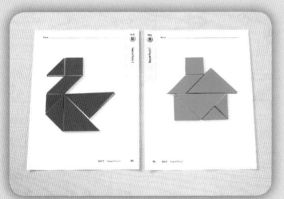

3. Have students fill in Tangram Puzzle 1. Tell students that when they move the pieces from the square they made to the puzzle, they can only use slides, flips, and turns. Have them use the same process to fill in Tangram Puzzle 2.

Geometry

Tiling Patterns

Students develop a sense for spatial relationships by matching and correlating shapes, a skill that leads to the creation of patterns. Students are challenged to create tiling patterns by arranging two or more geometric shapes in repetitive mosaic patterns. In order to do this, students use their foundational knowledge of polygons. They must look at shapes' sides and angles to decide which ones will fit together in repeating patterns.

Try It! *Perform the Try It! activity on the next page.*

Objective

Explore tiling patterns.

Skills

- Identifying shapes
- Manipulating shapes
- Identifying patterns

NCTM Expectations

Geometry
- Investigate, describe, and reason about the results of subdividing, combining, and transforming shapes.
- Predict and describe the results of sliding, flipping, and turning two-dimensional shapes.
- Create and describe mental images of objects, patterns, and paths.

Talk About It

Discuss the Try It! activity.

- **Ask:** *What shapes did you use in your new tiling pattern?* Have volunteers from the groups share their tiling patterns with the class.

- **Ask:** *When you combined different shapes, what did you have to do to some of the shapes to make them fit together? Can you show me the Pattern Blocks that you had to flip? Turn?*

- **Say:** *Look at the shapes you used.* **Ask:** *Why did they fit together in the pattern?* Guide students to describe attributes of their shapes, such as the lengths of their sides and the sizes of their angles, to describe why they fit together well in a pattern.

Solve It

With students, reread the problem. Have students use blocks to make a new tiling pattern that could be used as a border. Then ask students to transfer their designs to paper, color them, and present them to the class.

More Ideas

For other ways to teach about tiling patterns—

- Cut construction paper into various shapes, such as three-quarter- or half-sheet sizes, and distribute to students. Challenge students to use Pattern Blocks to fill in the planes with tiling patterns.

- Have students use Color Tiles to create tiling patterns that focus on alternating colors. Students can also use two or more tiles of the same color to create rectangles or other irregular figures, and create patterns using these.

Standardized Practice

Have students try the following problem.

What two shapes make up this tiling pattern?

A. ○ ☐   B. △ ○   C. ☐ △   D. △ ⬡

Try It! 30 minutes | Groups of 3

Here is a problem about tiling patterns.

Every month, your teacher puts a new border around the bulletin board, and this month your teacher is letting students design it. The border should use two shapes in a repeating pattern. The shapes in the border should not overlap, and there should be no gaps between the shapes. What shapes could you use for your border?

Introduce the problem. Then have students do the activity to solve the problem. Give Pattern Blocks and paper to each group of students. Explain to students that they will make a tiling pattern, which is a pattern made from two or more repeating shapes where there are no gaps and no overlaps. Tell students that the pattern should fill up all the space on their paper and overrun if necessary.

Materials
- Pattern Blocks (90 of various shapes per group)
- paper (1 quarter sheet per group)

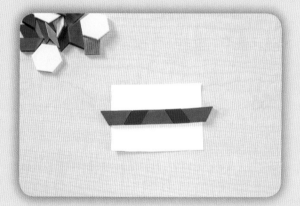

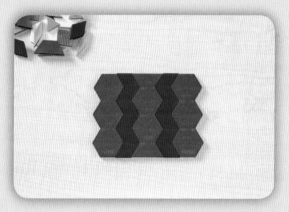

1. Say: *We're going to make a tiling pattern.* Demonstrate creating the beginning of a tiling pattern with the red trapezoid and blue rhombus blocks.

2. Have groups create the same pattern with their blocks. Then have them extend the pattern by adding blocks to fill up the space on their quarter sheets of paper. Emphasize that a tiling pattern is not just linear but should fill up the whole plane or extend in all directions.

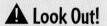

3. Have students work in pairs to make their own tiling patterns with two shapes.

⚠ Look Out!

Watch for students who don't repeat the shapes in their tiling patterns properly. For example, in a rhombus-triangle-rhombus-triangle pattern, a student might at one point set two rhombuses next to each other. Have students model the basic unit of their repeating pattern (for example, rhombus-triangle) and keep it apart from the tiling pattern itself. Students can use this model to stop and check whether they are correctly repeating the basic unit in the tiling pattern.

Geometry

Tessellations

A tessellation is a repeated geometric design that fills a plane without creating any gaps or overlaps. Regular tessellations are made with congruent regular polygons, such as equilateral triangles, that have congruent sides. However, not all regular polygons tessellate. Semiregular tessellations—also called *tiling patterns*—are made with combinations of two or more different regular polygons. Some irregular polygons, such as rectangles or trapezoids, also tessellate. Tessellations are an ideal opportunity to discuss congruence, as well as translation, reflection, and rotation, with students.

Try It! *Perform the Try It! activity on the next page.*

Talk About It

Discuss the Try It! activity.

- **Ask:** *Which Pattern Block shapes could you use to create a tessellation?* Students should conclude that they could use any of the blocks.
- **Ask:** *Which shape allowed you to cover the most space? Why?*
- **Ask:** *When you made your tessellation, were all of the shapes in the same position or did you have to turn them? How did turning the shapes help you make a tessellation?*

Solve It

With students, reread the problem. Have students describe in writing how they created a tessellation using one type of block.

More Ideas

For other ways to teach about creating a tessellation—

- Have students work in pairs to make a tessellation using Pattern Blocks. One student begins the tessellation by tracing blocks. Then the other student must identify the right block to use to continue the tessellation. Students switch roles and repeat the activity.
- Have students list the Pattern Block shapes that they know will tessellate. Distribute geoboards to pairs and challenge them to model other shapes, such as regular pentagons and octagons. Have students create cardboard models of these shapes, then trace them to test whether they tessellate.

Standardized Practice

Have students try the following problem.

Which figure shows a tessellation?

A.   B.   C.    D.

Objective

Investigate tessellations.

Skills

- Identifying shapes
- Manipulating shapes
- Identifying patterns

NCTM Expectations

Geometry
- Predict and describe the results of sliding, flipping, and turning two-dimensional shapes.
- Build and draw geometric objects.

Try It! 15 minutes | Groups of 3

Here is a problem about creating a tessellation.

Mrs. Winn is having a contest for her students. Each student has to create a puzzle using one Pattern Block shape. There cannot be any space between the shapes and they cannot overlap. What shapes can her students use?

Introduce the problem. Then have students do the activity to solve the problem. Distribute blocks to each group of students. Explain to students that when you make a pattern with one repeating shape, without any gaps or overlaps, you are making a tessellation. Point out to students that many shapes tessellate, but some shapes do not.

Materials
- Pattern Blocks

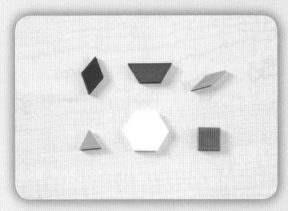

1. Say: *A tessellation is one single shape repeated over and over again.* Ask students which of the block shapes could be used to make a tessellation. Have them tell their predictions to the other students in their group.

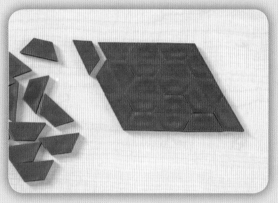

2. Ask each student in the group to choose a shape and use it to make a tessellation. Students should share their tessellations with their groups, then pick a new shape and make a new tessellation.

3. Once groups have tried all the shapes, ask students to check with the other group members to see which shapes worked to make a tessellation. They should find that all the block shapes could be used.

⚠ Look Out!

Students may try to create tessellations with gaps or overlaps in them or that use multiple shapes. Remind them that a tessellation must fill the space without gaps or overlaps. Stress that a tessellation uses only one shape repeated over and over. If more than one shape is used, it is a tiling pattern, not a tessellation. Show students examples of tessellation patterns and reinforce that there are no gaps or overlaps.

Geometry

Putting Shapes Together

Putting shapes together and taking them apart are important skills as students learn to find the area and volume of shapes. Working with shapes in this way will help students learn that the area of the original shape is equal to the sum of the areas of subdivided parts. If students can master this concept, they will come to understand that the volume of a subdivided solid is equal to the sum of the volumes of the subdivided parts.

Objective

Investigate and predict the results of putting together and taking apart plane shapes.

Skills

- Changing orientation of shapes
- Putting shapes together
- Taking shapes apart

NCTM Expectations

Geometry
- Investigate, describe, and reason about the results of subdividing, combining, and transforming shapes.
- Build and draw geometric objects.

Try It! *Perform the Try It! activity on the next page.*

Talk About It

Discuss the Try It! activity.

- **Say:** *Look at the two triangle tangram pieces you used to make a square.* **Ask:** *Can you use the same two pieces to make a new shape?* (larger triangle)

- **Say:** *Look at the red trapezoid Pattern Block.* **Ask:** *What shapes do you get if you break it apart? Is there more than one way to do this?* Students should notice that they can use either three triangles or one triangle and one blue parallelogram.

- **Ask:** *What were some of the shapes you made on your own with the blocks? What blocks did you use to make them?*

Solve It

With students, reread the problem. Have students draw a picture and write a sentence to describe what shapes Kim could have used to make the hexagon. Students might use a combination of trapezoids, triangles, or parallelograms.

More Ideas

For other ways to teach about putting shapes together or taking them apart—

- Have students use tangram pieces to make a variety of different shapes, such as rectangles, trapezoids, and parallelograms. Then challenge students to use all seven tangram pieces to make one large square.

- Have students use rubber bands on a geoboard to show how shapes can be combined and taken apart.

Standardized Practice

Have students try the following problem.

Which shapes can be put together to make a trapezoid like this one?

A.   B.  C.   D.

Try It! 20 minutes | Pairs

Here is a problem about putting shapes together and taking shapes apart.

During free time, Kim is playing with Pattern Blocks. She is making shapes out of smaller shapes. She puts two shapes together to make a hexagon. What two shapes did Kim use to make the hexagon?

Introduce the problem. Then have students do the activity to solve the problem. Distribute tangrams and Pattern Blocks to each pair of students. Explain to students that most shapes can be broken into smaller shapes or combined to make larger shapes.

> **Materials**
> - Tangrams (1 set per pair)
> - Pattern Blocks (5 of each shape per pair)

1. Have students use the square tangram piece. **Ask:** *What two tangram pieces can you use to make a square of the same size?*

3. Ask: *Can you use the tangram pieces to build a hexagon with six equal sides?* Guide students to see that they cannot. Have students select a yellow hexagon from the Pattern Blocks and challenge them to find smaller shapes that make the hexagon. **Ask:** *Can you make a hexagon using just one type of block? Using two different types? What shapes can you use?* Have students use the blocks to build other shapes, such as trapezoids.

2. Ask students to use the two large triangle tangram pieces to create a larger square. **Say:** *Use the five remaining tangram pieces to build a congruent square.* Have students list the shapes they used to build each square. Guide students to discuss how one shape may be made out of different sets of smaller shapes.

⚠ Look Out!

Look out for students who have difficulty selecting which shapes to put together to make a hexagon. Have students experiment with placing trapezoid, triangle, and parallelogram blocks directly on top of the yellow hexagon block.

Geometry

Flips (Reflections)

In geometry, a flip is when an object is transformed across a line. The side of the object closest to the line, when flipped, is the same distance from the line, but on the other side of the line. After the object is flipped, it appears as a mirror image of the original object. Flipping a flipped object over the original line will result in the original image.

Objective

Demonstrate flips (reflections) with physical models.

Skills

- Representing flips using geometric models
- Representing reflections using geometric models and mirrors

NCTM Expectations

Geometry
- Predict and describe the results of sliding, flipping, and turning two-dimensional shapes.
- Describe location and movement using common language and geometric vocabulary.

Try It! *Perform the Try It! activity on the next page.*

Talk About It

Discuss the Try It! activity.

- Have students look at the Pattern Blocks and drawn representations used in the Try It! activity.
- **Ask:** *How did you show the first row of shapes? Did every group's shapes look exactly the same?*
- **Say:** *Explain how you and your partner demonstrated what the second row of shapes would look like.*
- **Ask:** *Why did modeling two rows of the pattern speed up the process of reflecting the pattern in the mirror?*

Solve It

With students, reread the problem. Ask students to write a few sentences to answer the following question. *How many more times would Destiny have to use a mirror to show 16 rows of her pattern?*

More Ideas

For other ways to teach about flips (reflections)—

- Have students continue Destiny's pattern to make more rows of shapes, and describe the pattern of the rows in writing. (Extension: Predict what the 10th row would look like.)
- Have students use other manipulatives, such as tangrams, to build more composite shapes, and then show their reflection over a line.

Standardized Practice

Have students try the following problem.

Draw a picture of the following shapes flipped over the lines.

1. 　　2. 　　3.

Try It! 30 minutes | Pairs

Here is a problem using reflection.

Destiny painted a four-row pattern on her bedroom wall. She painted a parallelogram, a triangle, and a trapezoid in the first row. Then she painted a line 2 inches below the figures. She flipped the figures over the line to create the next row. Then she repeated the process. Show how the four rows of shapes looked.

Introduce the problem. Then have students do the activity to solve the problem.

Follow the steps below to show Destiny how the four rows of shapes looked.

Materials
- Reflect-It™ Hinged Mirror
- Pattern Blocks
- ruler
- scissors
- white paper/one-inch isometric dot paper

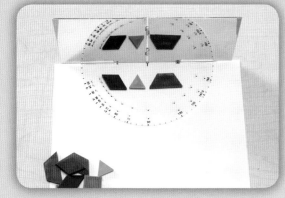

1. Choose Pattern Blocks to represent the pattern Destiny painted in the first row on her wall. Place the blocks 2 inches away from the Mirror.

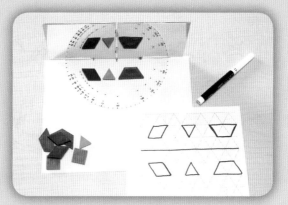

2. Draw the first row of the pattern on a piece of paper. Draw a line 2 inches from the first row. Draw the second row of the pattern as it is seen in the Mirror.

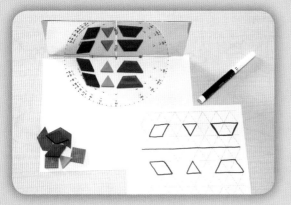

3. Use blocks to model the first two rows of Destiny's pattern. The reflection, as seen in the Mirror, shows the third and fourth rows of the pattern.

⚠ Look Out!

Watch for students who use the Mirror correctly but fail to draw a representation accurately. Encourage them to focus on drawing sides and vertices of each shape one at a time, exactly as they see them in the Mirror.

Rotational Symmetry

Rotational symmetry describes the property of an object to match itself, or show symmetry, when rotated a certain number of degrees around a central point. The number of times the object has the same orientation as the original object designates the "order" of the rotational symmetry. For example, when rotating an equilateral triangle, the triangle will appear the same as the original orientation 3 times, so it has rotational symmetry of order 3. An object with rotational symmetry may or may not have line symmetry.

Objective

Identify figures with rotational symmetry using physical models.

Try It! *Perform the Try It! activity on the next page.*

Skills

- Identifying the geometric center of figures
- Identifying which geometric figures have rotational symmetry

NCTM Expectations

Geometry
- Identify and describe line and rotational symmetry in two- and three-dimensional shapes and designs.
- Recognize geometric ideas and relationships and apply them to other disciplines and to problems that arise in the classroom or in everyday life.

Talk About It

Discuss the Try It! activity.

- Have students look at the figures they used in the Try It! activity.
- **Ask:** *What figures can Horatio use as the outline of his stepping stones?*
- **Ask:** *What are the orders of rotational symmetry of the figures Horatio can use?*
- **Ask:** *Can you make a guess about the types of figures that Horatio can use?* **Say:** *Explain.*

Solve It

With students, reread the problem. Ask students to draw pictures and write a few sentences to answer the following question. *Suppose Janie wants to rotate the rectangular mattress on her bed. How many ways can the mattress be rotated (but not flipped) and still fit in the frame that sits on the floor? Explain.*

More Ideas

For other ways to teach about rotational symmetry—

- Have students color each side of a polygon with a different color marker to help find the orders of rotational symmetry of different shapes. Have students physically rotate their polygons.
- Have students find pictures of real-life objects that have rotational symmetry.
- Have students draw letters and trace Pattern Blocks on a sheet of paper. Have students categorize the shapes and letters by their types of symmetry.

Standardized Practice

Have students try the following problem.

Draw pictures or cut to solve. What is the order of rotational symmetry of the shape below?

Try It! 30 minutes | Pairs

Here is a problem using rotational symmetry.

Horatio wants to create a decorative design that will appear in a stepping stone when viewed from different orientations. Identify several shapes he can use as the base shape of the stepping stone.

Introduce the problem. Then have students do the activity to solve the problem.

Follow the steps below to show Horatio several shapes he can use for his stepping stone.

Materials
- Reflect-It™ Hinged Mirror
- Pattern Blocks
- straightedge
- white paper/one-inch isometric dot paper

1. Choose a Pattern Block to represent the outline of the base of Horatio's stepping stone. Trace the block on a piece of paper. Find the center of the shape, using a straightedge and the vertices.

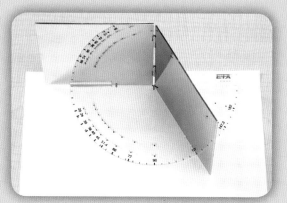

2. To find the angle at which you will set the Mirror, divide 360° by the number of sides of the figure. For example, a triangle has 3 sides, so you would set the Mirror at 120° (360° ÷ 3 = 120°). Set the Mirror to the proper degree setting.

⚠ Look Out!

Watch for students who do not find the correct center points of their traced figures. Remind these students to count the number of sides of their figures again, and use the appropriate rule for finding the centers.

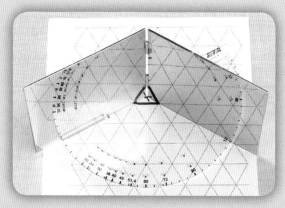

3. Place the vertex of the Mirror on the center of your traced figure. Align the bottom edge of each side of the mirror along one of the lines you drew. If the original figure shows in the mirror, the figure has rotational symmetry.

Geometry

Vertical and Horizontal Line Symmetry

An object has vertical line symmetry when a vertical line drawn through the middle of an object creates two halves that are reflections of each other. These halves are symmetrical. Horizontal symmetry describes the same result from a horizontal line through an object. Line symmetry can be confirmed by folding the object in half and aligning the halves or by holding a mirror on the line of symmetry to compare the reflection. An object may have only a vertical line of symmetry, only a horizontal line of symmetry, both vertical and horizontal lines of symmetry, or no lines of symmetry.

Objective

Demonstrate vertical and horizontal line symmetry with physical models.

Skills

- Demonstrating reflections using geometric models
- Identifying symmetry in geometric models

NCTM Expectations

Geometry
- Identify and describe line and rotational symmetry in two- and three-dimensional shapes and designs.
- Recognize geometric ideas and relationships and apply them to other disciplines and to problems that arise in the classroom or in everyday life.

Try It! *Perform the Try It! activity on the next page.*

Talk About It

Discuss the Try It! activity.

- Have students look at their Pattern Blocks and draw representations used in the Try It! activity.
- **Ask:** *What types of shapes could Flora use on her quilt?*
- **Say:** *Demonstrate how to prove that one of your shapes has vertical and horizontal symmetry.*

Solve It

With students, reread the problem. Ask students to answer the following question. *What other shape could Flora use on her quilt? Draw the shape showing the lines of symmetry. Write a few sentences explaining how you know the shape will work for Flora's quilt.*

More Ideas

For other ways to teach about vertical and horizontal line symmetry—

- Have students explore and draw lines of symmetry other than vertical and horizontal lines of symmetry.
- Have students go on a "symmetry hunt" to find shapes with symmetry in the classroom.
- Have students create patterns with vertical or horizontal line symmetry, using Pattern Blocks or Attribute Blocks.

Standardized Practice

Have students try the following problem.

Draw the lines of symmetry on these shapes.

Try It! 30 minutes | Independent

Here is a problem using line symmetry.

Flora wants to make a quilt with one large shape in the middle. She also wants the shape to have vertical and horizontal line symmetry so she can fold it either way on her bed and the sides will be the same. Which Pattern Block shapes could Flora use for her quilt?

Introduce the problem. Then have students do the activity to solve the problem.

Follow the steps below to show Flora which shapes she could use for her quilt.

Materials
- Reflect-It™ Hinged Mirror
- Pattern Blocks
- white paper

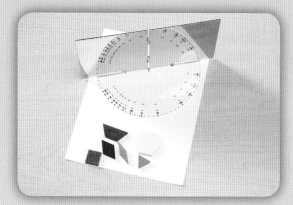

1. Choose a block to check for vertical symmetry. Place the mirror along a vertical line through the center of the block. Check to see if the half of the block in front of the mirror and the reflection in the mirror are the same.

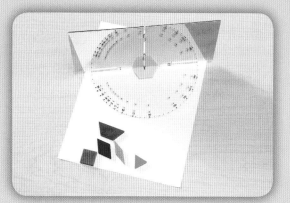

2. Use the same block to check for horizontal symmetry. Place the mirror along a horizontal line through the center of the block. Check to see if the half of the block in front of the mirror and the reflection in the mirror are the same.

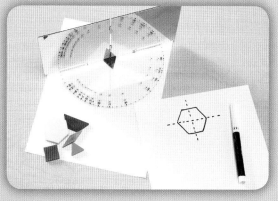

3. Draw pictures to show all the block shapes Flora could use on her quilt. Draw lines on the figures to show the lines of symmetry. Repeat the activity until you have all the shapes that have line symmetry.

⚠ Look Out!

Watch for students who think blocks with rotational symmetry (such as a rhombus) have line symmetry. Demonstrate rotational symmetry, but then emphasize the lack of line symmetry by both folding a paper shape and showing the reflection in the Reflect-It Mirror.

Geometry

Locating Points on a Coordinate Grid

A coordinate grid is formed by two perpendicular number lines, which are used to locate and name ordered pairs. The horizontal number line is referred to as the *x*-axis. The vertical number line is referred to as the *y*-axis. The two axes intersect at the origin. The origin is labeled with the ordered pair (0, 0). When naming ordered pairs, the *x*-axis coordinate is first, followed by the *y*-axis coordinate. The ordered pair is written with the *x* and *y* coordinates separated by a comma in a set of parentheses. For example, the ordered pair for the point five units right of (0, 0) (along the *x*-axis) and three units above (0, 0) (along the *y*-axis) is written as (5, 3).

Try It! *Perform the Try It! activity on the next page.*

Talk About It

Discuss the Try It! activity.

- Have students look at their coordinate grids.
- **Ask:** *How did you know where to mark the final ordered pair?*
- **Ask:** *What ordered pair marks the location of Sean's final cone?*

Solve It

With students, reread the problem. Suppose Sean wanted to alter his course to form a square. How could he move two points on his grid to make a square course? Name all four ordered pairs.

More Ideas

For other ways to teach about coordinate grids—

- Have students mark on a Coordinate Grid (BLM 10) ordered pairs that form a simple picture. Have students create a set of directions for other students to replicate the picture.
- Have students play "battleship" with Coordinate Grids; one student secretly marks locations of ships.

Standardized Practice

Have students complete the following activity.

Name a point A *on the coordinate grid as an ordered pair. Mark a second point* B *on the grid that has a location of (5, 2).*

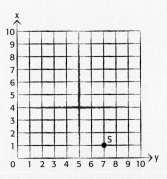

Objective

Locate and name points in the first quadrant of a coordinate grid.

Skills

- Locating and marking points on a coordinate grid
- Naming points on a coordinate grid

NCTM Expectations

Geometry
- Make and use coordinate systems to specify locations and to describe paths.
- Find the distance between points along horizontal and vertical lines of a coordinate system.

Try It! 30 minutes | Pairs

Here is a problem using a coordinate grid.

Sean wants to set up an obstacle course in his backyard. He wants to put cones at four corners of the course to make a rectangle. He makes a grid to mark the course. He marks the ordered pairs (2, 2), (10, 2), and (2, 8) as locations for placing cones. At which ordered pair should he place the final cone?

Introduce the problem. Then have students do the activity to solve the problem.

Follow the steps below to show Sean where to place the final cone.

Materials
- *XY* Coordinate Pegboard and pegs
- rubber bands
- paper

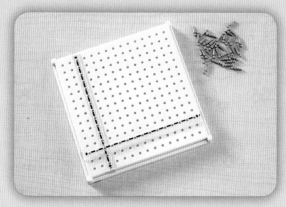

1. To begin, have students slide the bars that represent the horizontal and vertical number lines (axes) so the intersection of the lines is near the bottom left of the grid.

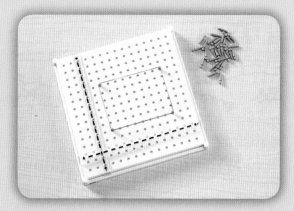

3. Determine the location of the fourth vertex that completes the rectangle. Determine its horizontal and vertical coordinates. Place a peg at the location of the ordered pair. Use a rubber band to check that your figure is a rectangle.

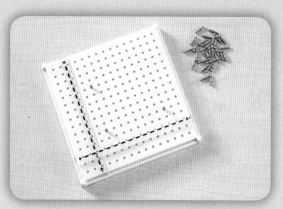

2. Have students use the pegs to mark the cones Sean has already set. Make sure they remember to start at the origin (the intersection of the axes) and count across the horizontal axis the number of units given first in each ordered pair, then up the number of units given second in the ordered pair.

⚠ Look Out!

Watch for students who interchange the horizontal and vertical coordinate values when reading or writing ordered pairs. Remind them to start by moving left or right the distance specified by the first number and then going up or down the distance specified by the second number.

Objective

Follow and create directions between points in the first quadrant of a coordinate grid.

Skills

- Locating and marking points on a coordinate grid
- Naming points on a coordinate grid
- Following directions to arrive at an unknown point
- Creating directions to arrive at a given point

NCTM Expectations

Geometry
- Describe location and movement using common language and geometric vocabulary.
- Make and use coordinate systems to specify locations and to describe paths.

Geometry

Directions on a Coordinate Grid

Each location on a coordinate grid is unique. An ordered pair names the specific location on the grid. There are numerous paths that can be followed from one ordered pair to another.

Try It! *Perform the Try It! activity on the next page.*

Talk About It

Have students look at the marked grids and written directions used in the Try It! activity on the next page to explore following directions on coordinate grids.

- **Ask:** *What ordered pair represents the location of Laura's friend's house?*
- **Ask:** *Which other way could Laura locate her friend's house on the map?*

Solve It

With students, reread the problem. After leaving her friend's house, Laura decides to walk to the library, which is located at (3, 6) on the map. Write a sentence giving her directions to find the library from her friend's house and then from the library back to her house.

More Ideas

For other ways to teach about directions on coordinate grids—

- Have students make coordinate grids and maps of the classroom or school on Centimeter Grid Paper (BLM 17) and write directions to and from various locations.
- Have students label a city street map (real or fictional) as a coordinate grid. They should write and follow directions to and from certain locations.
- Have students conduct an archeological "dig" (or other similar activity) using square netting with lines labeled as a coordinate grid to document the locations of "important findings."

Standardized Practice

Have students complete the following activity.

Write directions to get from (3, 10) to (7, 5) on a coordinate grid.

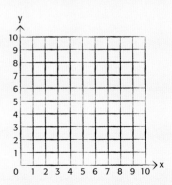

Try It! 30 minutes | Pairs

Here is a problem using a coordinate grid.

Laura is trying to get from her house to a friend's house by looking at the grid on a map. Laura's house is located at (4, 1). Her friend told her to follow the map up seven blocks and right four blocks. At what ordered pair on the map is her friend's house located?

Introduce the problem. Then have students do the activity to solve the problem.

Follow the steps below to show Laura how to get to her friend's house.

Materials
- *XY* Coordinate Pegboard and pegs
- notebook or paper
- pencils

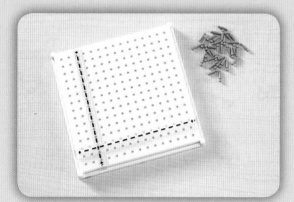

1. Slide the bars that represent the horizontal and vertical number lines (axes) so the intersection of these lines is near the bottom left of the grid.

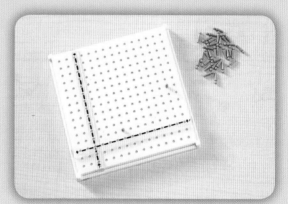

2. Use a peg to mark the location of Laura's house. From the peg, follow the directions to find the location of Laura's friend's house. Name the ordered pair that represents the location of her friend's house.

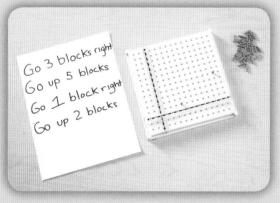

3. Write a set of alternative directions to locate Laura's friend's house on the map.

⚠ Look Out!

Watch out for students who reverse the directions. Remind them that you can start all sets of directions from the origin (0, 0). Also, look out for students who reverse the order of the coordinates.

Go 3 blocks right
Go up 5 blocks
Go 1 block right
Go up 2 blocks

Reflections on a Coordinate Grid

Every ordered pair on a coordinate grid is at the intersection of a vertical and a horizontal line. These lines can be used as lines of reflection. A point and its reflection are the same distance from a line of reflection, but on opposite sides of that line of reflection. If a line of reflection is a vertical line, then a point and its reflection have the same *y*-coordinate. If a line of reflection is a horizontal line, then a point and its reflection have the same *x*-coordinate.

Try It! *Perform the Try It! activity on the next page.*

Talk About It

Have students look at the grids used in the Try It! activity.

■ **Ask:** *What are the coordinates of the vertices of the triangle?*

■ **Ask:** *What are the coordinates of the vertices of the reflected triangle?* Have students compare the two sets of coordinates. **Ask:** *What is different between the sets of coordinates? What is the same?*

■ **Ask:** *How can you verify that the reflection is correct?*

Solve It

With students, reread the problem. Suppose Evan decided to flip his triangle over a horizontal line at *y* = 6. What happens to the ordered pair (6, 6)? Find the vertices of this reflected triangle.

More Ideas

For other ways to teach about coordinate grids—

■ Have students make coordinate grids on grid paper and flip Pattern Blocks over lines, recording the locations of the original and reflected shapes.

■ Have students draw simple pictures on Coordinate Grids (BLM 10) and then draw the reflection over a line.

■ Have students use a compass to mark reflected points: place the stationary tip on the reflection line, mark a point on one side of the line, and "flip" the compass to mark the reflection on the other side.

Standardized Practice

Have students complete the following activity.

Point A is located at (2, 3). What are the coordinates of the point reflected over the vertical line at x = 5? *What are the coordinates of the point reflected over the horizontal line at* y = 4?

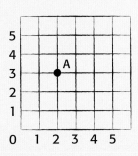

Objective

Reflect points over a line in the first quadrant of a coordinate grid.

Skills

- Locating and marking points on a coordinate grid
- Naming points on a coordinate grid
- Finding the reflections of points on a coordinate grid

NCTM Expectations

Geometry
- Describe location and movement using common language and geometric vocabulary.
- Make and use coordinate systems to specify locations and to describe paths.
- Predict and describe the results of sliding, flipping, and turning two-dimensional shapes.

Try It! 30 minutes | Groups of 3 or 4

Here is a problem using a coordinate grid.

Evan wants to flip a triangular chalk drawing over the other side of his driveway, but he is not sure where to draw the lines. He makes a coordinate grid and marks the vertices at (5, 7), (5, 9), and (6, 6). He draws a vertical line at x = 4 on the grid. What are the coordinates of the vertices of the reflected triangle?

Introduce the problem. Then have students do the activity to solve the problem.

Follow the steps below to show Evan how to flip his chalk drawing.

Materials
- *XY* Coordinate Pegboard and pegs
- rubber bands
- white paper

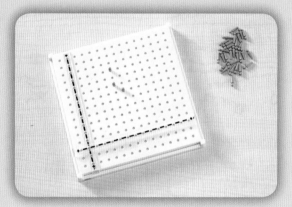

1. Slide the bars that represent the horizontal and vertical number lines so the intersection of these lines is near the bottom left of the grid. Place pegs to represent the vertices of Evan's triangle.

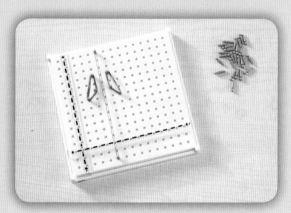

3. Pick one of the three vertices of Evan's triangle. Place a peg in a location with the same *y*-coordinate and with *x*-coordinate the same distance from, but on the other side of, the line of reflection. Repeat for the other two vertices. Stretch rubber bands around the pegs representing the original triangle and around the pegs representing the reflected triangle. Are the triangles reflections of each other over the line x = 4?

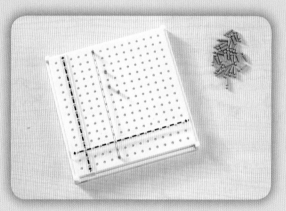

2. Place a peg at the bottom-most hole of the column of pegs representing x = 4. Place a peg at the upper-most hole of the column of pegs representing x = 4. Stretch a rubber band around these two pegs. This rubber band represents the line of reflection.

⚠ Look Out!

Watch out for students who change both coordinates when reflecting a point over a vertical or horizontal line. Remind them that a reflection over a horizontal line has the same *x*-coordinate as the original point.

Algebra

Algebra uses symbols to show mathematical relationships and to solve problems. The study of algebra in the elementary grades includes investigating relationships among quantities, finding ways of representing mathematical relationships, and analyzing change. Algebra builds on students' experiences with numbers and is closely linked to geometry and data analysis. In this way, the ideas taught in algebra help to unify the elementary mathematics program.

As students progress through the intermediate grades, two very important uses for algebra emerge. First, students begin to use algebra to mathematically model real-world phenomena. At Grades 3 and 4, students use these models to draw conclusions, make predictions, or better understand situations that can be quantified. Second, third- and fourth-grade students begin to look more closely at change. At this level, students use graphs and tables to notice change and distinguish between arithmetic and geometric growth.

The Grades 3 – 5 NCTM Standards for Algebra suggest that students should:

- Understand patterns, relationships, and functions
- Represent and analyze mathematical situations and structures using algebraic symbols
- Use mathematical models to represent and understand quantitative relationships
- Analyze change in various contexts

At Grades 3 and 4, algebraic reasoning becomes a large part of mathematical investigations and discussions. The discussions at this level provide rich contexts for advancing students' understanding of mathematical concepts, as well as a strong foundation for future, more formal, algebra instruction. At this level, students use algebraic concepts to investigate numerical and geometric patterns. They use words and symbols to express their findings, organize information, and make generalizations about the relationships they find within patterns. Students also gain a deeper understanding of multiplicative processes and strategies through investigation and discussion of the properties of multiplication. Internalization of these strategies gives students the ability to apply their understandings across situations. The following are activities involving manipulatives that third- and fourth-grade students can use to develop skills in **Algebra.**

Algebra

Contents

Algebra

Extend Patterns

Although patterns were introduced in kindergarten, they have become much more complex—involving multiple shapes, colors, and numbers—as students have grown older. By the time students reach third and fourth grade, they should be able to express descriptions of patterns in words and in numbers. Students who understand a pattern will be able to extend the pattern.

Try It! *Perform the Try It! activity on the next page.*

Objective

Recognize and extend a geometric pattern.

Skills

• Identifying a pattern
• Representing a pattern
• Extending a pattern

NCTM Expectations

Algebra
• Describe, extend, and make generalizations about geometric and numeric patterns.
• Represent and analyze patterns and functions, using words, tables, and graphs.

Talk About It

Discuss the Try It! activity.

■ **Ask:** *Which shapes make up the pattern you made? What order are they in?*

■ **Say:** *Look at the pattern you made by following another group's directions.* **Ask:** *Could you extend the pattern for another 20 shapes? How far could you keep going?* Help students to conclude that the pattern can repeat forever—or until they run out of Attribute Blocks.

■ **Ask:** *What can you do to change the pattern?*

Solve It

With students, reread the problem. Have students draw the pattern of shapes their group made. Then challenge students to extend the activity by coloring in the shapes with crayons or markers. Have students repeat the pattern four more times. **Say:** *The colors must repeat the same way the shapes do.*

More Ideas

For other ways to teach about identifying and extending a pattern—

■ Have students use Centimeter Cubes to practice making patterns of different-sized and different-colored stacks.

■ Set up a learning center with rectangles created from Color Tiles that follow a color pattern. For example, you might make a 3 × 5 rectangle in which there is a color pattern in each row. Remove tiles from each rectangle and have students take turns finding the pattern and filling in the missing tiles.

Standardized Practice

Have students try the following problem.

Identify the next four shapes in the pattern.

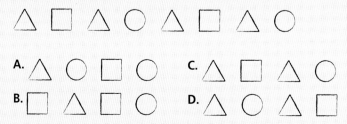

Try It!   20 minutes | Groups of 4

Here is a problem about recognizing and extending a geometric pattern.

Mr. Williams is having his class play a game with Attribute Blocks. Each group makes a pattern that is four shapes long, and repeats it four times. Then the students write a list of directions on how to re-create the pattern. Other class members will have to follow the directions to re-create the pattern. What pattern can a group make with the Attribute Blocks?

Introduce the problem. Then have students do the activity to solve the problem. Distribute Attribute Blocks, paper, and pencils to groups of students.

Materials
- Attribute Blocks
- paper
- crayons

1. Have one student in each group make a shape pattern that is four blocks long. Then have students repeat the pattern with blocks and two more times on their papers. **Ask:** *What shapes are repeated? What order are they in?*

2. Have students identify the original part of the pattern that repeats and trace it with their fingers. **Ask:** *Is the original part of your pattern repeated exactly? Are the shapes in the same order every time the pattern repeats?* Direct students to work as a group to write directions on how to form their pattern.

3. Have groups exchange directions with one another and then work to find the pattern with their blocks and on paper.

⚠ Look Out!

Students may have difficulty recognizing a pattern composed of more than two shapes. Suggest that students use string or yarn to circle what they think is the original part of the pattern.

Ask: *How many shapes are there?* If students say "four," have them look at the next four shapes. **Ask:** *Do these four match the first four exactly, in both the shapes used and the order they're in?*

Algebra

Identify the Rule

Patterns are the basis of algebra. In third and fourth grade, students should be able to identify geometric patterns of several shapes that are repeated and be able to generalize to find a rule for the pattern. With a rule for the pattern, students will be able to correctly extend the pattern indefinitely. Students apply these skills to identify numeric patterns and rules and to extend them using calculations or models.

Objective

Identify patterning rules to extend a numerical pattern.

Try It! Perform the Try It! activity on the next page.

Skills

- Understanding a pattern
- Identifying a rule
- Extending a pattern

Talk About It

Discuss the Try It! activity.

■ **Say:** *There are different ways to describe this pattern.* **Ask:** *How could you describe the pattern with numbers?* (Each group has 2 more Pattern Blocks than the previous group.)

■ **Ask:** *What is the rule for the pattern?* (Add 2 to each group.) **Say:** *Suppose the pattern was reversed and started with 16, then 14, then 12, and so on.* **Ask:** *Would the rule be the same or would it change? How can you tell?* Students should see that the rule is to subtract 2. Discuss the difference between growing patterns and decreasing patterns.

■ **Say:** *Explain how you used the "add 2" rule to predict the next three numbers in the pattern.*

NCTM Expectations

Algebra
- Describe, extend, and make generalizations about geometric and numeric patterns.
- Represent and analyze patterns and functions, using words, tables, and graphs.

Solve It

With students, reread the problem. Have students extend the pattern by drawing a picture to figure out how many plants Ms. Chin would have in the tenth section of the garden. Then have students write to explain how they drew their conclusions.

More Ideas

For other ways to teach about pattern rules and extending patterns—

■ Have students work in pairs. Ask one student in a pair to create a growing or decreasing pattern using stacks of one color of Color Tiles. Then have his or her partner describe the rule and extend the pattern.

■ Give students a pattern such as 2, 3, 5, 9, 17 (double the number and subtract 1). Have them show the pattern with Centimeter Cubes, find the rule, and extend the pattern.

Standardized Practice

Have students try the following problem.

Identify the next three numbers in the pattern below.

30, 29, 27, 24, 20, _____ , _____ , _____

A. 16, 12, 8   **B.** 15, 9, 2   **C.** 15, 10, 5   **D.** 24, 27, 29

Try It! 25 minutes | Groups of 4

Here is a problem about identifying pattern rules.

Ms. Chin and her students are planting a vegetable garden in the corner of the schoolyard. She put 2 plants in the first section, 4 in the second section, and 6 in the third section. What is the rule for the pattern? Can you find how many plants she will put in the tenth section?

Introduce the problem. Then have students do the activity to solve the problem. Distribute Pattern Blocks to each group of students.

Materials
• Pattern Blocks

1. Ask students to create the pattern 2, 4, 6 with blocks as shown in the photograph. You may wish to draw the pattern on the board to show students how to arrange their blocks.

2. Have students describe the pattern to their groups. **Ask:** *What is the rule for this pattern?* Students should recognize that each group of blocks has two more blocks than the previous group.

3. Say: *Now that you know the rule, you can predict what comes next in the pattern.* Ask students to predict the next three steps in the pattern and extend the pattern using blocks.

⚠ Look Out!

Students may be confused by patterns that descend in size if they have only seen ascending patterns. Write out the pattern 15, 13, 11, 9, 7, 5, 3, 1, and then use Color Tiles to model the pattern and show students the visual decline in the pattern corresponding to the numerical values.

Algebra

Square Numbers

Students need to understand that square numbers are the product of a number multiplied by itself. It is often helpful if students memorize square numbers from $1 \times 1 = 1$ to $12 \times 12 = 144$. They should also understand that they can divide a square number into two equal factors. Understanding square numbers becomes increasingly important for future work in algebra with the quadratic formula and the distance formula, which rely on being able to accurately find square roots and square numbers.

Try It! *Perform the Try It! activity on the next page.*

Talk About It

Discuss the Try It! activity.

- **Say:** *We have been working with square numbers.* **Ask:** *How would you describe a square number? What is the rule for making a square number?*
- **Ask:** *What numbers can be multiplied by themselves to make square numbers?*
- **Say:** *You made several models of square numbers using Color Tiles.* **Ask:** *What did you notice about the shape of your arrays? Is 20 a square number? What shape would an array for the number 20 be?*

Solve It

With students, reread the problem. Have students draw models to show the three square numbers from the problem. Then have them draw a model to answer the question. Invite students to label each drawing with a multiplication problem.

More Ideas

For other ways to teach about square numbers—

- Ask students to use Centimeter Cubes to create square numbers up to 144 and record the value of each square in a table. Then have students mark their answers on a Hundred Chart (BLM 3).
- Have students use Two-Color Counters to work backward to find the factors of square numbers. Students should build large squares with the counters, then count two sides of the squares to find the factors.

Standardized Practice

Have students try the following problem.

Which array shows the square number 16?

A. ⁞⁞⁞ B. ⁞⁞⁞⁞ C. ⁞⁞⁞⁞⁞ D. ⁞⁞⁞⁞⁞⁞⁞

Objective

Investigate square numbers.

Skills

- Identifying a pattern
- Multiplying numbers
- Representing numbers

NCTM Expectations

Algebra
- Describe, extend, and make generalizations about geometric and numeric patterns.
- Represent and analyze patterns and functions, using words, tables, and graphs.

Try It! 30 minutes | Pairs

Here is a problem about square numbers.

Mrs. Zuniga wants to arrange the chairs in the classroom into squares for a game. She starts with 1 chair, then she uses 4 chairs to make a square that is 2 chairs by 2 chairs, and 9 chairs to make a square that is 3 chairs by 3 chairs. If the pattern continues, how many chairs will make up the next square?

Introduce the problem. Then have students do the activity to solve the problem. Explain to students the concept of a square number: A square number is a number that can be represented by a square array. Distribute Color Tiles to each pair of students.

Materials
• Color Tiles (50 per pair)

1. Tell students to use their tiles to make squares that represent square numbers. Ask students to model the square numbers 1, 4, and 9 with their tiles. Remind them to check their squares to make sure that each side is the same length.

2. Say: *Look at the pattern in tiles.* **Ask:** *What do you think is the next square number in this pattern? Can you build a square with 12 tiles?* Have students model the square number 16 with tiles.

3. Have students continue the pattern by modeling square numbers, such as 25, 36, and 49. For numbers greater than 49, pairs will need to form groups of four to combine tiles.

⚠ Look Out!

Because of their studies in geometry, students may associate the term *square* with *even* and think that square numbers are only even numbers, such as 10 or 40. Demonstrate to students that square numbers are both even and odd by making a list of the square numbers—including the products and their factors—from 1 to 144 and having students identify the odd numbers.

Algebra

Identifying Change

Qualitative and quantitative change are important concepts in statistics. Students should learn that qualitative change can be described in general non-numerical terms (e.g., growing taller), and quantitative change is described in precise numerical terms (e.g., growing 3 inches). Often quantitative change is precise enough to make a prediction about what is going to happen. The first inclination of students may be to describe change qualitatively, but it is important to encourage students to make quantitative statements about change.

Try It! *Perform the Try It! activity on the next page.*

Talk About It

Discuss the Try It! activity.

- **Say:** *Describe the pattern 1, 2, 4, 7, 11, 16 in a qualitative way.*
- **Say:** *We talked about two types of change.* **Ask:** *When we discovered that we were adding 1, then 2, then 3, then 4, then 5—always adding the previous number added plus one—was that a qualitative or quantitative change? Why?*
- **Ask:** *What is another example of quantitative change? What is another example of qualitative change?*

Solve It

With students, reread the problem. Ask students to write a short paragraph to explain the pattern of can collection in the problem, and then identify how many cans will be collected by the third-grade class on the sixth day.

More Ideas

For other ways to teach about qualitative and quantitative change—

- Have one student in a pair create a numeric pattern with Color Tiles. Have the other student in the pair describe the pattern in qualitative and quantitative ways. Then partners switch roles.
- Divide the class into pairs. One partner should work out the first five steps of a pattern and then challenge his or her partner to predict what the eighth step would be in the pattern. Have students use Centimeter Cubes to model the pattern and describe the pattern qualitatively and quantitatively.

Standardized Practice

Have students try the following problem.

Look at the pattern below. What are the next three numbers?

1, 4, 7, 10, 13, _____ , _____ , _____

A. 16, 19, 22   **B.** 17, 22, 28   **C.** 15, 17, 19   **D.** 23, 39, 62

Objective

Identify qualitative and quantitative change.

Skills

- Identifying patterns
- Understanding patterns
- Describing change

NCTM Expectations

Algebra
- Describe, extend, and make generalizations about geometric and numeric patterns.
- Represent and analyze patterns and functions, using words, tables, and graphs.

Try It! 20 minutes | Pairs

Here is a problem about qualitative and quantitative change.

Third graders are recycling aluminum cans. They collected 1 can on the first day, 2 cans on the second day, 4 cans on the third day, and 7 on the fourth day. If this pattern continues, how many cans would they collect on the sixth day?

Introduce the problem. Then have students do the activity to solve the problem. Distribute Two-Color Counters to each pair of students.

Materials
- Two-Color Counters (65 per pair)
- paper and pencil (1 of each per pair)

1. Have students model the numbers 1, 2, 4, and 7 with counters. **Ask:** *What changes do you see from the number of counters in one group to the next?* The number of counters is increasing in a growing pattern. Explain to students that this change is qualitative because it is being described in general terms with words, not specific numbers.

2. Say: *A quantitative change is change that can be described with numbers.* **Ask:** *How can we find the quantitative change?* Guide students to see that they must find the number of counters each group increases by in the pattern. Have students count the counters in each group. They should see that there is one more counter in the second group than in the first. Have them write an addition problem to express this change.

⚠ Look Out!

Students may confuse quantitative and qualitative change. Emphasize that the word "quantitative" is related to the word "quantity" and the word "qualitative" is related to the word "quality."

3. Have students write addition problems to show the change from group to group. **Ask:** *What is the quantitative change in this pattern? How many counters will be in the next group?* Have students model the next two numbers in the pattern.

Objective

Model and identify the Commutative Property of Addition.

Skills

- Adding
- Applying the Commutative Property
- Understanding sums

NCTM Expectations

Algebra
- Identify such properties as commutativity, associativity, and distributivity and use them to compute with whole numbers.

Algebra

Commutative Property of Addition

The Commutative Property of Addition states that addends added in any order will still have the same sum. For any two values, *a* and *b*, $a + b = b + a$. The Commutative Property of Addition is important for numeric values, but it also sets the stage for working with equations in algebra adeptly and flexibly.

Try It! *Perform the Try It! activity on the next page.*

Talk About It

Discuss the Try It! activity.

- **Say:** *Look at your first pair of number sentences.* **Ask:** *How are the addends, or the numbers being added, in each number sentence similar? How are they different?*
- **Ask:** *What did you notice about the sums of your two number sentences?* Discuss the Commutative Property of Addition with students.
- **Ask:** *What happened when we added three numbers in different orders? Did the Commutative Property of Addition work for three numbers?*

Solve It

With students, reread the problem. Ask students to explain in writing the Commutative Property of Addition. Tell students to use this property to explain how Teams A and B got the same answer to the problems.

More Ideas

For other ways to teach about the Commutative Property of Addition—

- Have students create number sentences with three addends. Then have them use one size of Three Bear Family® Counters to model the number sentences and reorder the addends.
- Have pairs of students use the Bucket Balance and Color Tiles to create equalities in which the addends are on the left side of the balance and the sum is on the right side of the balance. For example, have students put 8 tiles on the right side. Have them add 5 tiles to the left side, then 3 tiles to make both sides even. Students should remove tiles from the left side, then add tiles in reverse order, first 3, then 5.

Standardized Practice

Have students try the following problem.

According to the Commutative Property of Addition, which of the following means the same as 2 + 3 = 5?

A. $3 + 2 = 5$ **B.** $5 - 2 = 3$ **C.** $2 + 3 + 2 = 7$ **D.** $3 \times 2 = 5$

Try It! 20 minutes | Groups of 3

Here is a problem about the Commutative Property of Addition.

Mr. Samuel divided his class into two teams to practice addition problems. He asked Team A to solve 7 + 2. He asked Team B to solve 2 + 7. What answers did the two teams get?

Introduce the problem. Then have students do the activity to solve the problem. Distribute Cuisenaire® Rods, Centimeter Grids (BLM 17), and paper to groups of students.

Materials
- Cuisenaire® Rods (half a set per group)
- Centimeter Grid (BLM 17; 1 per group)
- paper (1 sheet per group)
- crayons

1. Ask students to find the Rod that is equal to 7. Students should use the white Rods to measure, if necessary. Then have students find the Rod equal to 2. **Say:** *Now find the Rod that is equal to 7 plus 2.* Have students write an addition number sentence to show their model.

2. Have students reverse the order of the black and red Rods to show 2 + 7. **Say:** *Now build a train to show 2 + 7.* Have students write an addition number sentence to show their model. Have students compare the answers of the two addition sentences.

3. Ask: *What if we added three numbers together? Does the order of the addends change the answer we get?* Have students model adding 3 + 1 + 4 with Rods, then 1 + 4 + 3. They should reach the conclusion that the numbers can be added in any order. Explain to students that this is because of a rule called the Commutative Property of Addition.

⚠ Look Out!

Students may mistakenly think that they can use the Commutative Property of Addition to switch any two numbers in an addition problem. Reaffirm that only the addends can shift places without changing the problem. Demonstrate by showing students that only the numbers to the left of the equal sign may be switched. Also, some students may overgeneralize, thinking that the property can also be applied to subtraction. Demonstrate with Rods that changing the number order in a subtraction problem will change the outcome.

Algebra

Commutative Property of Multiplication

The Commutative Property of Multiplication states that you can multiply factors in any order and get the same product. For any two values, *a* and *b*, $a \times b = b \times a$. Students will apply the Commutative Property in their work in algebra with variables.

Try It! *Perform the Try It! activity on the next page.*

Talk About It

Discuss the Try It! activity.

- **Ask:** *What answer did you get for 3 × 6? 6 × 3?*
- **Ask:** *What numbers can you change the order of using the Commutative Property of Multiplication? Can you switch a factor and the product? Why or why not?* Model for students what will happen if a product is changed for a factor. For example, write on the board 3 × 4 = 12. **Ask:** *If you change the number sentence to 3 × 12 = 4, is it still true?*
- **Ask:** *Do you think the Commutative Property of Multiplication works for multiplication sentences with more than two factors?* Encourage students to test the property using number sentences with three factors.

Solve It

With students, reread the problem. Have students write two multiplication sentences that could be used to find the amount of fruit each class has. Then ask them to write a sentence telling why both multiplication sentences have the same answer.

More Ideas

For other ways to teach about the Commutative Property of Multiplication—

- Have one student model an array with Color Tiles. Then have his or her partner model an array that uses the same factors in a different order. Both students write multiplication sentences to represent the arrays.
- Prepare a paper bag that contains different multiplication sentences written on slips of paper. Have students pick a slip from the bag without looking and rewrite the multiplication sentence using the Commutative Property. Students should make arrays of Centimeter Cubes for both sentences.

Standardized Practice

Have students try the following problem.

What is another way to write 10 × 12 = 120?

A. 12 + 10 = 120 **B.** 1 × 10 = 10 **C.** 12 × 10 = 120 **D.** 2 × 20 = 120

Objective

Model and identify the Commutative Property of Multiplication.

Skills

- Multiplying
- Applying the Commutative Property of Multiplication
- Understanding products

NCTM Expectations

Algebra
- Identify such properties as commutativity, associativity, and distributivity and use them to compute with whole numbers.
- Represent the idea of a variable as an unknown quantity using a letter or a symbol.

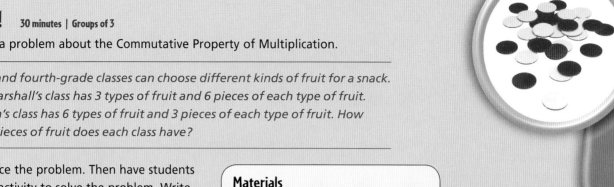

Try It! 30 minutes | Groups of 3

Here is a problem about the Commutative Property of Multiplication.

Third- and fourth-grade classes can choose different kinds of fruit for a snack. Mrs. Marshall's class has 3 types of fruit and 6 pieces of each type of fruit. Mr. Kim's class has 6 types of fruit and 3 pieces of each type of fruit. How many pieces of fruit does each class have?

Introduce the problem. Then have students do the activity to solve the problem. Write 3 × 6 = _____ and 6 × 3 = _____ on the board. Distribute Two-Color Counters to each group of students. Define the terms *factor* and *product*.

Materials
- Two-Color Counters (40 per group)

1. Have students model 3 groups of 6 using counters in an array. The array should have 3 rows with 6 counters in each row. Ask students to find the product. Fill in the answer for 3 × 6 on the board.

2. Have students model 6 groups of 3 using counters in an array. The array should have 6 rows of counters with 3 in each row. Ask students to find the product. Fill in the answer for 6 × 3 on the board.

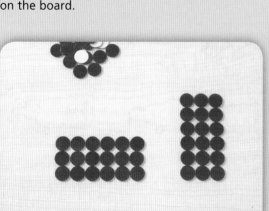

3. Ask students to compare the arrays they have made to confirm that both have the same number of counters. Explain that the factors in the number sentence can be switched because of the Commutative Property of Multiplication. Have students compare the two arrays side-by-side to see that they reflect the same quantities.

⚠ Look Out!

Students may believe that they can use the Commutative Property of Multiplication to exchange the product with one of the factors. Reinforce that the Commutative Property of Multiplication says that you can change the order of the factors with one another but not with the product. Use arrays of counters to show that when a factor and product are switched, the resulting number sentence will be incorrect. Also, be aware that some students may overgeneralize and try to use the Commutative Property to do division. Demonstrate with counters that when the order of numbers in a division sentence is changed, the answer is changed as well.

Algebra

Associative Property of Addition

The Associative Property of Addition allows you to group and regroup addends without changing the sum: $(a + b) + c = a + (b + c)$ for any three values, a, b, and c. Students will find that the Associative Property allows them to add compatible numbers more easily by regrouping a series of addends when finding the sum.

Objective

Model and identify the Associative Property of Addition.

Skills

- Adding
- Applying the Associative Property of Addition
- Understanding sums

NCTM Expectations

Algebra
- Identify such properties as commutativity, associativity, and distributivity and use them to compute with whole numbers.
- Represent the idea of a variable as an unknown quantity using a letter or a symbol.

Try It! *Perform the Try It! activity on the next page.*

Talk About It

Discuss the Try It! activity.

- Display $4 + 3 + 2 =$ _____ . **Say:** *A train of purple, green, and red Cuisenaire® Rods shows $4 + 3 + 2$. A blue Rod shows the sum.* **Ask:** *What is the sum?*

- Display $(4 + 3) + 2 =$ _____ . Remind students that they should do the work inside the parentheses first. **Ask:** *What train did we use to show that we added the 4 and 3 first?* (the black Rod and the red Rod) **Ask:** *When we added the 4 and the 3 first, did we still get 9 as the sum?*

- Display $4 + (3 + 2) =$ _____ . **Ask:** *What train did we use to show that we added the 3 and the 2 first?* (the yellow Rod and the purple Rod) **Ask:** *When we added the 3 and the 2 first, did we still get 9 as the sum?*

Solve It

With students, reread the problem. Ask students to explain in writing how they used the Associative Property to write two addition sentences to show the total weight of Tricia's books.

More Ideas

For other ways to teach about the Associative Property of Addition—

- Have students work in pairs to represent number sentences using Three Bear Family® Counters. Students should draw large parentheses lengthwise on index cards and pick one size of Bear. Then one student should write a pair of number sentences, and the other student should place groups of Bears inside the parentheses to show the different groupings of addends.

- Have students use Centimeter Cubes to model two number sentences, such as $(7 + 9) + 6 =$ _____ and $7 + (9 + 6) =$ _____ . They should use a different color for each numerical value.

Standardized Practice

Have students try the following problem.

What is another way to write $8 + (9 + 4) = 21$ using the Associative Property?

A. $4 + 8 + 9 = 21$ C. $(8 - 4) + 9 = 21$

B. $(8 + 9) + 4 = 21$ D. $8 + (9 \times 4) = 21$

Try It! 20 minutes | Pairs

Here is a problem about the Associative Property of Addition.

Tricia's math book weighs 4 pounds. Her science book weighs 3 pounds, and her reading book weighs 2 pounds. Write two addition sentences that can be used to find the total weight of her books. Then solve to find the total weight.

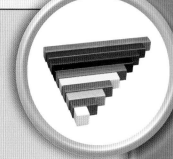

Introduce the problem. Then have students do the activity to solve the problem. Distribute materials to students. Review the meanings of *addend* and *sum*. Explain that each Rod represents a number. Have students count how many white Rods each Rod is made out of to find the number it represents.

Materials

- Cuisenaire® Rods (1 each of blue, black, yellow; 2 each of purple, light green; 3 red per pair)
- Associative Property Worksheet (BLM 13; 1 per pair)

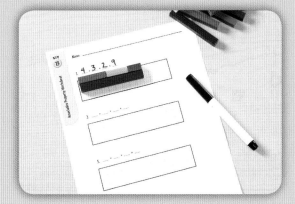

1. Ask students to model the addition number sentence 4 + 3 + 2 using a train of Rods to show the addends and find the Rod that shows the sum (blue). Have students complete the first section on their worksheets by writing the number sentence and sketching the Rods.

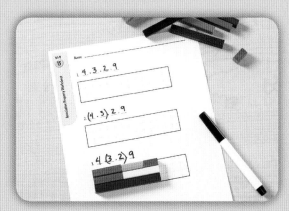

3. Have students make another purple, light green, and red train. Write the number sentence 4 + (3 + 2) = _____ on the board. Ask students to model this number sentence with Rods and fill in the third section on their worksheets.

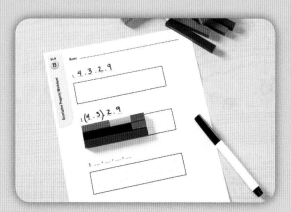

2. Have students make another purple, light green, and red train. Write the number sentence (4 + 3) + 2 = _____ on the board. Explain that the numbers in parentheses must be added first. Have students find a Rod the same length as the purple and green Rods combined (black) to show that these Rods are being added first. They should then combine the black Rod with the red Rod. Have students complete the second section on their worksheets.

⚠ Look Out!

Students may confuse the Commutative Property of Addition with the Associative Property of Addition. Emphasize that the use of parentheses tells students that they are grouping numbers together using the Associative Property; whereas the Commutative Property involves the order of numbers.

Objective

Model and identify the Associative Property of Multiplication.

Skills

- Multiplying three factors
- Applying the Associative Property of Multiplication
- Understanding products

NCTM Expectations

Algebra
- Identify such properties as commutativity, associativity, and distributivity and use them to compute with whole numbers.
- Represent the idea of a variable as an unknown quantity using a letter or a symbol.

Algebra

Associative Property of Multiplication

The Associative Property of Multiplication allows you to group and regroup the factors in a multiplication equation without changing the product. For any three values, *a*, *b*, and *c*, $(a \times b) \times c = a \times (b \times c)$. Students need to understand that regrouping numbers will allow them to multiply number pairs. The Associative Property is used in algebraic relations when working with equations.

Try It! Perform the Try It! activity on the next page.

Talk About It

Discuss the Try It! activity.

- **Ask:** *When you grouped the factors differently, did you get different products?* Emphasize that the Associative Property of Multiplication allows students to use different groups of factors to get the same product.

- **Ask:** *Which way was easier to multiply, 2 × (4 × 5) or (2 × 4) × 5? Why do you think the Associative Property is useful sometimes?* Guide students to understand that some number pairs are easier to multiply than others.

- **Ask:** *How is the Associative Property of Multiplication like the Associative Property of Addition? How are the properties different?*

Solve It

With students, reread the problem. Have students write to tell what products Jack and Meg calculated and explain why their answers were the same.

More Ideas

For other ways to teach about the Associative Property of Multiplication—

- Ask students to use Color Tiles to group factor arrays in different ways to get the same product. Have students draw large parentheses on paper to put around the tiles to show which factors are being multiplied first.

- Have students work in pairs with Color Tiles. Give students a product and have them work backward to find factors using the Associative Property. For example, if you gave students 50 as a product, they could come up with the number sentences (25 × 2) × 1 = 50 or (2 × 5) × 5 = 50.

Standardized Practice

Have students try the following problem.

What is another way to write (4 × 9) × 8 = 288 using the Associative Property of Multiplication?

A. 4 + (9 + 8) = 288   **C.** 4 × (9 × 288) = 8
B. 8 × 9 × 4 = 288   **D.** 4 × (9 × 8) = 288

Try It! **25 minutes | Groups of 3**

Here is a problem about the Associative Property of Multiplication.

Mrs. Larson's fourth-grade class is practicing multiplication. Mrs. Larson gives Jack the following problem to solve: 2 × (4 × 5) = _____ . She gives Meg another problem: (2 × 4) × 5 = _____ . What answers do the students get?

Introduce the problem. Then have students do the activity to solve the problem. Distribute Two-Color Counters to groups of students. Review the terms *factor* and *product* and the use of arrays if necessary. Write the problem 2 × 4 × 5 = _____ on the board.

Materials
- Two-Color Counters (80 per group)
- paper (1 sheet per group)
- pencils (1 per group)

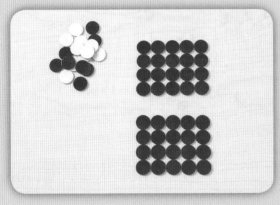

1. Have students model the number sentence 2 × (4 × 5) = _____ by showing 2 groups of 4 × 5 arrays. Then have them find the product.

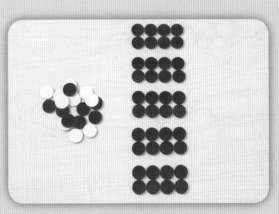

2. Have students model the number sentence (2 × 4) × 5 = _____ by showing 5 groups of 2 × 4 arrays. Then have them find the product.

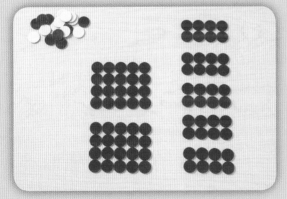

3. Have students compare the two sets of arrays they made out of counters. Ask them to write two number sentences to represent their models using parentheses to group the numbers that are multiplied first.

⚠ Look Out!

Students may confuse the Associative Property of Multiplication with the Commutative Property of Multiplication. Remind students that the Associative Property allows you to group numbers in different ways. The Commutative Property allows you to shift the factors' places in the number sentence. Also, watch for students who try to use the Associative Property when there is more than one operation present. For example, students may think that (6 + 4) × 3 is the same as 6 + (4 × 3). Model for students on the board that number sentences like this will have two different answers. It may be helpful to allow students to represent their products on grid paper.

Algebra

Distributive Property

The Distributive Property may be particularly challenging to students at this age because it involves more than one operation. The Distributive Property shows that, for the whole numbers a, b, and c: $(a \times b) + (a \times c) = a(b + c)$. While learning to apply the Distributive Property, students must address the order of operations and explore the consequences of ignoring it.

Try It! *Perform the Try It! activity on the next page.*

Talk About It

Discuss the Try It! activity.

■ **Say:** *First you made two rectangles.* **Ask:** *What part of the problem on the board does each model represent?*

■ **Say:** *Both rectangles had one side that was two Color Tiles long. Then you pushed the two rectangles together to make one.* **Ask:** *What number sentence shows the multiplication problem modeled by the tiles?*

■ **Say:** *The Distributive Property worked for (2 × 3) + (2 × 5) because the multiplication problems have a* common factor, *or one factor that is the same in both.* Have students identify the common factor (2).

Solve It

With students, reread the problem. Have students draw a picture of the tables and computers in the problem. **Say:** *Now draw a picture that shows the tables pushed together to make one long table.* Have students write a short paragraph telling how many computers there are in all.

More Ideas

For other ways to teach about the Distributive Property—

■ Discuss the order of operations with students. Write $3 \times 5 + 3 \times 4$ on the board. Have students use Centimeter Cubes to model each problem twice: once following the proper order of operations and once ignoring it. Have students use pencils or cut out parentheses to group the models. Then have students apply the Distributive Property and solve the problem.

■ Make two columns on the board. On the left, write $(5 \times 4) + (5 \times 2)$, $(3 \times 6) + (3 \times 5)$, and $(2 \times 8) + (2 \times 3)$. On the right, write $2(8 + 3)$, $5(4 + 2)$, and $3(6 + 5)$. Have groups of students use Color Tiles to model each problem. Then have students identify the equivalent models and problems.

Standardized Practice

Have students try the following problem.

Circle the choice that shows (3 × 2) + (3 × 4) rewritten using the Distributive Property.

A. $3(2 + 4)$ **B.** $2(3 \times 4)$ **C.** $4(3 + 2)$ **D.** $2(3 + 4)$

Objective

Model and identify the Distributive Property.

Skills

- Applying properties of operations
- Addition
- Multiplication

NCTM Expectations

Algebra
- Identify such properties as commutativity, associativity, and distributivity and use them to compute with whole numbers.

Number and Operations
- Understand the effects of multiplying and dividing whole numbers.
- Understand and use properties of operations, such as the distributivity of multiplication over addition.

Try It! 30 minutes | Pairs

Here is a problem about modeling and identifying the Distributive Property.

The computer lab at Lincoln Elementary School rearranged the computers. One table has 2 rows of 3 computers each, and the other table has 2 rows of 5 computers each. How many computers are there in all?

Introduce the problem. Then have students do the activity to solve the problem. Distribute Color Tiles to students. Write $(2 \times 3) + (2 \times 5) =$ _____ on the board. Remind students that the numbers within the parentheses should be multiplied before their products are added together.

Materials
- Color Tiles (30 of one color and 30 of another color per pair)

1. Tell students to use one color of tiles to model a 2×3 rectangle and another color to model a 2×5 rectangle. **Ask:** *How many counters are in each rectangle? How many in all?*

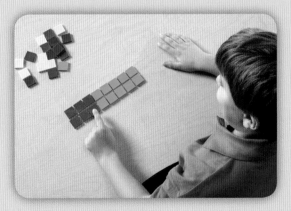

3. Say: *Your model shows one side that is 2 tiles long and another that is 3 + 5, or 8, tiles long.* Write 2(3 + 5) and 2 × 8 on the board. **Ask:** *How many tiles are there altogether?* Explain that their models show an example of the Distributive Property. **Say:** *Making a 2 × 3 array and adding it to a 2 × 5 array is the same as making a 2 × 8—or 2(3 + 5)—array.*

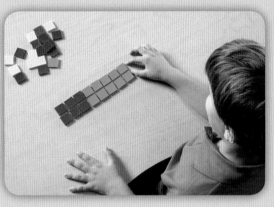

2. Point out that both rectangles have one side that is 2 tiles long, and explain that this means they can push the rectangles together to make one larger one. Have students push their 2 rectangles together to make one larger 2 × 8 rectangle.

⚠ Look Out!

Watch for students who try to push their models together into a shape that is not a rectangle. For example, students might make a shape that has four rows instead of two. Have students start over, then ask them to count to find the side that is the same length in both rectangles. Tell students to make these two sides meet when they push the rectangles together.

Algebra

Input/Output Tables

Students should have experiences applying their knowledge of operations in a variety of ways. Completing input/output function tables gives students the chance to use many different operations, and also gives them practice finding and using inverse operations. For example, if a student must add to get from the input number to the output number, then he or she must subtract to get from the output number to the input number. Using function tables also helps students find patterns and express patterns as rules, or functions, such as "add 3" or "multiply by 11."

Objective

Complete input/output function tables.

Try It! *Perform the Try It! activity on the next page.*

Talk About It

Discuss the Try It! activity.

- **Ask:** *How did you find the function, or rule, for this table?*
- **Ask:** *How can you find the output number if you know the input number? How can you find the input number if you know the output number?*
- **Say:** *Suppose your table had 3 more rows.* **Ask:** *What would be the input and output numbers for those 3 rows?*

Skills

- Multiplying
- Dividing
- Identifying functions

Solve It

With students, reread the problem. Have students write a short paragraph explaining to Mrs. Barr's students how to find the missing numbers in the Input/Output Table (BLM 14). Then have students extend the Input/Output Table by modeling the input numbers up to 10 with Centimeter Cubes and finding their corresponding output numbers.

NCTM Expectations

Algebra
- Describe, extend, and make generalizations about geometric and numeric patterns.
- Represent and analyze patterns and functions, using words, tables, and graphs.

Number and Operations
- Identify and use relationships between operations, such as division as the inverse of multiplication, to solve problems.

More Ideas

For other ways to teach about input/output function tables—

- Have students make their own input/output function tables using Cuisenaire® Rods. Instruct students to leave at least two spaces blank on their tables. Tell them to exchange tables with a partner, and have partners determine the functions of the tables and fill in the missing Rods.

- Divide students into groups of four. Have them use large sheets of poster board, markers, and Base Ten Blocks to create large input/output function tables. Challenge students to use functions that involve multiples of 10.

Standardized Practice

Have students try the following problem.

Which number completes the table?

A. 25
B. 29
C. 35
D. 40

Input	Output
4	28
5	?
6	42

Try It! 30 Minutes | Pairs

Here is a problem about completing input/output function tables.

Every day, Mrs. Barr has "secret numbers of the day." She gives her class clues. Today's clue is an input/output table, and the "secret numbers of the day" are the two missing numbers in the table. How can the students find the missing numbers?

Introduce the problem. Then have students do the activity to solve the problem. Distribute Centimeter Cubes and an Input/Output Table (BLM 14) to each pair. Draw the table shown at the right on the board. **Say:** *This is called an Input/Output Table. The purpose of the table is to show how the input number changes to the output number.*

Materials

- Centimeter Cubes (80 per pair)
- Input/Output Table (BLM 14; 1 per pair)
- paper and pencils

Input	Output
2	4
?	5
4	6
5	?

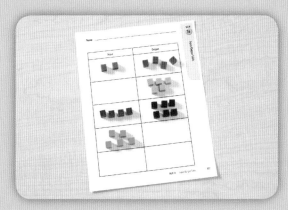

1. Say: *Look at the table on the board.* Have students use cubes to model the table from the board on their Input/Output Tables.

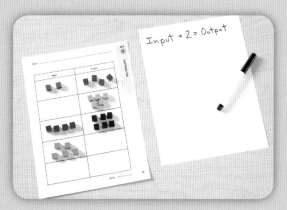

2. Ask: *If we started with 2 cubes, how did we get 4 cubes? How did we get from 4 cubes to 6?* Have students examine the rows of cubes to find the pattern. Tell students that this change can be expressed using operations and numbers. Guide students to record the change, + 2.

⚠ Look Out!

Students may not see that they have to use the function's inverse operation when finding an input number. Explain that if you add to go from the input number to the output number, then you must subtract to go from the output number to the input number.

3. Ask: *Now that we know about the change, how can we find the missing numbers?* Instruct students to use cubes to fill in the blank boxes.

Algebra

Addition and Subtraction

As students become fluent in computation, they begin to apply their understanding of operations to problem-solving situations. Students address equations that have an unknown number and learn to work backward by using the inverse operation to solve for the missing number. In this lesson, students model addition and subtraction number sentences and experience firsthand how the two operations are related.

Objective

Solve addition and subtraction number sentences.

Skills

- Adding
- Subtracting
- Problem solving

NCTM Expectations

Algebra
- Express mathematical relationships using equations.
- Model problem situations with objects and use representations such as graphs, tables, and equations to draw conclusions.

Number and Operations
- Identify and use relationships between operations, such as division as the inverse of multiplication, to solve problems.
- Develop fluency in adding, subtracting, multiplying, and dividing whole numbers.

Try It! *Perform the Try It! activity on the next page.*

Talk About It

Discuss the Try It! activity.

- **Ask:** *How did you use subtraction to find a missing addend—or adding number—in an addition sentence? How did you use addition to solve a subtraction problem?*

- **Ask:** *How can you use subtraction to find out what number plus 13 equals 29?* Write _____ + 13 = 29 on the board. Students should explain that they would subtract 13 from 29. Write 29 − 13 = _____ on the board. Invite students to solve.

- **Ask:** *How can I use addition to show what number minus 23 equals 18?* Write _____ − 23 = 18 on the board. Students should explain that they would add 23 and 18 to find the answer. Write 18 + 23 = _____ on the board. Invite students to solve.

Solve It

With students, reread the problem. Have students explain in writing how they solved the problem. Then have students show the solution using both an addition and a subtraction sentence.

More Ideas

For other ways to teach about addition and subtraction number sentences—

- Invite students to solve additional problems using Base Ten Blocks and the Missing Numbers Worksheet (BLM 15). Have students record their completed addition and subtraction sentences for each problem.

- Have students write their own addition and subtraction problems involving families of bears. Have students exchange problems with a partner. Then partners use the inverse operation and Three Bear Family® Counters to model and solve the problems.

Standardized Practice

Have students try the following problem.

Circle the addition sentence that solves this problem: _____ − 29 = 16

A. 10 + 6 = 16   **B.** 16 + 29 = 45   **C.** 13 + 16 = 29   **D.** 29 + 29 = 58

Try It! 25 minutes | Groups of 4

Here is a problem about addition and subtraction number sentences.

Of the 18 students in our class, 7 students have perfect attendance so far this year. How many students do not have perfect attendance?

Introduce the problem. Then have students do the activity to solve the problem. Distribute Cuisenaire® Rods and Missing Numbers Worksheets (BLM 15) to students. Remind students that white Rods have a value of 1, orange Rods have a value of 10, and other colors have values in between.

Materials

- Cuisenaire® Rods (half a set per group)
- Missing Numbers Worksheet (BLM 15; 1 per group)

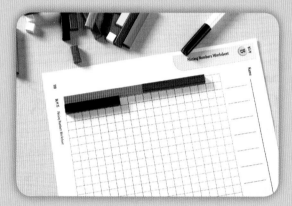

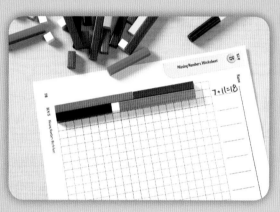

1. Say: *Look at the Missing Numbers Worksheet.* **Ask:** *How can you use it to find what number you would add to 7 to get 18?* Have students use Rods to model the addition problem on the worksheet.

2. Ask: *How can we solve this addition number sentence?* Guide students to see that they should subtract to find the missing number. Have students complete the train on the second line to match the first train.

3. Have students use Rods to solve a subtraction problem. Then write 20 − _____ = 14 on the board. **Ask:** *How can we solve this subtraction number sentence?* Have students model the problem on their worksheet and use addition to solve it.

⚠ Look Out!

Watch out for students who seem to start over from scratch when forming a subtraction problem to solve for a missing addend in an addition problem. Point out that the numbers in both problems should be identical; only their positions and the operation change. Demonstrate by showing how Rods placed on the Missing Numbers Worksheet change places.

Objective

Solve problems using either multiplication or division.

Skills

- Multiplying
- Dividing
- Problem solving

NCTM Expectations

Algebra
- Express mathematical relationships using equations.
- Model problem situations with objects and use representations such as graphs, tables, and equations to draw conclusions.

Number and Operations
- Understand various meanings of multiplication and division.
- Identify and use relationships between operations, such as division as the inverse of multiplication, to solve problems.

Algebra

Multiplication and Division

Beginning with concrete models and moving on to paper and pencil experiences, students begin to develop computational fluency. The more they work with numbers, the stronger this foundation becomes. Using the inverse operation of a problem as a means of checking answers is another way to practice computations and build fluency. In this lesson students identify whether multiplication or division should be used to solve problems and then create arrays to model and find the answers.

Try It! *Perform the Try It! activity on the next page.*

Talk About It

Discuss the Try It! activity.

- **Say:** *Look at the multiplication problem you wrote.* **Ask:** *How did you turn it into a division problem to find the missing factor?*
- **Ask:** *What two multiplication problems describe the array you made with the Color Tiles?* Students should conclude that 4×7 and 7×4 describe the array.
- **Ask:** *How can you use multiplication to make sure you perform division problems correctly?*

Solve It

With students, reread the problem. Have students write instructions telling how to solve the problem using multiplication, and then how to solve it using division. Then have students illustrate the solution on paper.

More Ideas

For other ways to teach about solving problems using multiplication or division—

- Display the following multiplication problems on the board: $6 \times$ _____ $= 42$, $7 \times$ _____ $= 35$, $9 \times$ _____ $= 27$, and $3 \times$ _____ $= 45$. Have students model and solve each problem using Centimeter Cubes. Then find the corresponding division problems.
- Have one student write a multiplication or division problem and model it using Color Tiles. Then direct his or her partner to make an inverse model to find the same answer.

Standardized Practice

Have students try the following problem.

Which of the following is another way to write and solve $20 \times$ _____ $= 80$?

A. $2 \times 80 = 160$
B. $80 \div 20 = 4$
C. $80 - 20 = 60$
D. $80 + 20 = 100$

Try It! 25 Minutes | Pairs

Here is a problem about using either multiplication or division.

There are 28 desks in the classroom. If we arrange the desks evenly in 4 rows, how many desks will there be in each row?

Introduce the problem. Then have students do the activity to solve the problem. Distribute Color Tiles, paper, and pencils to pairs of students.

Materials
- Color Tiles (50 per pair)
- paper (1 sheet per pair)
- pencils (1 per pair)

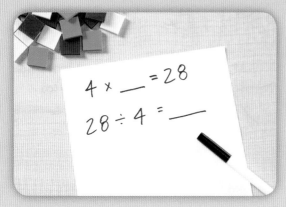

1. Say: *We know that there are 28 desks arranged evenly in 4 rows.* Write 4 × _____ = 28 on the board, and have students write it on their papers. **Say:** *We want to find the missing number.* **Ask:** *What kind of problem can we write to find how many desks will be in each row?* Guide students to conclude that they should write a division problem. Write 28 ÷ 4 = _____ on the board, and have students write it on their papers.

2. Tell students that they can make an array using the tiles to solve a division problem. **Ask:** *How many tiles will you use in your array?* Students should see that they will use 28 tiles, since that is the number they want to divide. **Ask:** *How many rows of tiles will there be in the array?* Guide students to conclude that there will be 4 rows. Have students make the array.

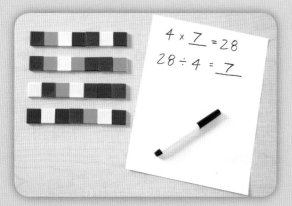

3. Ask: *How can you use the array to find the answer to 28 ÷ 4 = _____ .* Have students count the rows to solve and then fill in the blanks in the multiplication and division problems on their paper.

⚠ Look Out!

Look out for students who have difficulty formulating a division problem to solve a multiplication problem. Write 4 × 5 = 20 and 20 ÷ 4 = 5 on the board. Point out how the same three numbers are used in both problems, and how they are related. Invite students to write their own pairs of simple, corresponding division and multiplication problems.

Objective

Apply mathematical processes and concepts using concrete objects.

Skills

- Finding ratios
- Comparing weight
- Using tools for measuring weight

NCTM Expectations

Algebra
- Describe, extend, and make generalizations about geometric and numeric patterns.
- Represent and analyze patterns and functions, using words, tables, and graphs.
- Model problem situations with objects and use representations such as graphs, tables, and equations to draw conclusions.
- Investigate how a change in one variable relates to a change in a second variable.

Measurement
- Understand the need for measuring with standard units and become familiar with standard units in the customary and metric systems.

Algebra

Mathematical Reasoning

The use of concrete objects helps students to understand mathematical concepts by grounding abstract ideas in real-world experience. Comparing and ordering objects by weight allows students to apply their understanding of *greater than* and *less than* in a new context. Finding how many of one object equal the weight of another object by removing the same amount from both sides of a balance prepares them for later understanding of algebraic expressions.

Try It! *Perform the Try It! activity on the next page.*

Talk About It

Discuss the Try It! activity.

- With students, discuss the relationship between the weights of the Three Bear Family® Counters. Have students demonstrate each relationship with the Bucket Balance and Bears. **Ask:** *How many Mama Bear™ Counters equal 1 Papa Bear™ Counter? How many Baby Bear™ Counters equal 1 Mama Bear Counter? How many Mama Bear Counters equal 1 Papa Bear Counter? How can you tell?*

- On the board, write 1 Papa + 2 Mama = 3 Baby + 2 Mama. **Ask:** *How can we show in writing that we are taking 2 Mama Bear Counters away from each side?*

Solve It

With students, reread the problem. Then have students write step-by-step directions telling Matt how to find how many Baby Bear Counters equal 1 Papa Bear Counter.

More Ideas

For other ways to teach about mathematical reasoning—

- Once students have established the ratios among the Three Bear Family Counters, challenge them to figure out how many Bears it would take to balance the scale given a certain number on one side. For example, ask students how many Baby Bear Counters it would take to balance 2 Papa Bears.

- Instruct students to use the Bucket Balance to find out how many Centimeter Cubes weigh the same as given classroom objects. For example, how many cubes weigh the same as a pair of scissors? Have students list the objects in order of weight.

Standardized Practice

Have students try the following problem.

Three plums weigh the same as one apple. Two apples weigh the same as one orange. Which lists the fruits from heaviest to lightest?

A. orange, plum, apple   **C.** apple, orange, plum

B. orange, apple, plum   **D.** plum, orange, apple

Try It! 15 minutes | Pairs

Here is a problem about applying mathematical processes and concepts using concrete objects.

Matt has a Bucket Balance. One side of the balance has 1 Papa Bear™ Counter and 2 Mama Bear™ Counters. The other side has 3 Baby Bear™ Counters and 2 Mama Bears. How can Matt find out how many Baby Bears equal 1 Papa Bear?

Introduce the problem. Then have students do the activity to solve the problem. Place a balance and Three Bear Family® Counters at three different stations in the math center or in three locations in the classroom.

Materials
- Three Bear Family® Counters (12 each Papa Bear™ Counters and Mama Bear™ Counters, and 25 Baby Bear™ Counters per math center station)
- Bucket Balance (one balance per math center station)

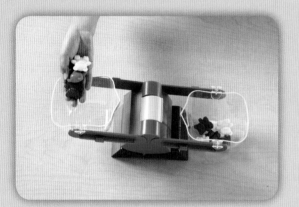

1. Have students place 1 Papa Bear and 2 Mama Bears on one side of the balance and 3 Baby Bears and 2 Mama Bears on the other side. **Say:** *Look at the arrows on the scale.* **Ask:** *Is the scale balanced? When the scale is balanced, what do we know about the objects in the buckets?*

3. Direct students' attention to the Bears that remain in the balance. **Ask:** *How many Baby Bears equal the weight of one Papa Bear?* Have students work with other combinations of Bears to find the relationships between their weights.

2. Ask: *Are there any Bear Counters that are on both sides of the balance?* Instruct students to remove 2 Mama Bears from one side. **Ask:** *Is the scale balanced now? What would we have to do to the other side of the scale to make it balance again?* Guide students to understand that they would have to remove 2 Mama Bears. **Say:** *When we do something to one side of the scale, we have to do the same thing to the other side to keep the scale balanced.*

⚠ Look Out!

Encourage students to use the appropriate weight terms when discussing the activity. Remind students that the balance shows that the large Bear is *heavier* than the small Bear. Students may say that the large Bear is *bigger* than the small Bear. While this is true, *bigger* does not always mean *heavier*. Students need to use terms such as *heavier* and *lighter* when discussing weight and the results discovered by using a scale.

Measurement

Measurement is the assignment of a value to an attribute of an object, such as length, area, or mass. In the elementary grades, students first learn to determine what a measurable attribute is. Next, they must become familiar with the units and processes of measuring. Finally, students must become proficient in using the tools, techniques, and formulas used in measurement.

Measurement is a practical and pervasive part of everyday life. In the school setting, measurement connects several areas of mathematics—number operations, geometry, and statistics—as well as connecting to other subject areas such as social studies, science, art, and physical education. The study of measurement lends itself to the use of manipulatives and concrete objects. It is nearly impossible for a student to gain a full understanding of measurement without handling materials, making physical comparisons, and using measuring tools.

The Grades 3–5 NCTM Standards for Measurement suggest that students should:

- Understand measurable attributes of objects and the units, systems, and processes of measurement
- Apply appropriate techniques, tools, and formulas to determine measurements

The focus in Grades 3 and 4 is on deepening and expanding students' understanding and use of measurement. Students at this level develop benchmarks and strategies for estimating, focus more on using standard units of measure, and measure and represent changes in attributes. Through practice and discussion, students understand that real-life measurements are often approximations, thus focusing more on accurate measurements. Third- and fourth-grade students also begin to discover and use formulas in place of standard measuring tools. Lastly, students in the intermediate grades begin to express measurements in equivalent forms, learning more about the metric and U.S. Customary systems. The following are activities involving manipulatives that third- and fourth-grade students can use to develop skills in **Measurement.**

Measurement

Contents

Measurement

Telling Time

Time is a very abstract concept. We live in a digital world; therefore, students have less and less exposure to analog clocks. Teachers can help make the concept more understandable if they incorporate time into their classes on a daily basis. Experience using an analog clock shows a child that time is divided up into smaller units. In this lesson students will tell time to the hour, half hour, quarter hour, and minute.

Objective

Tell time to the hour, half hour, quarter hour, and minute on analog and digital clocks.

Skills

- Telling time
- Modeling time
- Writing time

NCTM Expectations

Measurement
- Select and apply appropriate standard units and tools to measure length, area, volume, weight, time, temperature, and size of angles.

Try It! *Perform the Try It! activity on the next page.*

Talk About It

Discuss the Try It! activity.

- Review the terms *quarter after* and *half past*. **Ask:** *What do you think it means if the time is a quarter to 12:00?* Have students compare $\frac{1}{4}$ Fraction Circles to Write-On/Wipe-Off Clocks and identify and model 11:45.

- **Ask:** *How can we tell if a written time is in the morning or at night?* Discuss the difference between A.M. and P.M. Have students model and write 9:00 A.M. and then 9:00 P.M. on their clocks.

Solve It

With students, reread the problem. Have students make a schedule of picture times. They should list each in digital form and draw a picture of a clock face to show each in analog form. **Say:** *Mrs. Kennedy wants to add another picture time at quarter to 11:00 in the morning.* Have students add this time in analog and digital forms to their picture schedules.

More Ideas

For other ways to teach about telling time—

- Have students create their own movie schedule with at least seven movies. On the schedule, there must be at least one movie in the morning, one in the afternoon, one that starts before the half hour, one that starts past the half hour, one that starts at a quarter after the hour, and one that starts at a quarter to the hour. After students write their schedule using digital forms, have them model each time on the Write-On/Wipe-Off Clocks.

- Have students work in pairs to take turns quizzing each other about telling time. One student models a time on the analog clock, and the other writes the time in digital form. Then the first student provides a digital time and the partner models the analog. Then students switch roles.

Standardized Practice

Have students try the following problem.

Mrs. Barnes told her class that lunch is at a quarter after twelve. What is another way to write the time for lunch?

A. 11:45 A.M.   **B.** 12:15 P.M.   **C.** 12:30 P.M.   **D.** 12:45 P.M.

Try It! 30 Minutes | Groups of 4

Here is a problem about telling time.

Mrs. Kennedy's class is going to have their school pictures taken. The first group will go at a quarter after 11:00 A.M., the second will go at half past 1:00 P.M., and the third will go at 2:55 P.M. How can the students tell the picture times on both the round clock on the wall and the digital clock on Mrs. Kennedy's desk?

Introduce the problem. Then have students do the activity to solve the problem. Distribute Write-On/Wipe-Off Clocks and Fraction Circles to students. Write the three picture times on the board: *quarter after 11:00 A.M., half past 1:00 P.M., and 2:55 P.M.*

Materials
- Write-On/Wipe-Off Clocks (1 per student)
- Fraction Circles (1 set per group)
- paper (1 sheet per group)
- markers (1 per student)

1. Say: *"Quarter after"* is a way of saying that one quarter, or one-fourth, of an hour has passed. Have students compare the $\frac{1}{4}$ circle pieces to the clock face. **Ask:** *Where should the minute hand on the clock be when one quarter of an hour has passed?* (on 3) **Ask:** *If the time is quarter after 11:00, where should the hour hand be?* (just past 11) Guide students to write the time in digital form under the clock: 11:15.

2. Ask: *What do you think "half past 1:00 P.M."* means? Have students compare the $\frac{1}{2}$ circle pieces to the clock to see that *half past 1:00 P.M.* means that one half of an hour has passed since 1:00. **Ask:** *Where should the hands be to show half past 1:00?* Help students model and write 1:30 on their clocks.

3. Ask: *Where should the minute hand be for 2:55? Where should the hour hand be?* Have students model and write 2:55 on their clocks.

⚠ Look Out!

Watch out for students who successfully move the minute hand but do not correctly advance the hour hand to correspond. For example, when showing 1:30, students may move the minute hand to the 6 but point the hour hand directly at the 1 instead of midway between the 1 and the 2. Help students identify the correct placement of the hour hand. Point out that 1:30 is halfway between 1:00 and 2:00, so the hour hand should be halfway between the numbers 1 and 2 on the clock.

Measurement

Elapsed Time

In grades 3 and 4, students begin to deepen their understanding of time. They start to move from simply telling time to calculating elapsed time. Since the school day is driven by a schedule, real-life opportunities arise during the day for students to calculate elapsed time.

Objective

Find elapsed time.

Skills

- Telling time
- Calculating elapsed time
- Adding and subtracting

NCTM Expectations

Measurement
- Select and apply appropriate standard units and tools to measure length, area, volume, weight, time, temperature, and the size of angles.

Try It! Perform the Try It! activity on the next page.

Talk About It

Discuss the Try It! activity.

- Tell students that the time between a start time and an end time is called elapsed time. **Ask:** *Why do we need to be able to figure out elapsed time?* Discuss with students the importance of knowing how long activities last.

- **Ask:** *When you have a start time and an end time, how can you figure out elapsed time?*

- **Ask:** *When you have a start time, and you know how long something lasts, how can you find the end time?*

- **Ask:** *If we know the time something ends and how long it lasts, how can we figure out what time it starts?* Guide students to use their Write-On/Wipe-Off Clocks to model.

Solve It

With students, reread the problem. Have students write a paragraph telling how they found the elapsed time of the three movies and which movie the students decided to see at the museum.

More Ideas

For other ways to teach about elapsed time—

- Have students make a schedule of their evening activities for a specific day of the week and use Write-On/Wipe-Off Clocks to find the amount of time spent doing each activity. Students should identify start time, end time, and elapsed time and use the clocks to model each.

- Have students keep track of a whole day at school and use Write-On/Wipe-Off Clocks to figure out the amount of time spent doing each activity.

- Have students work in pairs. One partner uses a Write-On/Wipe-Off Clock to show a start time. The other partner models an end time on a second clock. Partners look at both clocks to find the elapsed time.

Standardized Practice

Have students try the following problem.

The baseball game started at 4:30 P.M. It lasted for 1 hour and 15 minutes. What time did the game end?

A. 3:15 P.M.   **B.** 4:45 P.M.   **C.** 5:30 P.M.   **D.** 5:45 P.M.

Try It! 30 minutes | Pairs

Here is a problem about finding elapsed time.

Miss Gabowski took her class to a science museum on a field trip. The students were allowed to spend 1 hour and 15 minutes watching a movie at the museum. They looked at a movie schedule. Weather Mysteries *was playing from 12:45 to 2:30.* The Moon *was playing from 1:30 to 2:30.* Trees, Trees, Trees *was playing from 2:15 to 3:30. The students decided to see the movie that was exactly 1 hour and 15 minutes long. Which movie did they see?*

Introduce the problem. Then have students do the activity to solve the problem. Distribute Write-On/Wipe-Off Clocks to pairs of students. Model for students how to use the clocks.

Materials
• Write-On/Wipe-Off Clocks (1 per student)

1. Have one partner set their clock to the 12:45 start time and the other to the 2:30 end time of the *Weather Mysteries* movie. Guide students to compare the two clocks and rotate both hands of the start time clock to match the end time, counting by fives to track the elapsed time.

2. Ask: *How long is the movie* The Moon? *Use your clocks to find out.* Students should use the clocks to find the elapsed time from 1:30 to 2:30. Then have students find the length of *Trees, Trees, Trees* (2:15 to 3:30).

3. Ask: *What if* Trees, Trees, Trees *started at 2:15 and lasted 2 hours? What time would the movie end?* Have students use the clocks to count ahead 2 hours to find the end time (4:15).

⚠ Look Out!

Watch for students who do not realize that they must move the hour hand as well as the minute hand to accurately show time on the clocks. If applicable, you may wish to point out an analog clock in the classroom to show students that the hour hand moves from one number to the next over the course of the hour. Also, watch for students who have trouble finding elapsed time when the start time is A.M. and the end time is P.M., or vice-versa. Guide students to keep counting as they move the clock's hands past the 12.

Estimating and Measuring

Students in the intermediate grades are exposed to measurement daily at school and at home. At school, measurement encompasses several areas of math. By this age, students should have experienced measuring objects with standard units. This exposure has formed a foundation of reference points that students can draw upon to make logical estimates and pick the best tools for measuring.

Objective

Estimate and measure in customary and metric units.

Skills

- Estimating
- Measuring
- Comparing

NCTM Expectations

Measurement
- Understand the need for measuring with standard units and become familiar with standard units in the customary and metric systems.
- Select and apply appropriate standard units and tools to measure length, area, volume, weight, time, temperature, and the size of angles.

Try It! Perform the Try It! activity on the next page.

Talk About It

Discuss the Try It! activity.

- **Ask:** *How many inches long did you estimate that the pencil would be? How many inches was it when you measured with 1-inch Color Tiles?*
- **Ask:** *What was your estimate of the length of the pencil in centimeters? How many centimeters was it when you measured it with Centimeter Cubes?*
- **Ask:** *How did you use the measurement of the pencil to help you estimate the length of the piece of paper? Did you use the measurements of the paper or pencil to help you estimate the length of the eraser? Why or why not?*
- Discuss with students the similarities and differences between inches and centimeters. Emphasize that inches and centimeters are both accurate ways to measure because they are both standard units.

Solve It

With students, reread the problem. Have students write a letter to Clyde explaining how he can measure in inches the same way he would measure using centimeters. They should tell Clyde how inches and centimeters are similar and different.

More Ideas

For other ways to teach about measuring in customary and metric units—

- Have students work in groups to trace outlines of their bodies on large sheets of paper and then measure from their feet to the top of their heads using both Color Tiles and Centimeter Cubes.
- Have one student look around the room and select an object, estimating how long it is in inches or centimeters. Then have the student tell the class the estimate, using only the number and not the unit. The class then guesses the unit. Students then measure the object using Color Tiles and Centimeter Cubes to find how close the estimate was.

Standardized Practice

Have students try the following problem.

Which is a good estimate of the length of your thumb?

A. 1 cm   **B.** 4 cm   **C.** 6 inches   **D.** 12 inches

Try It! 35 Minutes | Pairs

Here is a problem about measuring in customary and metric units.

Mr. Rossi asked his students to measure objects in inches. Clyde is a new student in Mr. Rossi's class. He is from England. He told Mr. Rossi that people use centimeters to measure in England. Mr. Rossi told Clyde to measure the objects with Centimeter Cubes while his partner measured with 1-inch Color Tiles. Who used more units to measure?

Introduce the problem. Then have students do the activity to solve the problem. Distribute Centimeter Cubes, Color Tiles, and Measurement Recording Sheets (BLM 16) to students. Tell students that a tile is 1 inch long and a cube is 1 centimeter long. Explain that in the United States, we usually measure with customary units, such as inches and feet, but most other countries in the world use metric units, such as centimeters and meters.

Materials

- Centimeter Cubes (30 per pair)
- Color Tiles (15 per pair)
- Measurement Recording Sheet (BLM 16; 1 per pair)
- unsharpened pencil (1 per pair)
- $8\frac{1}{2}" \times 11"$ piece of paper (1 per pair)

1. Have students estimate the length of the unsharpened pencil in tiles, then measure. Students should record the estimate and measurement on the recording sheet. They should then repeat the process with cubes.

2. Have students use their measurement of the pencil to estimate the length of a piece of paper in inches. Students should measure with tiles and record the numbers. Have students repeat the activity for centimeters.

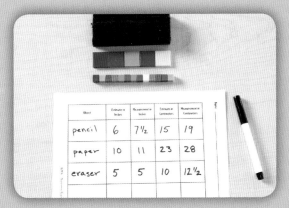

3. Have students repeat the steps of the activity to estimate and measure the length of a chalkboard eraser, and record their measurements.

⚠ Look Out!

Some students may have trouble measuring accurately using cubes and tiles. Make sure students are lining up manipulatives correctly with the objects being measured. They should also be careful not to leave gaps between the units of measure. Demonstrate for children that they will get a more accurate answer if the tiles and cubes are lined up correctly.

Perimeter of Shapes

Perimeter is the distance around a two-dimensional shape. When finding perimeter, students use geometry by relying on their knowledge of shape attributes while measuring. Once they have had a lot of hands-on exposure, they start to create formulas for finding perimeter. In this lesson students will find the perimeter of a shape using a geoboard.

Objective

Find the perimeter of a shape using a geoboard.

Skills

- Measuring
- Adding
- Spatial Visualization

NCTM Expectations

Measurement
- Understand the need for measuring with standard units and become familiar with standard units in the customary and metric systems.
- Select and apply appropriate standard units and tools to measure length, area, volume, weight, time, temperature, and the size of angles.

Try It! *Perform the Try It! activity on the next page.*

Talk About It

Discuss the Try It! activity.

- **Ask:** *How can we figure out the perimeter of a rectangle or square without using a geoboard?* Discuss how rulers and other tools can be used to measure the perimeter of shapes that are not made on a geoboard.

- **Ask:** *What if the shape was 3 units by 4 units? What would the perimeter be then?* Have students model the new shape and find the perimeter.

- **Ask:** *When might it be important to figure out the perimeter of something?* Discuss real-life situations involving perimeter, such as making a frame or building a fence.

Solve It

With students, reread the problem. Have students explain in writing how many inches of ribbon are needed and how they found the perimeter of the invitation.

More Ideas

For other ways to teach about finding the perimeter of a shape—

- Students can use Centimeter Cubes to find the perimeter of a book cover, box top, or similar object using standard metric units. Make sure students understand that 1 cube equals 1 centimeter. Have students estimate the perimeter of each object before measuring.

- Students can use Color Tiles to find the perimeter of classroom items such as a piece of paper or folder using standard customary units. Make sure students understand that each tile equals 1 inch. Have students estimate perimeters before measuring. Also watch that students only measure edges, not corners, using tiles.

Standardized Practice

Have students try the following problem.

What is the perimeter of a 3 inch by 3 inch square?

Try It! 25 Minutes | Pairs

Here is a problem about finding the perimeter of a shape.

The students in Mr. Woodley's class are having a play. The students made invitations to send home to their parents. The invitations are 4-inch by 4-inch squares. The students decided to put ribbon around the edges of the invitations. How many inches of ribbon are needed for one invitation?

Introduce the problem. Then have students do the activity to solve the problem. Distribute geoboards and rubber bands to students.

Materials
- Geoboards (1 per pair)
- rubber bands (4 per pair)
- paper (1 sheet per pair)
- pencils (1 per pair)

1. Say: *Place a rubber band around two pegs to show 1 unit. Now stretch the rubber band to show 2 units.* Guide students to repeat the process for 3 and 4 units, identifying the number of units each time the rubber band moves.

2. Say: *I want you to make a square that is 2 units by 2 units.* Students work with their partners to make the shape. **Ask:** *How do we find the perimeter of this shape?* Remind students, if needed, that perimeter is the distance around a two-dimensional shape.

3. Have students find the perimeter of the shape. Repeat the activity for a 3-unit by 2-unit rectangle and a 3-unit by 3-unit square. Guide students to write number sentences representing the perimeters they calculated on the geoboards.

 Look Out!

Watch for students who count the number of pegs versus the space between pegs as a unit. If students are confused by this, have them put two fingers on the two pegs to show 1 unit, and move the fingers along as they count. Stress that the unit is the space between the two fingers. Also watch for students who call the units inches. Use Color Tiles to show that geoboard units are not equal to inches. In addition, some students may attempt to calculate area (length times width) instead of perimeter. Emphasize that students should be measuring the distance around the shape, not the number of square units inside the shape.

Objective

Build a shape with a given perimeter.

Skills

- Adding
- Measuring
- Spatial visualization

NCTM Expectations

Measurement
- Understand the need for measuring with standard units and become familiar with standard units in the customary and metric systems.
- Explore what happens to measurements of a two-dimensional shape such as its perimeter and area when the shape is changed in some way.
- Develop strategies for estimating the perimeters, areas, and volumes of irregular shapes.
- Select and apply appropriate standard units and tools to measure length, area, volume, weight, time, temperature, and the size of angles.

Measurement

Building Perimeter

Having a student measure the perimeter of a shape is the first step in understanding the concept of perimeter. The next step is requiring students to apply their knowledge in order to create a shape with a given perimeter. This shows a higher level of understanding. In this lesson students will use Pattern Blocks to create a shape with a given perimeter.

Try It! *Perform the Try It! activity on the next page.*

Talk About It

Discuss the Try It! activity.

- **Say:** *Everyone made a shape with a perimeter of 8, but groups made different shapes.* **Ask:** *How is it possible for different shapes to have the same perimeter?*

- **Ask:** *As the size of the perimeter increased, did the number of Pattern Blocks in the shape increase? Why or why not?*

- **Ask:** *What if you kept the same blocks in your design but moved them around to make a different design? Would you still have the same perimeter?*

- **Ask:** *What if you measured the last shape you made using a different tool, such as a ruler? Would it still have a perimeter of 30? Why or why not?* Stress that when measuring anything, it is important that units are established.

Solve It

With students, reread the problem. Distribute a Centimeter Grid (BLM 17) to each student, and have them use it to draw a possible shape for the garden. Explain that in this case 1 cm—or one edge of one square in the grid—equals 1 unit (foot), so the perimeter should be 30 cm.

More Ideas

For other ways to teach about building a shape with a given perimeter—

- Direct students to use geoboards to create irregular shapes and find the perimeter. The space between two pegs equals 1 unit.

- Have students make shapes using Centimeter Cubes and find the perimeter. Then have students measure the shapes using Color Tiles, where one edge of one tile equals 1 unit. Have students compare the measurement in cubes to the measurement in tiles.

Standardized Practice

Have students try the following problem.

Which arrangement of blocks has a perimeter of 12 units?

A. B. C. D.

Try It! 30 Minutes | Groups of 4

Here is a problem about building a shape with a given perimeter.

Washington School decided to plant a garden. The students want to put a fence around the garden to keep out rabbits. They have 30 feet of fence. How can the students make a garden that measures 30 feet around?

Introduce the problem. Then have students do the activity to solve the problem. Pass out an assortment of Pattern Blocks with at least one square and one triangle to each group.

1. Say: *For this activity, one side of the green triangle equals 1 unit.* **Ask:** *What is the perimeter of the triangle? What is the perimeter of a square?* Have students establish that the triangle has a perimeter of 3, and the square has a perimeter of 4.

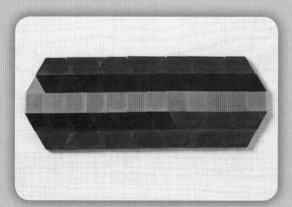

3. Say: *Now, create a shape that has a perimeter of 30 units.* Have groups create a shape. Encourage students to use many different blocks to make their shape. **Say:** *Take a green triangle. Find a group that made a different design. Use the green triangle to check the perimeter by measuring the other group's design.*

2. Say: *With your group, make a shape that has a perimeter of 8 units.* Students should work with their groups to make shapes. Remind students that only the outside edges count in the perimeter. **Say:** *Let's see the different shapes you made.* Draw some of the different shapes students made on the board, and count to establish each shape's perimeter. Repeat the process, having students create shapes with perimeters of 20 units.

⚠ Look Out!

Some students think that a triangle included in the shape they make automatically adds three sides to the perimeter, or that a square adds four sides to the perimeter. Point out that not all of the sides are on the outside of the shape, so they are not all part of the perimeter. Remind students that perimeter is the distance around the outside edges of the shape only. Also, look out for students who think you can only measure perimeter on squares or triangles. Model how an irregular shape can have the same perimeter as a regular square or rectangle.

Measurement

Finding Area

Students have already had some experience with the ideas of shape, perimeter, and area in their geometry lessons, although they may not have learned the terminology or formally addressed the concepts. Area is an aspect of measurement that is connected to other areas of math, such as geometry and algebra. Here students explore finding a shape's area by simply counting the square units that make it up, but this lays the groundwork for using formulas and calculations such as multiplication to measure and find area and perimeter.

Objective

Find the area of a shape using a geoboard.

Skills

- Counting
- Measuring
- Spatial visualization

NCTM Expectations

Measurement
- Understand such attributes as length, area, weight, volume, and size of angle and select the appropriate type of unit for measuring each attribute.
- Understand the need for measuring with standard units and become familiar with standard units in the customary and metric systems.
- Select and apply appropriate standard units and tools to measure length, area, volume, weight, time, temperature, and the size of angles.
- Develop, understand, and use formulas to find the area of rectangles and related triangles and parallelograms.

Try It! *Perform the Try It! activity on the next page.*

Talk About It

Discuss the Try It! activity.

- **Ask:** *How did you check to make sure the shape you made had an area of 6 units?*
- Have pairs of students form groups to compare the shapes they made on their geoboards. **Ask:** *Can shapes that look different have the same area?*
- **Ask:** *Do you think a shape could have an area that includes half units?* Guide students to model a shape with an area of $5\frac{1}{2}$ units on their geoboards.

Solve It

With students, reread the problem. **Ask:** *What if Ms. Liu wanted the name tags to be a different size?* Display a geoboard with a rubber band stretched in a rectangle with an area of 8 square units. Have students replicate the shape on their own geoboards and then calculate its area in square units.

More Ideas

For other ways to teach about finding the area of a shape—

- Have students take turns with partners using their geoboards to explore making figures that have half square units. Challenge students to each make a shape that includes at least two half square units. **Say:** *When you count the square units, don't forget to add the two halves to make one.*
- Tell students that Color Tiles are also square units. Have students build shapes from tiles and count tiles to find the shapes' areas. Remind students to describe a shape's area by saying how many "square units" it has.

Standardized Practice

Have students try the following problem.

What is the area of this shape?

A. 16 square units
B. 18 square units
C. 20 square units
D. 22 square units

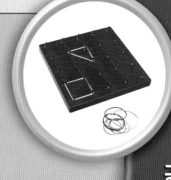

Try It! 25 Minutes | Pairs

Here is a problem about finding the area of a shape.

A new student is joining Ms. Liu's class tomorrow, so she asks every student to make a name tag to wear. To show the size the name tags should be, Ms. Liu makes a rectangle on a geoboard by stretching a rubber band around 2 rows made of 3 units each. How many square units will make up the area of the name tags?

Introduce the problem. Then have students do the activity to solve the problem. Distribute geoboards and rubber bands to students.

Materials
- Geoboards (1 per pair)
- rubber bands (1 per pair)

1. Model 1 square unit on a geoboard by stretching a rubber band around 4 pegs, and guide students to do the same. **Say:** *The area of the square is the part inside the rubber band. The area of this square is 1 square unit.*

2. Move the rubber band to stretch around 2 rows of 2 units each. **Ask:** *How many square units is this shape?* Help students see there are now 4 square units in this shape. Have students replicate the shape on their geoboards and trace over the 4 square units with their fingers.

3. Say: *With your partner, make a rectangle on the geoboard that is 2 units high and 3 units wide.* Have students work with their partners to create the rectangles. **Ask:** *How many square units make up the area of your rectangle?* Students should count to find that the area of their rectangles is 6 square units.

⚠ Look Out!

Watch out for students who confuse area with perimeter. Make a square on a geoboard and point out that the rubber band is the shape's perimeter, and that all the red space enclosed by the rubber band is the shape's area. Have students draw several shapes. Then have them use one color marker or crayon to trace each shape's perimeter and another color to shade in its area.

Measurement

Area of Irregular Figures

Students should already be familiar with standard measurement tools, such as rulers or metersticks, used to measure linear distances. However, students must develop strategies for measuring with nonstandard tools, as well as for measuring the area of regular and irregular figures. Students need to understand that familiar measurement tools and strategies may not be appropriate for every situation, especially for irregular figures. Estimating and finding the area of irregular figures offers students the opportunity to discover techniques for finding area when a standard measure cannot be applied, and it will deepen their understanding of measurement and area.

Objective

Estimate and find the area of irregular figures.

Skills

- Estimation
- Exploring area
- Measurement

NCTM Expectations

Measurement
- Understand such attributes as length, area, weight, volume, and size of angle and select the appropriate type of unit for measuring each attribute.
- Understand the need for measuring with standard units and become familiar with standard units in the customary and metric systems.
- Develop strategies for estimating the perimeters, areas, and volumes of irregular shapes.
- Select and apply appropriate standard units and tools to measure length, area, volume, weight, time, temperature, and the size of angles.

Try It! *Perform the Try It! activity on the next page.*

Talk About It

Discuss the Try It! activity.

- **Say:** *Look at your hand tracing.* **Ask:** *Why do we call this an "irregular figure"?*
- **Ask:** *How is finding the area of an irregular figure similar to finding the area of a rectangle? How is it different?*

Solve It

With students, reread the problem. Have students explain in writing how they used Centimeter Cubes to find the area of a hand tracing. Then have the class work together to order their tracings from smallest to largest.

More Ideas

For other ways to teach about finding the area of irregular figures—

- Have students make a design using a geoboard and then estimate the area. Tell students to count the units in the design to check their estimates.
- Have students estimate and then measure to find the number of Centimeter Cubes necessary to cover various Attribute Blocks. Point out that some of the cubes will probably hang over the edge of the block. Have students count these as $\frac{1}{2}$ or $\frac{1}{4}$ units, depending on how much is on the block.

Standardized Practice

Have students try the following problem.

If each square is 1 square inch, what is the estimated area of this puddle?

A. 10 square inches
B. 16 square inches
C. 21 square inches
D. 25 square inches

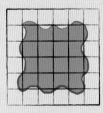

Try It! 20 minutes | Pairs

Here is a problem about finding the area of an irregular figure.

Your class is making a wall display of handprints. Each student will trace, cut out, and decorate his or her handprint. Your teacher wants to measure the area of each handprint and display them from smallest to largest. How large do you think the area of your handprint is? How can you find the area?

Introduce the problem. Then have students do the activity to solve the problem. Distribute Centimeter Cubes and Centimeter Grids (BLM 17). Introduce and discuss the term *irregular figure* and explain that a handprint is an example of an irregular figure.

Materials
- Centimeter Cubes (80 per pair)
- Centimeter Grid (BLM 17; 2 per pair)
- paper (2 sheets per pair)
- pencils (2 per pair)

1. Ask: *How many cubes do you think it will take to cover your hand?* Introduce and discuss the term *estimate*. Have students write down their estimates. Then instruct them to trace their hands onto the Centimeter Grid.

2. Have students take turns using cubes to find the area of their hands on the Centimeter Grid.

3. Have students write down the actual number of cubes it took to cover their hand tracings. **Ask:** *How does your estimate compare to the actual area of your hand?*

⚠ Look Out!

When finding the area of irregular figures using Centimeter Grids, students will discover that many of the squares have been split by the outline of the figure. Watch out for students who disregard these partial squares. Explain that to accurately find the area, students will need to decide whether enough of the square is included to be counted. Encourage students to count halves of squares as $\frac{1}{2}$ and to combine parts of squares when possible to count as one whole.

Measurement

Building Area

Students benefit from having concrete experiences working with measurement before being expected to comprehend measurement formulas, such as $l \times w$ for finding area. By building shapes with a given area, students are able to explore ways to manipulate figures so that their appearance is altered but their area remains constant. They will discover that as some measurements increase, others must decrease if the area of the figures is to stay the same. Such generalizations provide the foundation for later understanding of the standard formula for area.

Try It! Perform the Try It! activity on the next page.

Objective

Build a shape with a given area.

Skills

- Composing and decomposing figures
- Exploring area
- Measurement

NCTM Expectations

Measurement

- Understand such attributes as length, area, weight, volume, and size of angle and select the appropriate type of unit for measuring each attribute.
- Understand the need for measuring with standard units and become familiar with standard units in the customary and metric systems.
- Develop strategies for estimating the perimeters, areas, and volumes of irregular shapes.
- Select and apply appropriate standard units and tools to measure length, area, volume, weight, time, temperature, and the size of angles.

Talk About It

Discuss the Try It! activity.

- **Ask:** *How many Color Tiles did you use to cover 4 square inches? What about the shapes you made that had areas of 6 and 10 square inches?*
- **Say:** *Remember, you can also find the area of squares and rectangles by multiplying the length of the shape times the width.* Have students make several square and rectangle shapes and check the area using the $l \times w$ formula.
- **Say:** *Suppose you used blocks to make a figure with an area of 12 square inches. Then you rearranged those blocks into a different design without adding or removing any blocks.* **Ask:** *Would the area change?* Have students model the two shapes using blocks and find the area of both.

Solve It

With students, reread the problem. Have students describe in writing how they used tiles to fill up 6 square inches. They should then explain how they can check the area of their shapes using length times width if their design was a perfect square or rectangle.

More Ideas

For other ways to teach about building shapes with a given area—

- Distribute geoboards to the class. Have students work with a partner to make 4 different shapes or designs with the same area.
- Have students use Pattern Blocks and Inch Grid Paper (BLM 18) to try to create patterns given a target area (i.e., make a design that covers 8 square inches).

Standardized Practice

Have students try the following problem.

What is the area of the shape?

A. 5 square units   C. 9 square units

B. 7 square units   D. 12 square units

Try It! 25 minutes | Pairs

Here is a problem about building a shape with a given area.

The students in Miss Ling's class are going to make a mosaic using square tiles. Each student will have about 6 square inches to fill with a design. How can the students use squares to fill up 6 square inches?

Introduce the problem. Then have students do the activity to solve the problem. Distribute Color Tiles and Inch Grid Paper (BLM 18) to students.

Materials
- Color Tiles (24 per pair)
- Inch Grid Paper (BLM 18; 1 per pair)

1. Have students place a tile on the Inch Grid Paper. **Ask:** _How long is one side of the square?_ Have students use tiles to make a larger square that has an area of 4 square inches.

2. Instruct students to use tiles to create a design on the grid paper that has an area of 6 square inches. Have students compare designs to see the various ways the area can be shown.

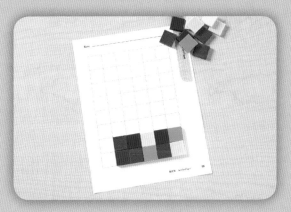

⚠ Look Out!

Watch for students who confuse perimeter and area. Remind students that perimeter is the distance around a shape, whereas area measures the space inside the shape. Have students use squares to build a shape and find both the perimeter and the area.

3. Next have students use tiles to create a rectangle with an area of 10 square inches on the grid paper. Have students compare their designs with that of another set of partners and check each other's designs to verify the area. Then guide students to use the formula $l \times w$ to check the area of their rectangles.

Measurement

Perimeter and Area

Students need to have concrete experiences discovering perimeter and area. Such opportunities will help them develop strategies for finding these measurements and build a deeper understanding of their meaning. Through hands-on exploration, students will come to understand that perimeter is one-dimensional, whereas area is two-dimensional. Looking for patterns in measuring the perimeter and area of shapes allows students to make generalizations about such measurements and prepares them for recognizing that their methods of measuring can be explained as mathematical formulas.

Try It! *Perform the Try It! activity on the next page.*

Objective

Recognize the relationship between perimeter and area.

Skills

- Measurement
- Exploring area
- Exploring perimeter

NCTM Expectations

Measurement
- Understand such attributes as length, area, weight, volume, and size of angle and select the appropriate type of unit for measuring each attribute.
- Explore what happens to measurements of a two-dimensional shape such as its perimeter and area when the shape is changed in some way.
- Select and apply appropriate standard units and tools to measure length, area, volume, weight, time, temperature, and the size of angles.
- Develop, understand, and use formulas to find the area of rectangles and related triangles and parallelograms.

Talk About It

Discuss the Try It! activity.

- **Say:** *Look at the information you recorded about the perimeter and area of the squares.* **Ask:** *What pattern did you notice in the perimeters as the squares were increased by 1 Color Tile? What pattern did you notice in the areas? If we continued to add to the 6 by 6 square, what would happen to the perimeters and areas of the new squares?*

- **Ask:** *Was there a square you built that had the same number for both area and perimeter? Which square was it?*

- **Say:** *Explain how you found the area and perimeter of each square.* **Ask:** *Were the equations helpful? Why or why not?*

Solve It

With students, reread the problem. Then have students use Inch Grid Paper (BLM 18) to draw a mural like the one the students were making in art class, and label the length of each side. Have students explain in writing how they found the area of the mural.

More Ideas

For other ways to teach about the relationship between perimeter and area—

- Have students work in pairs using geoboards to explore area and perimeter. One student should make a square or rectangle on the geoboard, and the other student should use equations to find the perimeter and area. Students then switch roles and repeat the activity.

- Have students work in groups using Color Tiles to measure the perimeter and area of classroom objects, such as the covers of books or the top of a desk. For each object, they should write down perimeter and area equations.

Standardized Practice

Have students try the following problem.

Draw a square that is 4 units long on each side. What is the perimeter of the square? What is the area?

Try It! 25 minutes | Groups of 4

Here is a problem about the relationship between perimeter and area.

In art class, students are making a mural. The mural will be a square shape. They want the perimeter to be 24 feet. How many feet across will the mural be? How many feet from top to bottom? What will be the area of the mural?

Introduce the problem. Then have students do the activity to solve the problem. Distribute Color Tiles and Inch Grid Paper (BLM 18) to each group. Have students build a square that is 2 tiles by 2 tiles on the grid paper. Explain that the perimeter equation for this square is $2 + 2 + 2 + 2 = 8$
(side length + side length + side length + side length = perimeter), and the area equation is $2 \times 2 = 4$ (side length $\times$ side length = area).

Materials
- Color Tiles (100 per group)
- Inch Grid Paper (BLM 18; 1 per group)
- paper (1 sheet per group)
- pencil (1 per group)

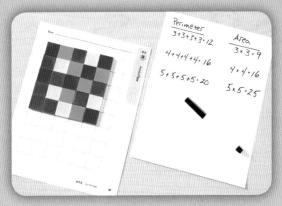

1. Have students make another square that is 3 tiles by 3 tiles on the grid paper. **Ask:** *What is the perimeter equation for this square? What is the area equation?* Remind students that they must add all the sides for the perimeter equation and multiply to find the area.

2. Have students grow the sides by 1 tile each time to build a 4 by 4 square, then a 5 by 5 square. They should write down the perimeter and area equations for both.

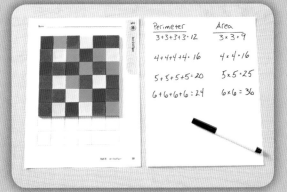

3. Finally, have students build a 6 by 6 square. They should write down the perimeter and area equations. Have groups check each other's squares and compare equations.

⚠ Look Out!

Watch for students who start to think perimeter and area are just for shapes with four sides (L + L + L + L = P). Guide students to make L-shaped figures and calculate perimeter using the formula to account for all sides. For area, have students divide the figure into two smaller rectangles or squares and combine the areas of each using the area formula twice.

Measurement

Finding Volume

Allowing students to have concrete experiences with abstract concepts such as volume not only helps them develop strategies for finding and understanding volume but also provides the opportunity for students to begin to generalize their discoveries about measurement and start to develop a formula based on patterns seen in the results of their measurement. Here students employ practical, concrete methods of measuring and comparing the volumes of solid objects.

> **Try It!** *Perform the Try It! activity on the next page.*

Talk About It

Discuss the Try It! activity.

- **Say:** *Look at your Relational Geosolids®. Turn them upside down. Now lay them on one side.* **Ask:** *Does moving or changing the position of a solid shape change its volume? How can you prove whether it does or doesn't?*

- **Ask:** *Were you able to predict which figure had a greater volume? Why might it be hard to compare the volumes of figures that have different shapes?*

- Discuss with students that volumes change when the size of the shape changes. **Ask:** *Is it possible to find a cube that has a bigger volume than anything we measured today?*

Solve It

With students, reread the problem. Have students write instructions that Paul and Rihana should follow to find whose solid has the greater volume. Then have students find a triangular prism with a greater volume than a cube and a cube with a greater volume than a triangular prism in a set of Solids.

More Ideas

For other ways to teach about the volume of cubes and prisms—

- Have students use Centimeter Cubes to build solid shapes to match Relational Geosolids. Have students estimate the volume of each shape in cubes.

- At a center, set up four cube and rectangular prism Relational Geosolids. Have students predict which of the four Solids has the greatest volume and which has the least. Have students measure the volume using rice, water, or sand, and order the shapes based on results.

Standardized Practice

Have students try the following problem.

If a box can hold 8 pounds of pebbles, and a bucket can hold 6 pounds of pebbles, which container has the greater volume?

Objective

Estimate and find the volume of cubes and prisms.

Skills

- Estimation
- Exploring volume
- Measuring volume

NCTM Expectations

Measurement
- Understand such attributes as length, area, weight, volume, and size of angle and select the appropriate type of unit for measuring each attribute.
- Select and apply appropriate standard units and tools to measure length, area, volume, weight, time, temperature, and the size of angles.
- Develop strategies to determine the surface areas and volumes of rectangular solids.

Try It! 25 minutes | Groups of 4

Here is a problem about estimating and finding the volume of cubes and prisms.

Rihana and Paul are comparing the attributes of two solid shapes, a cube and a triangular prism. Rihana thinks her cube has the greater volume, and Paul thinks his triangular prism does. How can Rihana and Paul find out which of their shapes has greater volume?

Introduce the problem. Then have students do the activity to solve the problem. Distribute two cube or prism Relational Geosolids®, one cup of rice, and one Bucket Balance to each group. Groups may need to share balances, and water or sand may be substituted for rice.

Materials
- Relational Geosolids® (2 per group)
- Bucket Balance (1 per group)
- cups of uncooked rice (1 per group)
- paper and pencils (1 per student)
- funnel (optional; 1 per group)

1. Explain that *volume* is the room inside a solid figure, or the space taken up by a solid figure. **Ask:** *Which Solid do you predict has the greater volume? Why?* Tell students to write down their predictions.

2. Tell students that they can use the rice to compare the volumes of their Solids. Have students fill up both Solids with rice.

3. Have groups compare the volumes of their Solids by emptying each one into one of the balance's buckets. **Say:** *You can compare the volumes by reading the numbers on the sides of the buckets.* Have students write down which of their Solids has the greater volume.

⚠ Look Out!

Some students may confuse volume with weight. Explain that volume measures the amount of space inside a shape, or how much it can "hold," regardless of weight. Have students fill one bucket of the balance with tissues and the other with pebbles. Make sure both buckets are filled to the 500 mL line, then explain that although both buckets have the same volume, they have different weights. Have students fill both buckets with pebbles to the 500 mL line and explain that now the buckets have both the same volume and the same weight.

Objective

Use metric units to estimate and measure weight (grams).

Skills

- Estimating
- Using metric measurement
- Using measurement tools

NCTM Expectations

Measurement
- Understand such attributes as length, area, weight, volume, and size of angle and select the appropriate type of unit for measuring each attribute.
- Understand the need for measuring with standard units and become familiar with standard units in the customary and metric systems.
- Understand that measurements are approximations and understand how differences in units affect precision.
- Select and apply appropriate standard units and tools to measure length, area, volume, weight, time, temperature, and size of angles.
- Select and use benchmarks to estimate measurements.

Measurement

Measure Weight

Estimation is an important mathematical skill for students to develop. Establishing benchmarks by which students can compare the weights of items is a strategy that will help them make more reasonable estimates. Students also need opportunities to work with a variety of measurement tools and to recognize that slightly different measurements may be found for the same items. It is important for students to experience both customary and metric units of measurement.

Try It! Perform the Try It! activity on the next page.

Talk About It

Discuss the Try It! activity.

- **Ask:** *Why do you think it's important to put the Centimeter Cubes into the Bucket Balance one at a time?*
- **Ask:** *How many grams did the Papa Bear™ Counter weigh? Mama Bear™ Counter? Baby Bear™ Counter? Did anyone find a different weight for any of these?*
- **Say:** *Grams are a good unit of measurement for small items like the Three Bear Family® Counters.* **Ask:** *Do you think grams would be practical for measuring the weights of larger items, such as your desk? Why or why not?*

Solve It

With students, reread the problem. Have students explain in writing how Jessica should measure each Bear Counter to find its weight.

More Ideas

For other ways to teach about estimating and measuring weight—

- Provide a Bucket Balance and Centimeter Cubes at the math center. Instruct students to find items they believe to weigh approximately 1, 50, 100, and 500 grams. Have students use the balance and cubes to check the weights of the items and select new items as needed. Instruct students to list the items discovered for each of the target weights.

- Challenge students to use the weights of the Three Bear Family Counters and the Centimeter Cubes to create problem-solving opportunities (1 Baby Bear = 4 grams, 1 Mama Bear = 8 grams, and 1 Papa Bear = 12 grams). Example: What combination of Bears weighs 24 grams (cubes)? What other combinations of Bears weigh 24 grams (cubes) total?

Standardized Practice

Have students try the following problem.

Which item weighs about 5 grams?

A. a pencil   **B.** an apple   **C.** a box of crayons   **D.** a dictionary

Try It! 20 minutes | Groups of 4

Here is a problem about using metric units to estimate and measure weight.

Jessica's teacher says that a Papa Bear™ Counter, a Mama Bear™ Counter, and a Baby Bear™ Counter all have different weights. How can Jessica measure them to find out how much each one weighs?

Introduce the problem. Then have students do the activity to solve the problem. Distribute Bucket Balances, Three Bear Family® Counters, and Centimeter Cubes to groups. Groups may have to share balances. Explain that a gram is a metric unit used to measure the weight of an object. Hold up one cube and explain that each cube weighs one gram.

Materials
- Bucket Balance (1 per group)
- Three Bear Family® Counters (20 per group)
- Centimeter Cubes (100 per group)
- paper and pencils (1 each per group)

1. Have students select three Bear Counters, one of each size. **Say:** *A paper clip weighs about 1 gram. A textbook weights about 435 grams.* **Ask:** *How much do you think each of the Bears weighs?* Have students make a simple chart with one column for the Bear name, one for their estimate, and one for the actual weight. Then have them fill in their estimates.

2. Have students measure the Baby Bear first. Tell them to put the Bear in one bucket and then place cubes in the other bucket one at a time. **Say:** *When the buckets are balanced, count the cubes and record the weight in your chart.*

⚠ Look Out!

Students may use arbitrary numbers when estimating the weights of classroom objects. Remind students of the weights of the textbook and the paper clip discussed in Step 1. Give students one cube to hold and use as they start to estimate. Then have them hold 10, and then 20, and compare how the different weights feel. Also, watch that students' buckets are balanced before they begin weighing. Have students check that the buckets are level, and discuss how having unlevel buckets can affect their measurements.

3. Have students continue by measuring the other two Bears and then comparing their estimated weights with their actual weights.

Data Analysis and Probability

The study of **Data Analysis and Probability** at the elementary-grade level has several purposes. These subject areas teach students how to ask questions, collect data, and organize and display the data in a chart or graph that answers the original questions. Students at this level also learn methods for analyzing the data to make inferences and draw conclusions. This learning, spanning from pre-kindergarten through high school, allows students to become informed citizens and intelligent consumers.

The study of data analysis connects to ideas and procedures from number, algebra, measurement, and geometry. It is also a natural way to connect mathematics instruction to student's daily lives. To develop statistical ideas, students must work directly with data. In the lower elementary grades, this may mean using census data of students in the classroom. As students progress through school, the types and uses of data become more sophisticated.

The Grades 3–5 NCTM Standards for Data Analysis and Probability suggest that students should:

- Formulate questions that can be addressed with data and collect, organize, and display relevant data to answer them
- Select and use appropriate statistical methods to analyze data
- Develop and evaluate inferences and predictions that are based on data
- Understand and apply basic concepts of probability

At Grades 3 and 4, students become more adept at using data sets to draw conclusions and answer specific questions. At this level, students pose questions not only about themselves but also about the greater community around them. Students are able to develop a plan for collecting data that will answer the questions they pose, discriminate between different representations of data, and choose the one that best reflects the answer to their question. Probability instruction at this level focuses more on quantifying the likelihood of an event. Third and fourth graders learn to express likely outcomes by means of fractions. The following are activities involving manipulatives that third- and fourth-grade students can use to develop skills in **Data Analysis and Probability.**

Data Analysis and Probability

Contents

Objective

Explore the meaning of average (mean).

Skills

- Analyzing data
- Using measures of central tendency
- Discovering statistical characteristics

NCTM Expectations

Data Analysis and Probability
- Use measures of center, focusing on the median, and understand what each does and does not indicate about the data set.

Data Analysis and Probability

Find the Average

By this age, students are familiar with recognizing and representing individual pieces of data on a graph and making comparisons between these values. Students now need to learn to view sets of data as a whole and to use statistical characteristics to analyze and compare these sets. They also need to recognize that samples of data are often representative of the data of a larger population. Measures of central tendency, such as mean, median, and mode, need to be introduced, applied, and explained in terms of real-life applications.

Try It! Perform the Try It! activity on the next page.

Talk About It

Discuss the Try It! activity.

- **Say:** *We practiced using Color Tiles to find the average of a set of numbers.* **Ask:** *What does the word* average *mean? What is another way to find averages?* Discuss the algorithm students used in Step 3.
- Have students make an array with the tiles to find the average of the numbers 3, 4, 5, and 6. **Ask:** *What happened when you tried to make 4 even rows of tiles?* Students should note that the tiles do not distribute evenly into 4 rows. Explain that students should use rounding rules to find the average: if more than half the rows have 4 tiles, round the average down to 4; if exactly half or more than half the rows have 5 tiles, round the average up to 5. **Ask:** *What is the average?*

Solve It

With students, reread the problem. Have students draw basketballs to represent the arrays they made. Then have students explain in writing how they found the average.

More Ideas

For other ways to teach about finding the average—

- Instruct students to work in groups and take turns pulling a handful of Three Bear Family® Counters from a paper bag and recording the number. Then have students model the Bears to find the average number pulled.
- Have each student in a small group use Centimeter Cubes to measure the lengths of pencils. Then instruct students to make an array to find the average length of the pencils in the group. Have students use the algorithm to check their work.

Standardized Practice

Have students try the following problem.

Shelby read 7 pages on Monday, 3 pages on Tuesday, and 8 pages on Wednesday. What was the average number of pages she read each day?

A. 3   **B.** 4   **C.** 5   **D.** 6

Try It!   25 minutes | Pairs

Here is a problem about finding the average.

At recess, six students were playing basketball. They recorded the number of baskets each student made. Hannah made 3 baskets. Emily made 6 baskets. Micah made 7 baskets. Jeremy made 2, Philip made 8, and Brittany made 4. What was the average number of baskets made by the students?

Introduce the problem. Then have students do the activity to solve the problem. Assign students to work in pairs and distribute Color Tiles.

Materials
- Color Tiles (65 tiles per pair)
- paper (1 sheet per pair)
- pencils (1 per pair)

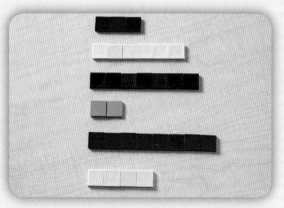

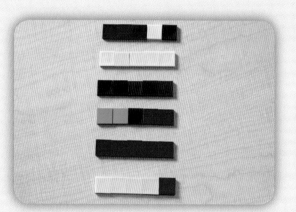

1. Instruct students to model the numbers 3, 6, 7, 2, 8, and 4 using tiles. Tiles should be placed in 6 rows, and each row should have tiles that are the same color.

2. Ask: *How many rows do you have?* Explain that to find the average number of tiles, there must be the same number of tiles in each row. Instruct students to rearrange tiles so that each of the 6 rows has the same number of tiles.

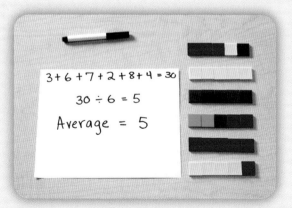

⚠ Look Out!

When rearranging the tiles to make equal rows, students may eliminate some rows completely or make new rows. Explain that the number of rows must remain the same. For example, in the second step of the Try It! activity, students must have 6 rows in order to find the correct answer.

3. Ask: *How many tiles are in each row now?* Explain that 5 is the *average* of 3, 6, 7, 2, 8, and 4. Tell students that they can also find averages using addition and division. Guide students to add the 6 numbers together, and then divide the total by the number 6. Explain that the answer is the average of the 6 numbers.

Data Analysis and Probability

Pictographs

Students need regular opportunities to perform investigations in which they collect, analyze, display, and interpret data. They should also explore different ways of displaying this data, such as creating pictographs.

Try It! *Perform the Try It! activity on the next page.*

Objective

Use tallies to collect data and construct a pictograph.

Skills

• Graphing
• Representing data
• Analyzing data

NCTM Expectations

Data Analysis and Probability
• Represent data using tables and graphs such as line plots, bar graphs, and line graphs.
• Describe the shape and important features of a set of data and compare related data sets, with an emphasis on how the data are distributed.

Talk About It

Discuss the Try It! activity.

■ **Ask:** *During which week were the most teddy bears collected? The least? How can you tell?* Students should recognize that they can compare the number of teddy bears collected each week by identifying the rows with the greatest and least number of Baby Bear™ Counters.

■ **Ask:** *What if 8 teddy bears, not 5, were collected during Week 1? How could you show that?* Students should conclude that they could draw one full Bear and a partial Bear Counter to represent 8 teddy bears.

Solve It

With students, reread the problem. Have students write out directions to Miss Roberts's class, telling the class how to show the number of teddy bears collected during each week of the toy drive on a pictograph. Then have students use Graphing Grids (BLM 19) to draw pictographs to show the data.

More Ideas

For other ways to teach about collecting data and constructing a pictograph—

■ Provide students with the following data about a school doughnut sale: Class A sold 39 doughnuts, Class B sold 36, and Class C sold 42. Have groups create pictographs using Pattern Blocks, where 1 hexagon equals 6 doughnuts sold. Have students trace the hexagons and color their graphs. Tell students to use $\frac{1}{2}$ or $\frac{1}{4}$ hexagons to show amounts of doughnuts smaller than 6.

■ Divide the class into four groups and assign each group a number. Poll groups to find how many books the students in the group read altogether during a week. Display the data in a tally chart, and have individuals use it to make pictographs using Color Tiles. Tell students to make a key, such as 1 tile equals 3 books read, before they begin.

Standardized Practice

Have students try the following problem.

How many apple juice boxes were sold during lunch?

A. 5
B. 9
C. 12
D. 15

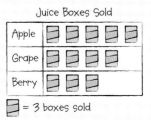

Try It! 30 minutes | Groups of 4

Here is a problem about collecting data and constructing a pictograph.

Miss Roberts's class had a month-long toy drive. Students collected 5 teddy bears during the first week, 15 during the second week, 25 during the third week, and 10 during the fourth week. How can Miss Roberts's students make a pictograph to show how many teddy bears were collected each week?

Introduce the problem. Then have students do the activity to solve the problem. Distribute Graphing Grids (BLM 19) and Baby Bear™ Counters to groups.

Materials

- Three Bear Family® Counters (15 Baby Bear™ Counters per group)
- Graphing Grid (BLM 19; 1 per group)
- paper (1 sheet per group)
- pencils (1 per group)

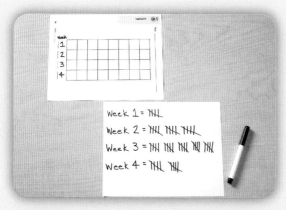

1. Instruct students to make a tally sheet to show how many teddy bears were collected during each week. Tell students that they will use Bear Counters to construct a pictograph horizontally on the Graphing Grid. Students should label four rows on the grid with the week numbers.

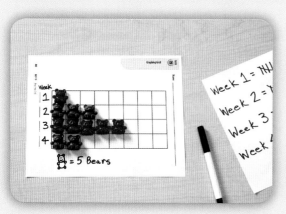

3. Point out that the color of the Bear Counters isn't important in this pictograph, only that there is 1 Bear to represent every 5 teddy bears collected. Instruct students to complete their pictographs by filling in all of the rows.

2. Explain that pictographs use pictures to represent data. Have students study their tally sheets to see that the teddy bear collection numbers are already grouped into 5s. **Say:** *Let's use 1 Bear Counter to represent every 5 bears collected in the toy drive.* Have students make a key for their pictograph to show that each Bear represents 5 bears collected in the toy drive. **Ask:** *How many Bears should go in the first row?* Have students complete the first row of the pictograph. Then they should place the appropriate number of Bears in each row.

⚠ Look Out!

Watch out for students who think that 1 Bear Counter equals 1 teddy bear from the toy drive. Remind students that they created a key to show that each Counter represents 5 teddy bears. Reinforce by having students compare their completed pictographs with their tally sheets.

Data Analysis and Probability

Bar Graphs

Students need to be given opportunities to collect, display, compare, and interpret data on a regular basis in order to become familiar with the process of gathering and analyzing information. The results of these investigations should be represented using a variety of graphs and tables. Students' involvement in the collection of data and the creation of the graphs will help them see the connection between the information and the way it is displayed.

Objective

Make and interpret a bar graph.

Skills

• Data collection
• Data representation
• Comparing sets of data

NCTM Expectations

Data Analysis and Probability
• Design investigations to address a question and consider how data-collection methods affect the nature of the data set.
• Collect data using observations, surveys, and experiments.
• Represent data using tables and graphs such as line plots, bar graphs, and line graphs.
• Describe the shape and important features of a set of data and compare related data sets, with an emphasis on how the data are distributed.

Try It! *Perform the Try It! activity on the next page.*

Talk About It

Discuss the Try It! activity.

■ Invite students to look at their bar graphs. **Ask:** *What does the graph show? Which type of shoe was worn the most? The least? How can you tell?*

■ **Ask:** *If students in another class made a graph of their shoes, would the graph look the same or different from the one you made? Why?*

■ **Ask:** *Why is it important to have a title on a graph? Why is it important to label each bar? What would happen if these were left out?*

Solve It

With students, reread the problem. Then have students write directions for Tomas. They should tell him how to gather the information, how to keep track of it, and how to show it on a bar graph.

More Ideas

For other ways to teach about bar graphs—

■ Ask several teachers from a variety of grade levels if your students can collect data from their classes. Then send pairs of students to ask what the students' favorite after-school activities are. Choices could include *reading, playing sports, riding bikes,* and *playing video games.* Have students pose the questions, tally the results, and make a bar graph using Color Tiles to display the results. Compare the results gathered from each class.

■ Pose a survey question to the class and give four answer choices. Have students write their choices on slips of paper, and then collect them and tally the results. Then have each student create a bar graph using Color Tiles. Remind students to label their graphs.

Standardized Practice

Have students try the following problem.

Which fruit is the favorite of the most students?

A. apples   C. oranges
B. bananas   D. grapes

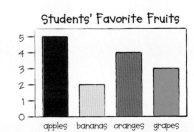
Students' Favorite Fruits

Try It! 30 minutes | Pairs

Here is a problem about bar graphs.

Tomas wants to find out what kinds of shoes the students in his class are wearing. He asks the students what shoes they are wearing. The choices are "sneakers," "sandals," "boots," and "other." How can Tomas show what kinds of shoes the class is wearing by using a bar graph?

Introduce the problem. Then have students do the activity to solve the problem. Distribute Color Tiles and Graphing Grids (BLM 19) to pairs. Explain that students will make a graph to show the types of shoes they are wearing.

Materials

- Color Tiles (60 per pair)
- Graphing Grid (BLM 19; 2 per pair)
- plain paper (1 sheet per pair)
- pencils (1 per pair)

1. Instruct students to label the columns on the Graphing Grid with the following shoe types: *sneakers, sandals, boots, other.* Have students write a title at the top of the graph.

2. Have students collect data about shoe type from their classmates and tally the results on a tally chart. Then students should use tiles to construct a bar graph to display the data.

3. Point out that each tile represents one student wearing one type of shoe. **Ask:** *What if we had colored in bars instead of using tiles?* Lead students to conclude that they should also label the side of the graph with numbers. Have students do so. Then have them discuss their data.

⚠ Look Out!

Students may not remember to label the graph and include a title. Explain the importance of including this information so that readers correctly understand and interpret the data displayed.

163

Data Analysis and Probability

Circle Graphs

A circle graph, also known as a *pie graph* or *pie chart,* represents data by comparing information in terms of its relationship to the whole. The information is reported as fractions, percents, or decimals. As students continue to gather, analyze, and compare data, it is important that they become familiar with a variety of representations of the results of their investigations.

Try It! *Perform the Try It! activity on the next page.*

Talk About It

Discuss the Try It! activity.

- **Say:** *Explain the information shown on your circle graph.* **Ask:** *Why does each mode of transportation get its own section of the circle?*
- **Ask:** *Why did you have to title and label your circle graphs?*
- **Ask:** *How is a circle graph different from a bar graph or a pictograph? How is it the same?*

Solve It

With students, reread the problem. Have students transfer their circle graphs to a new sheet of paper and shade each section a different color. Remind students to include labels and a title. Then have students write a short summary about what they can conclude from their graph.

More Ideas

For other ways to teach about circle graphs—

- Have students survey six classmates to find how many walk, bike, ride in a car, or ride the bus to school every day. Have groups of students use Color Tiles to represent this data in a bar graph. Then have them trace Fraction Circles to make circle graphs. Have students compare the different representations of the same information.
- Distribute Fraction Circles to groups of four students. Have students create circle graphs using eighths and trace them onto their paper. Then have students divide each section so the circle graph shows 16 equal sections. Conduct a survey of 16 students, tally the information on the board, and have students color their graphs to display the data.

Standardized Practice

Have students try the following problem.

What type of weather occurred the least in April?

A. cloudy   B. rainy   C. foggy   D. sunny

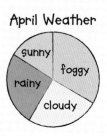

April Weather

Objective

Make and interpret a circle graph.

Skills

- Gathering and representing data
- Fractions
- Percentages

NCTM Expectations

Data Analysis and Probability
- Design investigations to address a question and consider how data-collection methods affect the nature of the data set.
- Collect data using observations, surveys, and experiments.
- Represent data using tables and graphs such as line plots, bar graphs, and line graphs.
- Describe the shape and important features of a set of data and compare related data sets, with an emphasis on how the data are distributed.

Try It!   25 minutes | Groups of 4

Here is a problem about making and interpreting circle graphs.

*Carter Elementary School's dance club has 8 members. After each meeting,
2 students walk home, 1 rides a bike home, 2 ride in a car home, and 3 ride
the bus home. How can the students use a circle graph to show how many
club members use each mode of transportation?*

Introduce the problem. Then have students
do the activity to solve the problem.
Distribute Fraction Circles to groups. Explain
that a circle graph is like a pie that is cut
into different-sized pieces. Each piece
represents a part, or fraction, of the whole circle.

Materials
- Fraction Circles (1 set per group)
- paper (2 sheets per group)
- pencil (1 per group)

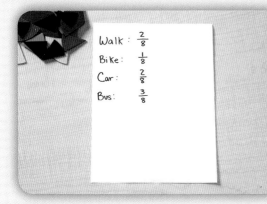

1. List the data on the board: 2 walk, 1 bike,
2 car, 3 bus. Tell students that they will be
making a circle graph to show the data. Have
students begin by converting the problem data
into fractions and listing the fractions.

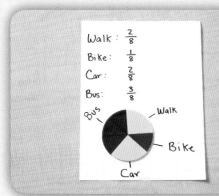

3. Have students represent with fraction pieces
and label the $\frac{1}{8}$ who bike, the $\frac{2}{8}$ who ride in a
car, and the $\frac{3}{8}$ who ride the bus. Students should
notice that there is no other fraction piece that
equals $\frac{3}{8}$. Tell students to use three $\frac{1}{8}$ pieces
pushed closely together to form one section.
Have students title their graphs.

2. Say: *All of the fractions are eighths, so start
by finding the eighths fraction circle.* Have
students arrange the eight $\frac{1}{8}$ pieces in a circle in
the center of a piece of paper and then identify
the pieces that show the fraction of students
who walk home: $\frac{2}{8}$. **Ask:** *Can you find another
fraction piece equal to these two pieces?* Have
students exchange one $\frac{1}{4}$ piece for two $\frac{1}{8}$ pieces
and label this section "Walk."

⚠ Look Out!

Students may struggle with converting data to
fractions when creating circle graphs. Review
the steps for converting data to fractions. Tell
students that first they should find the total
number of data that will be shown in the
graph, such as 8. Explain that this number will
be the denominator for their fractions because
it represents the whole, or total. Provide
students with sets of data they can use to
practice converting to fractions.

Data Analysis and Probability

Line Graphs

Students have already experienced many different ways of representing data, such as bar graphs, circle graphs, and pictographs, but line graphs can present a new challenge. Learning to represent data on a line graph provides students with a tool to show how data changes over time.

Try It! *Perform the Try It! activity on the next page.*

Talk About It

Discuss the Try It! activity.

- **Ask:** *How does your line graph show whether the number of Two-Color Counters flipped over was going up or down?* Discuss how line graphs are good at showing change.

- Invite students to compare their results. **Ask:** *Did you turn over more or fewer counters in 20 seconds than in 15? How can you tell?* Most students will have turned over more. **Ask:** *How many more did you turn over?*

Solve It

With students, reread the problem. Ask students to use their line graphs to determine the difference between how many counters were flipped over within 5, 10, 15, and 20 seconds. Then have students write to explain how graphing this data on a line graph helped them see the difference.

More Ideas

For other ways to teach about line graphs—

- Tell students that a cup of water that is left out will evaporate over time. Fill a plastic cup with water. Have volunteers measure the weight of the water using the Bucket Balance and Centimeter Cubes. (Remind students that each cube weighs 1 gram.) Have a volunteer weigh and record the amount of water left every morning until it is gone. Ask students to create a line graph to show the change in the amount of water every day.

- Have students keep track of how many homework assignments they get each day for a week. Then have students use geoboards to plot the data into a line graph. Have students use paper to label the horizontal and vertical axes with the days of the week and an appropriate range of numbers. Invite students to discuss their graphs.

Standardized Practice

Have students try the following problem.

Between which two weeks did the plant grow the most?

A. Weeks 1 and 2   C. Weeks 3 and 4
B. Weeks 2 and 3   D. None of the above

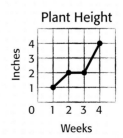

Plant Height

Objective

Make and interpret a line graph.

Skills

- Collecting data
- Representing data on a line graph
- Comparing and analyzing data

NCTM Expectations

Data Analysis and Probability
- Collect data using observations, surveys, and experiments.
- Represent data using tables and graphs such as line plots, bar graphs, and line graphs.
- Describe the shape and important features of a set of data and compare related data sets, with an emphasis on how the data are distributed.

Try It! **25 minutes | Pairs**

Here is a problem about making and interpreting line graphs.

Mrs. Stone's students want to know how many more Two-Color Counters they can flip over in 20 seconds than in 15, 10, or 5 seconds. How can Mrs. Stone's students graph their data and find the change in the number of counters flipped over each time?

Introduce the problem. Then have students do the activity to solve the problem. Pass out Two-Color Counters, Centimeter Cubes, and Graphing Grids (BLM 19) to pairs of students.

Materials
- Two-Color Counters (30 per pair)
- Centimeter Cubes (10 per pair)
- Graphing Grid (BLM 19; 1 per pair)
- paper and pencil (1 of each per pair)

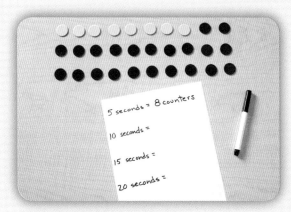

1. Instruct students to start with all the counters facing red-side up. Have one student in each pair be the timer while the other flips the counters. Tell students to see how many counters they can flip over in 5 seconds. Have students record the results and repeat for 10-, 15-, and 20-second intervals.

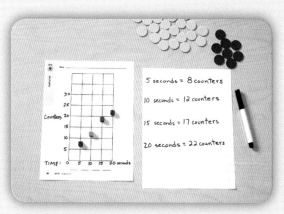

2. Guide students to label the bottom of their Graphing Grids with the time intervals (5, 10, 15, 20) and the left side with numbers 0–30 labeled by 5s (5, 10, 15, 20, and so on) to represent the counters students turned over. Show students how to use cubes to plot their results.

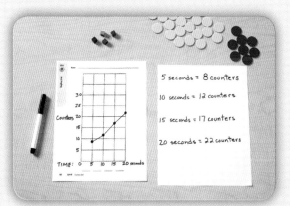

3. Have students replace each cube with a dot or point and connect the dots with lines to match the order in which they performed the experiment. Have them discuss the change in number of counters shown by the line.

⚠ Look Out!

Watch out for students who try to connect the dots in the wrong order. Stress that students should connect them in the same order as they performed the experiment: the 5 seconds, 10 seconds, 15 seconds, and then 20 seconds. If any students flipped over fewer counters in 10 seconds than in 5 seconds, they may be confused about their lines turning downward while other students' are going up. Explain that some line graphs go up, some go down, and some go up and down. Stress that what is important is that the graph accurately represents the data.

Objective

Explore outcomes with a probability experiment.

Skills

- Collecting data
- Recording results
- Analyzing data

NCTM Expectations

Data Analysis and Probability
- Collect data using observations, surveys, and experiments.
- Describe the shape and important features of a set of data and compare related data sets, with an emphasis on how the data are distributed.

Data Analysis and Probability

Probability

As children master data collection and comparison, they are ready to develop their knowledge of probability. This includes identifying the possible outcomes of an experiment, as well as performing and then analyzing the results of probability experiments. Students should identify the difference between the *probability* of a certain outcome and the actual outcome of the experiment.

Try It! *Perform the Try It! activity on the next page.*

Talk About It

Discuss the Try It! activity.

- **Ask:** *Did everyone have the same number of possible outcomes for their draws?* Students should explain that each pair had the same number of possible outcomes—3.

- Introduce the term *probability* to students and discuss how probability is often different from the actual outcome.

- **Say:** *Suppose we repeat the experiment and you draw the Three Bear Family® Counters from the bag 20 more times.* **Ask:** *Do you think your outcome will be the same? Why or why not?*

Solve It

With students, reread the problem. Have students explain in writing the possible outcomes each time they pulled a Bear from the bag.

More Ideas

For other ways to teach about probability—

- Have students repeat the experiment with different numbers of Three Bear Family Counter colors. Then have them try the activity with 25 tries. Invite students to discuss what parts of the experiment are the same or different from the first time they tried it and how it affected results.

- Set up a learning center with Color Tiles, bags, and tally charts with four columns labeled *green, yellow, red,* and *blue.* Combine different color combinations in different bags; for example, one bag could have 4 red, 4 green, 8 blue, and 2 yellow tiles, while another would have 2 of each color. Let students discover how having more or fewer of one color tile either increases or decreases the probability of drawing it.

Standardized Practice

Have students try the following problem.

Jason has a blue pen, a black pen, and two green pens in his desk. Without looking, he reaches into his desk for a pen. How many possible outcomes are there for what color pen he will pull out?

A. 2   **B.** 3   **C.** 4   **D.** 5

Try It! 20 minutes | Pairs

Here is a problem about probability.

Marta and Aiden want to perform an experiment with Papa Bear™ Counters. They have 3 different colors of Bears in a paper bag. They will take turns pulling out one Bear, recording its color, and replacing it in the bag. What are their possible outcomes each time they pull a Bear from the bag, and what will their results be after doing this 20 times?

Introduce the problem. Then have students do the activity to solve the problem. Give each pair of students 3 Papa Bears in 3 different colors, such as red, yellow, and green.

Materials
- Three Bear Family® Counters (3 Papa Bear™ Counters of 3 different colors per pair)
- bag (1 per pair)
- paper and pencil (1 of each per pair)

1. Ask each pair to lay their 3 Bears on the table and note their colors. Have students create a tally chart by labeling three rows or columns on a sheet of paper with the colors.

2. Say: *Put all 3 Bears in a bag and then draw one out without looking. Make a tally mark to show which color Bear you drew.* **Ask:** *What other colors could you have drawn?* Discuss the concept of possible outcomes.

⚠ Look Out!

Some students may think their results are wrong when they see that they differ from other pairs' tally sheets. These students may be uncomfortable with the absence of a foolproof formula or a "constant," such as a multiplication fact that always has the same answer. Explain that in a probability experiment like this one, there are no "sure" or "right" answers that will be the same every single time.

3. Remind students to place the Bear back in the bag before drawing again. Explore with students how not replacing the bear would change the experiment. Then instruct students to draw a Bear from the bag 19 more times, for a total of 20 draws. Invite students to compare their results when they've finished.

Data Analysis and Probability

Degrees of Probability

Students at this level come to understand that, although they cannot predict a single outcome, they can use information about the number and variety of choices in a probability experiment to describe choices as *certain, more likely, equally likely, less likely,* or *impossible.* This is a step toward being able to make predictions using a scale of numbers.

> **Try It!** *Perform the Try It! activity on the next page.*

Talk About It

Discuss the Try It! activity.

- **Ask:** *Why was it certain that you would pick a Centimeter Cube that was either red, blue, or yellow? Why was it impossible to pick a green cube?*

- Have students compare their results to their predictions. **Ask:** *Did your results match your predictions? Did anyone get results that were very different from their predictions? Why do you think an activity like this might not always turn out the way we predict?*

- **Say:** *We described the probability that you would choose a red cube as "more likely." We said the same about choosing a blue cube.* **Ask:** *Does that mean the red and blue cubes are equally likely? Why or why not? What if you had 5 blue cubes and 5 red? What would the probability be then?*

Solve It

With students, reread the problem. Have students explain in writing which color choices were more likely and which were less likely to be picked by the students.

More Ideas

For other ways to teach about degrees of probability—

- Have students use Color Tiles to explore degrees of probability by modeling situations in which one choice is *much more likely* and in which one choice is just *slightly more likely.*

- Challenge students to begin expressing probabilities as fractions. Give students Color Tiles in two colors. Have them arrange the tiles so that 7 are one color and 3 are the other color. Explain that the probability of choosing the first color is 7 out of 10, or $\frac{7}{10}$. Have students find the probability of choosing the other color and express it in fraction form.

Standardized Practice

Have students try the following problem.

Sarah has a bag with 3 red crayons, 4 blue crayons, 2 green crayons, and 7 yellow crayons. If she reaches into the bag without looking, which color crayon is she more likely to choose?

A. red **B.** blue **C.** green **D.** yellow

Try It! 30 minutes | Pairs

Here is a problem about probability.

Anne's class is choosing teams for a game by pulling colored chips out of a bag without looking. There are 6 red chips, 3 blue chips, and 1 yellow chip in the bag. What color chip are students more likely to pull? Less likely?

Introduce the problem. Then have students do the activity to solve the problem. Distribute Centimeter Cubes to pairs. Introduce the terms *certain, more likely, equally likely, less likely,* and *impossible* to students and list them on the board.

Materials
- Centimeter Cubes (6 blue, 3 red, and 1 yellow per pair)
- paper (1 sheet per pair)
- pencil (1 per pair)

1. Have students look at their cubes. **Ask:** *What is the probability that you will choose a cube that is either red, blue, or yellow?* (certain) **Ask:** *What is the probability that you will pick each color of cube?* Invite students to predict probability using the terms *certain, more likely, equally likely, less likely,* and *impossible*. Make sure students understand that they are most likely to pick a blue cube, as there are more of this color. Have them record their predictions.

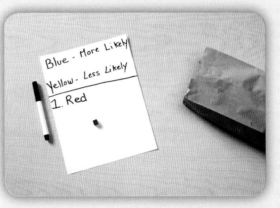

2. Have one student in each pair close his or her eyes, and direct the other partner to mix up the cubes. Tell the first partner to choose a cube. Direct students to record the color of the cube on paper, then replace the cube.

⚠ Look Out!

Some students may think that their choices need to match their predictions. Stress that there are no right or wrong results in an experiment like this. Make sure that students understand that probability tells us what we can expect, not necessarily what will happen.

3. Have students repeat Step 2 nine more times, recording the results each time. When finished, have students discuss and compare data.

Data Analysis and Probability

Predictions and Outcomes

At this point in their study of data analysis and probability, students should begin to go beyond just understanding or analyzing what their data shows. Their next step is comparing predictions they made to the actual outcomes.

Try It! *Perform the Try It! activity on the next page.*

Objective

Compare outcomes of experiments to predictions.

Skills

- Predicting
- Collecting and representing data
- Comparing

NCTM Expectations

Data Analysis and Probability
- Collect data using observations, surveys, and experiments.
- Represent data using tables and graphs such as line plots, bar graphs, and line graphs.
- Propose and justify conclusions and predictions that are based on data and design studies to further investigate the conclusions or predictions.
- Predict the probability of outcomes of simple experiments and test the predictions.

Talk About It

Discuss the Try It! activity.

- Have students discuss their results within their groups. **Ask:** *Did anyone get the results they predicted? Did anyone get the results that another group member predicted?*

- Survey students, asking them to compare their outcomes to the predictions they made.

- **Ask:** *Why do you think the actual results were often different from the predicted results?* Guide students in a discussion about chance.

Solve It

With students, reread the problem. Then have students draw on their activity experience to explain in writing whether Andre or Emily is probably right. Remind students to explain why the results at the fourth graders' booth might be different from their own group's results.

More Ideas

For other ways to teach about comparing outcomes to predictions—

- Have students compare the sizes of their hands and predict who can pick up the most Three Bear Family® Counters with one hand. Have them count the Bears picked up to see if the prediction is accurate. Invite students to then discuss the relationship between hand size related to the number of Bears that can be picked up.

- Have children predict and discover the relationship between different sizes of Three Bear Family counters. Use Centimeter Cubes and Bucket Balances to measure relationship (e.g., 3 Baby Bears equal 1 Papa Bear).

Standardized Practice

Have students try the following problem.

Tom reaches into a bag of 10 crayons 5 times to pull out a crayon. He pulls out blue crayons 4 times. He pulls out a red crayon 1 time. What is one possible reason for Tom's results?

A. There are no red crayons in the bag.
B. There are more blue than red crayons in the bag.
C. There are more yellow than blue crayons in the bag.
D. There are more red than blue crayons in the bag.

Try It! 20 minutes | Groups of 3

Here is a problem about comparing outcomes of experiments to predictions.

The fourth graders have a game booth at the school carnival. Students try to guess the order in which they will pull three Three Bear Family® Counters from a bag. Emily thinks that many students will guess correctly. Andre thinks that very few players will guess correctly. Who is right?

Introduce the problem. Then have students do the activity to solve the problem. Distribute Three Bear Family® Counters, Prediction/Result Recording Sheets (BLM 20), and paper bags to groups.

Materials

- Three Bear Family® Counters (3 different colors, all the same size per group)
- Prediction/Result Recording Sheet (BLM 20; 1 per group)
- paper bags (1 per group)

1. Tell students that first they will place all three Bears in the bag and pull them out one at a time. Have each student make a prediction about the order in which the Bears will be pulled from the bag. Have them record their predictions on their recording sheets.

2. Have one student in each group experiment by pulling the Bear Counters from the bag one by one and then recording the actual order on the recording sheet. Tell students to place the Bear Counters back in the bag.

3. When each of the other two group members has had a turn doing this, students compare their predictions to their actual results.

⚠ Look Out!

Look out for students who confuse this type of prediction with probability. Have students discuss probability experiments that they might conduct using the three Bears. Then point out that this activity is different because students are only making predictions about the order in which they will pull the Bears out of the bag, not the likelihood that they will pull one Bear or another.

Data Analysis and Probability

Fairness

The concept of fairness is a very important one to students at this age. They want fairness in all aspects of their lives and notice quickly when something seems unfair. Students already know that for something to be fair it must be absolutely equal for all parties or in all parts. Through a game activity, this lesson links fairness to the notion of mathematical probability.

Try It! *Perform the Try It! activity on the next page.*

Talk About It

Discuss the Try It! activity.

■ Ask each team to report its results.

■ Hold up an even spinner. **Ask:** *Is this spinner fair? Why?* Hold up an uneven spinner. **Ask:** *How many of you think this is fair? Why?*

■ **Ask:** *Which spinner was more likely to help you win the game? Is it impossible for a person to win with the uneven spinner? Why or why not?*

■ **Ask:** *What term would you use to describe the probability of winning the game if you have the uneven spinner?* Encourage students to use the phrase *less likely*.

Solve It

With students, reread the problem. Ask students to write a sentence telling how one of the spinners could be changed to make the game fair. Have them draw a picture of two spinners that would make the game fair.

More Ideas

For other ways to teach about fairness and probability—

■ Secretly place the following Three Bear Family® Counters in a bag: 7 blue, 2 red, and 1 green. Assign players in a group a color (blue, red, green, yellow). Have students take turns drawing a Bear out and awarding a point for each color drawn. After all the Bears have been drawn, have students discuss the fairness of the game and how it could be adjusted so that all players have equal chance to win.

■ Give each pair of students two paper bags with Pattern Blocks inside. One bag should have five each of two different shapes. The other bag should have nine of one shape and one of another. Tell students that the first person to pick both shapes wins the game. Have students take turns choosing shapes, replacing each shape after they have noted what it is. When a student has won, the pair should examine the contents of the bags, decide whether or not the game was fair, and explain why.

Standardized Practice

Have students try the following problem.

Dan and Maria are playing a game using this spinner. Maria wins if she spins a 1. Dan wins if he spins a 2. Is the game fair?

Objective

Explore and evaluate fairness.

Skills

• Predicting
• Testing predictions
• Evaluating

NCTM Expectations

Data Analysis and Probability
• Describe events as likely or unlikely and discuss the degree of likelihood using such words as *certain, equally likely,* and *impossible.*
• Predict the probability of outcomes of simple experiments and test the predictions.

Try It! 20 minutes | Pairs

Here is a problem about fairness.

John and Ali were playing a game during free time. They each used a spinner with four sections. The sections were colored red, blue, yellow, and green. Ali's spinner had large sections of red and yellow and small slivers of blue and green. John's spinner had equal sections of each color. Whoever spun all four colors first would win the game. Was the game fair?

Introduce the problem. Then have students do the activity to solve the problem. Distribute Color Tiles and Spinner Patterns (BLM 21) to students. Have students create two spinners — one with all four sections for the four colors (red, yellow, blue, green) equal, and the other with blue and green on the smaller sections. Allow students a few minutes to follow directions on the BLM to make and practice spinning the spinners. One student in each pair should have an equal spinner and the other student should have an unequal spinner.

Materials

- Color Tiles (1 each of red, blue, green, and yellow per student)
- Spinner Patterns (BLM 21; 1 per pair)
- crayons (1 each of red, blue, green, and yellow per student)
- pencil (1 per student)
- paper clip (1 per student)

1. Explain to students that they are going to play a game to see which partner can get all four colors first.

2. Have students take turns spinning their spinners and taking the tile indicated on the spinner. If a student spins a color they've already collected, play advances to the other player. The first person who makes a match for all four colors is the winner.

3. Help players compare their results. Request a show of hands. **Ask:** *How many thought the game was fair? Why or why not?*

⚠ Look Out!

Some students may object to being given the "unfair" spinner. Encourage them to express why they think this spinner will put them at a disadvantage, at the same time reminding them that this game is really an experiment and that their spinner will give important information.

Name

Standard Form	Word Form

Drawing	Expanded Form

Thousands	Hundreds	Tens	Ones

Name _____

1	2	3	4	5	6	7	8	9	10
11	12	13	14	15	16	17	18	19	20
21	22	23	24	25	26	27	28	29	30
31	32	33	34	35	36	37	38	39	40
41	42	43	44	45	46	47	48	49	50
51	52	53	54	55	56	57	58	59	60
61	62	63	64	65	66	67	68	69	70
71	72	73	74	75	76	77	78	79	80
81	82	83	84	85	86	87	88	89	90
91	92	93	94	95	96	97	98	99	100

Factor Pair	Rods

Name _____

Division Sentences	Multiplication Sentences

Name _____

Directions: Trace the fraction on the first cube. Trace the decimal on the second cube. Then write the fraction and the decimal on the blank lines, and fill in the circle with ‹ or ›.

_____ ◯ _____

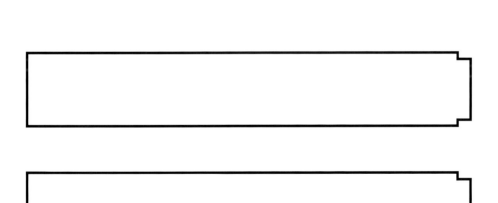

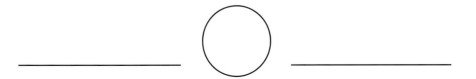

_____ ◯ _____

Name _____

Plane Shapes Recording Sheet

Name of Shape	Sketch of Shape	Number of Sides	Number of Vertices	Number of Parallel Sides

Geometric Solid Name	Number of Vertices	Number of Faces	Number of Edges	(V + F) = (2 + E)
				___ + ___ = 2 + ___ ___ = ___
				___ + ___ = 2 + ___ ___ = ___
				___ + ___ = 2 + ___ ___ = ___
				___ + ___ = 2 + ___ ___ = ___
				___ + ___ = 2 + ___ ___ = ___
				___ + ___ = 2 + ___ ___ = ___
				___ + ___ = 2 + ___ ___ = ___

Name _____

Nets Worksheet

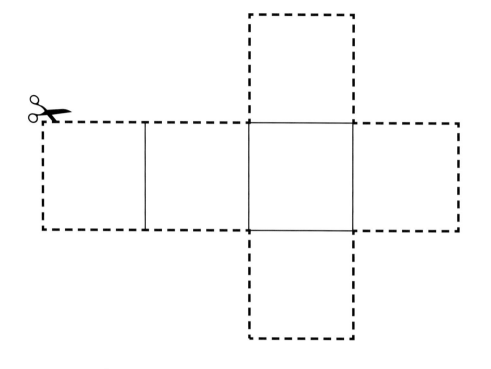

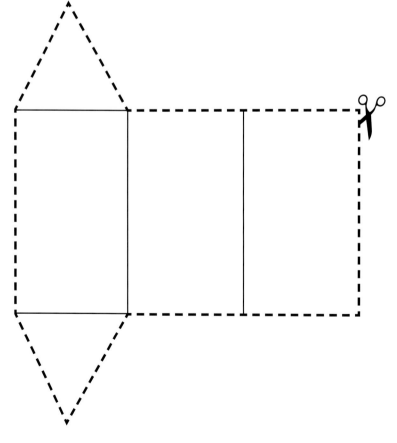

Name _____

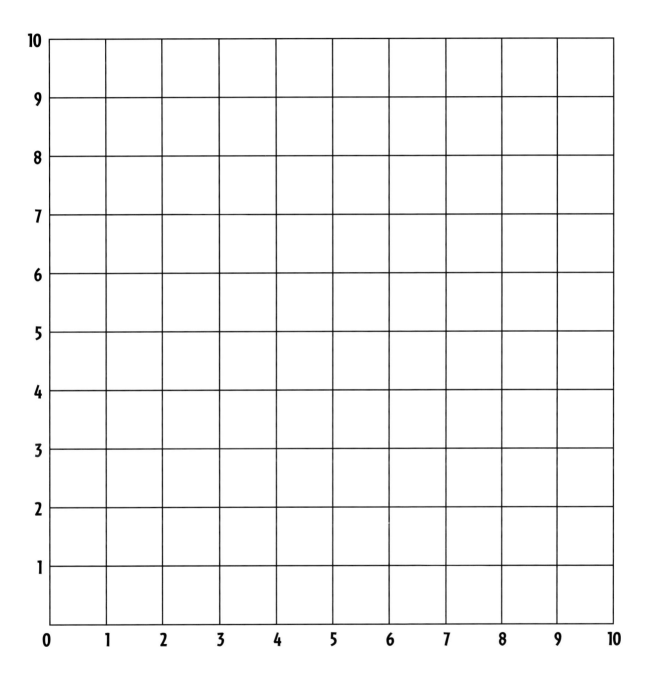

Name _____

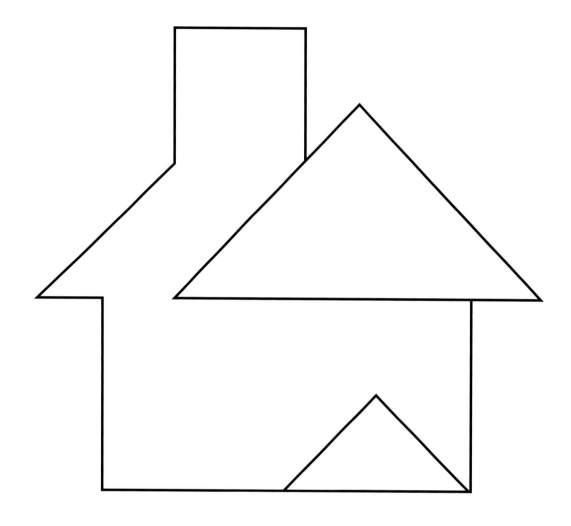

Name _____

1. ___ + ___ + ___ = ___

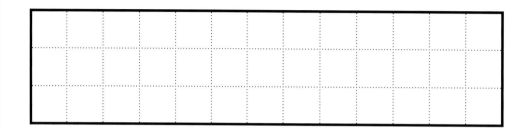

2. ___ + ___ + ___ = ___

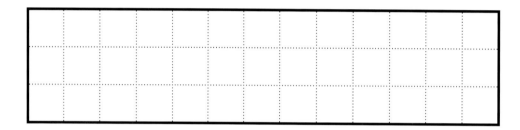

3. ___ + ___ + ___ = ___

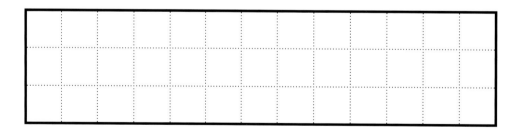

Name _____

Input	Output

Missing Numbers Worksheet

Name _____

BLM 15   Missing Numbers Worksheet

Object	Estimate in Inches	Measurement in Inches	Estimate in Centimeters	Measurement in Centimeters

Name _____

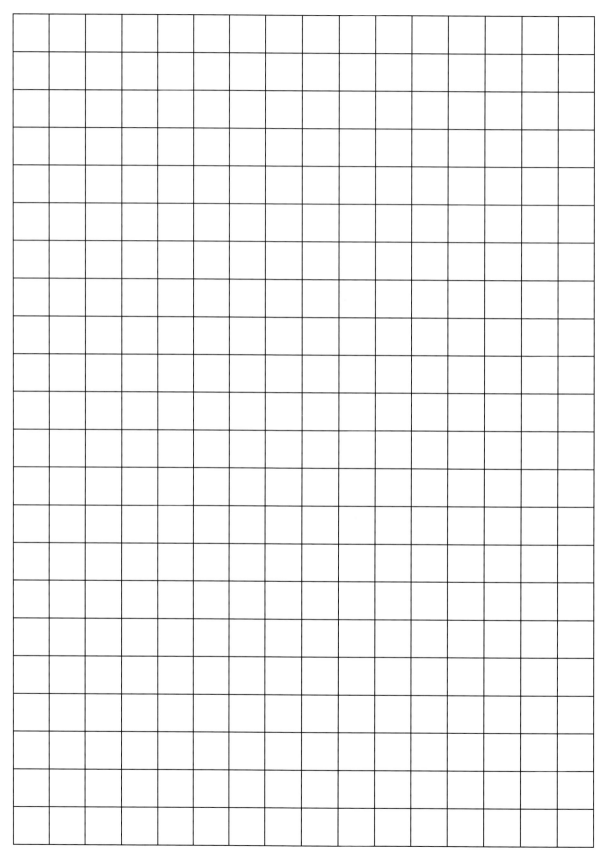

BLM 17   Centimeter Grid

Graphing Grid

Name _____

Name	Prediction	Result

Name _____

Directions: Cut out the Spinner Patterns. Color the sections. To make a spinner, place the end of a paper clip over the center of the spinner base. Put the point of a pencil through the end of the paper clip at the center of the spinner. Spin the paper clip around the pencil and see where it stops.

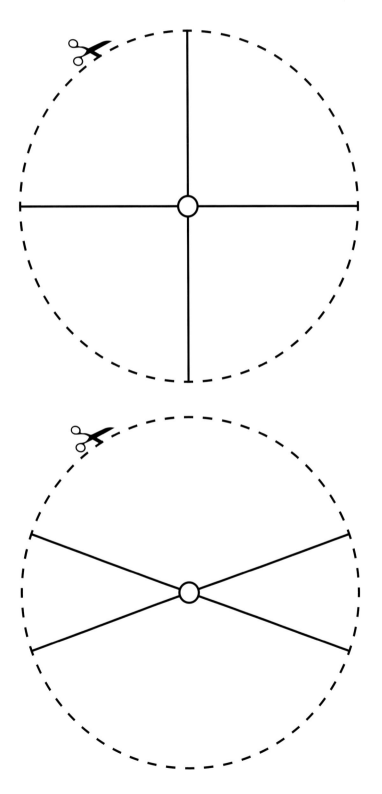

Glossary of Manipulatives

	Attribute Blocks The Attribute Blocks set includes five basic shapes (triangle, square, rectangle, circle, and hexagon) displaying different attributes. The basic shapes come in three different colors (red, blue, and yellow), two different sizes, and two different thicknesses. Attribute Blocks can be used to teach sorting, patterns, and identifying attributes.
	Base Ten Blocks Base Ten Blocks include cubes representing 1,000, flats representing 100, rods representing 10, and units representing 1. Blocks can be used to teach various number and place value concepts, such as the use of regrouping in addition and subtraction. Each unit measures 1 cm^2, making blocks ideal for measuring area and volume.
	Bucket Balance The Bucket Balance features removable $\frac{1}{2}$-liter buckets. The buckets are clear to help students get a visual idea of what they are measuring. Measures 16"L x 5.75"W x 5"H. The balance helps students explore the measurement of mass with accuracy to 1 gram.
	Centimeter Cubes These plastic cubes come in 10 colors. They can be used to teach counting, patterning, and spatial reasoning. They are also suitable for measuring area and volume.
	Color Tiles These 1" square plastic tiles come in four different colors: red, blue, yellow, and green. They can be used to explore many mathematical concepts, including geometry, patterns, and number sense.
	Cuisenaire® Rods Cuisenaire® Rods include Rods of 10 different colors, each corresponding to a specific length. White Rods, the shortest, are 1 cm long. Orange Rods, the longest, are 10 cm long. Rods allow students to explore all fundamental math concepts, including addition and patterning, multiplication, division, fractions and decimals, and data analysis.
	Fraction Circles Basic Fraction Circles have six circles that show halves, thirds, fourths, sixths, eighths, and one whole. Each circle is a different color, with plastic pieces that can be put together and taken apart to show different fractions. Circles are ideal for introducing students to basic fraction concepts.
	Fraction Tower® Equivalency Cubes Fraction Tower® Equivalency Cubes snap together to show fractions, decimals, and percents. Towers are divided into stacking Cubes that show halves, thirds, fourths, fifths, sixths, eighths, tenths, twelfths, and one whole, as well as equivalent decimals and percents. Each Cube is labeled to show the part of one whole that it represents. One side is labeled with the fraction, another with the decimal, and a third with the percent. Students can look at the three sides to see equivalency between the different representations of numbers less than one.
	Geoboards Double-sided geoboards are 7.5" square and made of plastic. One side has a 5 x 5 peg grid. The other has a circle with a 12-peg radius. Students stretch rubber bands from peg to peg to form geometric shapes. Geoboards can be used to study symmetry, congruency, area, and perimeter.

Pattern Blocks Blocks include six shapes in six different colors: yellow hexagon, red trapezoid, orange square, green triangle, blue parallelogram, and tan rhombus. The versatile blocks can be used to teach concepts from all strands of mathematics. Blocks illustrate algebraic concepts such as patterning and sorting. Students learn geometry and measurement concepts such as symmetry, transformations, and area. Blocks can also be used to show number concepts such as counting and fractions	
Reflect-It™ Hinged Mirror This mirror with hinge and clear protractor base allows you to see the multiple reflections created by controlling the angle size of the mirror. Create angles up to 180° using the base. Use the mirror without the base to hypothesize the properties of special angles; then draw conclusions and discover symmetry.	
Relational Geosolids® Relational Geosolids® are three-dimensional shapes made of transparent plastic. Shapes include prisms, pyramids, spheres, cylinders, cones, and hemispheres. Geosolids can be used to give students a concrete framework for the study of volume. They can be filled with water, sand, rice, or other materials to facilitate classroom demonstration and experimentation.	
Tangrams Tangrams are ancient Chinese puzzles made of seven three- and four-sided shapes. Each set of tangrams contains four tangram puzzles in four different colors. Each puzzle consists of five triangles (two small, one medium, and two large), a square, and a parallelogram. Tangrams can be used to solve puzzles in which all seven pieces must be put together to create a specified shape. Tangram puzzles teach many geometric concepts, including symmetry, congruency, transformations, and problem solving.	
Three Bear Family® Counters Bear Counters come in four colors and three different sizes and weights—Baby Bear™ (small), Mama Bear™ (medium), and Papa Bear™ (large). Bear Counters can be used to teach abstract concepts involving number sense and operations by allowing students to act them out. Use Bears to explore sorting and comparing sets, counting, estimating, addition and subtraction, patterning, and sequencing.	
Two-Color Counters These versatile counters are thicker than most other counters and easy for students to manipulate. They can be used to teach number and operations concepts such as patterning, addition and subtraction, and multiplication and division. Counters can also be used to introduce students to basic ideas of probability.	
Write-On/Wipe-Off Clocks These 4.5-inch-square clocks are laminated so that students can write the digital time below the moveable hands of the clock face. Clocks can be reused over and over again to give students plenty of hands-on practice measuring time. Clocks also help students practice addition, subtraction, and problem solving.	
XY Coordinate Pegboards XY Coordinate Pegboards can be used to graph coordinates in 1, 2, or 4 quadrants, show translations of geometric figures, display bar graphs and surveys, and graph lines.	

Index

Boldface page numbers indicate when a manipulative is used in the Try It! activity.